Like Father, Like Son

Like Father, Like Son

The Trinity Imaged in our Humanity

Tom Smail

WIPF & STOCK · Eugene, Oregon

Wipf and Stock Publishers
199 W 8th Ave, Suite 3
Eugene, OR 97401

Like Father Like Son
The Trinity Imaged in Our Humanity
By Smail, Tom
Copyright © 2005 Authentic All rights reserved.
Softcover ISBN-13: 978-1-7252-8175-2
Publication date 5/26/2020
Previously published by Paternoster, 2005

The Scripture quotations contained herein are from the New Revised Standard Version of the Bible, Anglicised Edition, copyright © 1989, 1995 by the Division of Christian Education of the National Council of the Churches of Christ in the United States of America, and are used by permission. All rights reserved.

For MARY DUNCAN,

My literary coadjutor
and
Our very good friend

If we are made in the image of God, we are made in the image of the Trinity; and the life of the Trinity must in some sort be reflected in the pattern of our human life.

> John F. X. Harriott

Contents

Preface   xi

1 Whose Image?   1
2 Biblical Image   38
3 God's Image   66
4 Human Image   108
5 Triune Image   153
6 Marred Image   201
7 Gendered Image   239
8 Incarnate Image   270

Notes   296
Select Bibliography   298
Index   301

Preface

This book is an attempt to discover what it might mean for our humanity that God is Trinity. According to one of the central affirmations of Christian theology, we are made in the image of God, so that what we say about God will be the determining factor in what we say about ourselves. If, in faithfulness to his revelation in Christ, we have to say that he is Father, Son, and Holy Spirit bound together in very specific relationships, we can go on to ask what that tells us about the relationships with God and with others that make up our human lives.

It is an old question, but we may nevertheless be able to give it a fresh answer. The renaissance of Trinitarian theology in the last fifty years, with its emphasis on the distinctness of the divine persons and the way they relate to one another, does, I believe, open the door to a genuinely fresh understanding of what it means to be human. The God who made us is three in one, and he made us like himself.

In Christ, this God has made himself accessible to us, and, therefore, what we say about him should be as accessible as we can make it. I have tried to explain what has been happening to Trinitarian doctrine in recent times in a way that will be comprehensible to people who have no reason to be familiar with the highly technical language it has often employed and that has often obscured it more than it has explained it. I have tried to show also how what we say about the triune God, far from being remote and irrelevant, has the most practical and down-to-earth implications for the way we react to the people and the situations we encounter every day.

The basis of the book is dogmatic rather than apologetic, in that it proceeds from and assumes a commitment to what might be loosely described as mainstream biblical and creedal orthodoxy, but it tries to show both to those who do and those who do not share that commitment, that this sort of Christianity has still a probing and revitalizing contribution to make to contemporary human concerns.

The book makes no claim to completeness. It concentrates on the relational center of the Christian doctrine of man at the expense of traditional concerns about the inner constitution of humanity as body, mind, and spirit. Its Trinitarianism is based on the Eastern Cappadocian rather than the Western Augustinian model, but, apart from distinguishing the one from the other, it tries as much as possible to avoid controversy, preferring rather to develop its own positive position with powerful help from the major theologians on whose work it depends.

The basic theology of the book was first presented in a more technical paper that ran the gauntlet of the late Professor Colin Gunton's post-graduate seminar in Kings College, London. It was developed in a course on Christian anthropology that I taught at Trinity College, Bristol, and I am grateful to that college and to Dr. James Steven for giving me scope to develop that course in a way that resourced this project. It has taken its present form partly as a result of fruitful discussions with Professors Andrew

Walker, Alan Torrance, and Christopher Seitz, and with Canon Val Hamer, who have all helped me to clarify my thoughts – sometimes in directions in which they would not wish to follow.

I owe much to the robust encouragement of Dr. Montagu Barker, and the whole-hearted and skilled help of Mary Duncan, to whom the book is dedicated, but most of all to the tolerance and support of my wife, who herself conducts her relationships with me and with many others in a way that genuinely mirrors the love that has its source in the triune God.

Tom Smail
London, Michaelmas 2004

1 Whose Image?

A fond new grandmother shows me a picture of her son's newborn baby and crows with delight that he is the spitting image of his father. How I react will depend on whether and how well I know the baby's father; if I do not know him at all, I can make no meaningful judgement about the alleged likeness and can only mutter, 'Really, how nice!' If, however, she then shows me another picture of the baby in his father's arms, I will be better placed to see any resemblance that there might be between them. Better still, if I live in the house next door, so that I can watch the baby day by day as he grows and develops, I will be able to see how much, not just in outward appearance, but in aptitudes habits and personality, he shows himself to be his father's son. To recognize the image, you must be able to see not just the reflection in the son but the original in the father, and the better you know the original, the better you will be able to compare the one with the other and to judge how alike and how different they are.

This book is about what it means for men and women to be made and remade in the image of God, which is, of course, one of the main ways in which Christian theology has tried to understand our humanity in its relationship to God. I will be affirming the continuing fecundity of that approach for us today. We will explore its biblical basis in the Old and New Testaments. We will also examine and reconsider the various issues it has raised as it has been developed in the different phases of the theological tradition. On this basis, we will argue that, far from being an entirely theoretical, overworked, and largely irrelevant theological category, the claim that the most important thing about us is that we are made in the image of God offers some innovatively fresh, specific, and practically important insights into the contemporary human situation that will inform and enrich our dealings with God, with one another, and with ourselves.

As a starting point for all this, we can see that in speaking of the image of God, we are committing ourselves on the theological level to the principle that we have already illustrated on the human level; what you can say about the image depends on what you know about the original. We can tell whether and in what ways we are like God, only if we also know what God himself is like.

To speak for once in traditional and non-inclusive terms, the Christian doctrine of man is related to and dependent upon the Christian doctrine of God. Anthropology depends on theology. And if that is true about the doctrine, it is because it is first true about the subjects with which the doctrine deals. If our humanity is constituted by the fact that we reflect God's divinity, then to know who we are, we must also know who he is. Our being is dependent on his being. As the psalmist puts it, "It is he who has made us and not we ourselves" (Ps. 100:2), a verse that Eugene Peterson renders even more pertinently: "He made us, we didn't make him."

Who made whom?

It is not hard to see that even at this basic level, we have started to say things that bring us into confrontation and controversy with the prevailing culture around us, which would contradict our first rendering of Psalm 100:2 in the name of a human autonomy that believes that it is we who at the end of a long evolutionary process have constructed our own humanity by and for ourselves and who are responsible for and to ourselves alone. Moreover, that same culture, on the evidence of the writings of many of its most influential representatives, would reverse the second rendering of the psalmist in the name of a skeptical atheism that has dismissed all theological claims as the projections and inventions of human imagination, so that he didn't make us but we made him; it is not that God has made us in his image, but rather that we have made him in ours.

The basic claim of modernity is that we do not need God either to be ourselves or to understand ourselves, that a relationship with God, far from being constitutive of and central to our humanity, is a largely peripheral religious extra for those inclined to that sort of thing but has little bearing on the realities of every day living. Part of the weakness and ineffectiveness of the churches in Western society is the extent to which these attitudes, in a largely unconscious way, have eroded the confidence of church people in the reality of their God and the relevance of their gospel when they are confronted with the apparently godless world of secular everyday life.

In the recent controversies about gay relationships and gay ordinations that have divided Christians and intrigued the media, I was more than a little disconcerted to discover that it had never occurred to many intelligent people who are regular worshippers in our churches, that the God whom they worship there might have a mind and a will that could conceivably be quite different from the mind and will of the society in which they lived and whose convictions on this issue they largely shared. They seemed to be unaware that, as committed Christians, they had a responsibility to be diligent in discerning that will and, when discerned, to act upon it.

The American WWJD (What would Jesus do?) movement may often be naive and subjective in its approaches and conclusions, but at least it makes it clear that as Christians there is something and somebody beyond ourselves and the culture that has shaped us, to whom we are bound and answerable, because our calling is not to be ourselves by and for ourselves, but to find ourselves beyond ourselves in becoming like him. "Do not be conformed to this world, but be transformed by the renewing of your minds so that you may discern what is the will of God – what is good and acceptable and perfect" (Rom. 12:2). Such a verse reminds us that the principle that requires the image to relate to the original operates not just theologically in terms of recognition, but rather dynamically and existentially in terms of transformation. Our humanity has, like a mirror, to be turned toward and focused upon God's divinity in order to catch and hold an authentic reflection of it.

When that humanity is instead turned in and focused on itself, our relationship to God becomes private and marginal, so that he ceases to exercise any real lordship over our lives or our society. It is then easy to advance from the practical atheism that so regards him and take the final step to the full blown theoretical atheism that extends our anthropological imperialism to the realm of the divine. Our claim to have created our own lives and our own world is easily extended to our religious experience, and we are invited to see the god it relates to as the work of our minds and the creation of our imaginations.

In Dr. Feuerbach's surgery

The first person to issue that invitation in this particular form was Ludwig Feuerbach (1804–72), who started life as a theological student but soon became the father of what has proved to be a highly influential brand of humanistic atheism. In his famous book *The Essence of Christianity* (1841) he tells us that "Anthropology is the essence of theology," that when we think we are talking about God, we are, in fact, just talking about ourselves. As autonomous human beings we have ideas about what it is to be spiritual, to be rational, to be powerful, to be good. We cannot bear to think that these ideas have no existence outside our own minds; we want and need them to characterize that ultimate reality that shapes our destiny here and hereafter. Just as a film projector throws images on to a blank screen, we project these ideas on to that ultimate reality and call them God.

But, just as there is nothing on the cinema screen except what the projector puts there, so there is no God in the heavens except the one that we have put there. The God that we imagine we can know and worship has no reality beyond our need and our wish that created him. As Hans Küng puts it, "The knowledge of God then is a gigantic floodlight. God appears as a projected, hypostatised reflection of man, behind which nothing exists in reality. The divine is the universally human projected into the hereafter. What are the attributes of the divine nature, love, wisdom, justice … ? In reality these are the attributes of man, of the human species. *Homo homini deus est,* man is god for man; here lies the whole mystery of religion" (Küng, 1980, p. 200).

Feuerbach's challenge to his contemporaries was that they should cease to be dependent upon and dominated by a god who was a man-made illusion and could do nothing for them, and should take the present and the future of themselves and their world into their own hands. Divine demise was good news because it opened the door wide to human advance; our salvation was no longer a gift to be prayed for from another, but a task to be accomplished for ourselves. Such a message found a ready response in the world of emancipated human optimism in which it was proclaimed, although Feuerbach's confident prophecy that as a result of his unmasking of the unreality of religion, it would in all its forms wither and die has hardly been fulfilled.

Political atheism

Feuerbach won influential disciples. Karl Marx started where Feuerbach ended and developed his basic insight in social and economic terms. His famous dismissal of religion as the opium of the people claims that its significance is to be understood in terms of the class struggle. Religion was the device by which capitalist property owners kept the masses in subjection, promising that submission in this life would be rewarded in the life to come. At the same time it was the tranquillizing drug by which the uncared-for masses comforted themselves with the hope that if there was no justice for them now, there was a righteous God who would ensure that there was justice in heaven. The oppressed, in their need and for their comfort, are compelled to invent a fantasy god who will save them from the bonds from which they have no power to save themselves. Marx was against this sort of religion for the very same reasons that all sensible people would be against any kind of opiate drug. By fostering theological illusions, it isolated people from their real situation and disabled them from recognizing and employing the remedy by which they could deal with their oppression – which was, of course, for Marx the proletarian revolution that would usher in the classless society in which there would be no need for religion because the conditions that created that need had been removed.

In Soviet Russia, where the Marxist philosophy was put to the test, religion proved more resilient and harder to eradicate than expected and has, indeed, outlasted its Marxist oppressors, while the classless society signally failed to appear, so that the question of just who was in touch with reality and who was promoting illusion remains much more open than Marx allowed.

Psychological atheism

Feuerbach's most influential disciple has, however, proved to be not Karl Marx, who applied his basic insights politically, but Sigmund Freud, who applied the same insights psychologically. Freud's work has changed human self-understanding more radically than almost anyone else in recent centuries, both by his exposure of the range and influence of the submerged world of the unconscious and by his understanding of our sexuality as something that permeates and affects our whole being in all its aspects. Freud also was an atheist who had studied in the school of Feuerbach. His attitude to religion is already apparent in an article he published in 1910.

> Psychoanalysis has made us familiar with the intimate connection between the father-complex and belief in God; it has shown us that a personal God is, psychologically, nothing other than an exalted father, and it brings us evidence every day of how young people lose their religious beliefs as soon as their father's authority breaks down. Thus we recognise that the roots of the need for religion are in the parental complex.
>
> (Freud, 1910, quoted in Küng, 1980, p. 281)

These ideas were systematically developed in his main critical work on religion published in 1927 and entitled significantly *The Future of an Illusion*. Religious ideas are not "precipitates of experiences or end-results of our thinking," but "illusions, fulfilments of the oldest, strongest and most urgent wishes of mankind." They arise from our never wholly overcome infantile awareness of helplessness and dependence on someone who is stronger than we are, who is to be feared because he holds our destiny in his hands, but for the same reason is to be placated so that we can be sure of his vindicating and life-giving protection. Out of the Oedipus complex in which the infant fears his father and yet longs for his love, all the gods are born.

For people caught in the illusions of religion, Freud's prescription is what he calls "education for reality." Hans Küng summarizes this as follows:

> Both for the individual human being and for mankind as a whole, religion is a pubertal, transitional phase of human development. Neither as an individual nor as a species can man remain a child for ever. He must grow up; he must master reality with his own resources and with the aid of

science and at the same time learn to resign himself to the inescapable necessities of fate. To leave heaven to the angels and the sparrows ... abandon expectations of a hereafter and concentrate all the resources thus released on earthly life – that is the task of the mature adult human being.

(Küng, 1980, pp. 285–86)

Optimistic autonomy

We have made the gods to meet our needs, but the gods we have made have failed us and we need to be liberated from the illusions of religion that have gathered round them. But we who have made them can be taught to unmake them; like Adam and Eve in Eden, we can become our own gods, the independent arbiters of what is good and what is evil for us, whose destiny is in our own hands. The humanistic atheism, thus sponsored by thinkers like Feuerbach, Marx, and Freud, looked, in the nineteenth century in which it was propounded, like the final victory of genuine human autonomy over unreal divine domination to be hailed with confidence and hope.

Nowadays, however, after the sobering experience of the actual exercise of human autonomy in the twentieth century, we are left asking not how we may be liberated from the gods, but how we may be liberated from ourselves now that the gods are gone. If our hope in them was illusion, our hope in ourselves has not served us any better; in the West at least, where the influences we have been describing have predominated for so long, we live in societies in which modern optimism and self-confidence are giving way to post-modern skepticism and despair. This is the point to which we have been led by the mindset to which our three protagonists gave classic expression and the question for the Christian community is how we should respond to it.

Toward a Christian response

The first answer is that we should not be mesmerized by it. The case for humanistic atheism is not as impregnable as it might at first sight seem. The godlessness it has recommended has not proved any more salvific than the religion it has deconstructed, leaving the suspicion that the confidence in human autonomy that was its basis might itself be a product of the very same process of wish fulfilment on which it relied for its dismissal of religion The same Freudian sauce that was designed to cook the theistic goose may also give a good grilling to the atheist gander! The declaration of independence that claims that we have it in us to be our own saviors without the gods, might itself have its roots in an adolescent rebellion against parental authority projected if not into the heavens, all over the earth.

Christians also have to ask whether the religion that the atheists criticized was, in fact, a credible description of the faith that we profess. The answer to that question is highly ambiguous, as we will see, but it is perfectly proper to confront Karl Marx with the Old Testament prophets with their denunciations of oppression and demands for social reform that are not entirely unlike his own and ask how the God of the Magnificat who "has brought down the powerful from their thrones and lifted up the lowly, who has filled the hungry with good things and sent the rich away empty" (Luke 2:52–53) – how such a God can be the source of the opiate religion he denounces.

What could he make of the Liberation theology of the twentieth century, which roots its revolutionary agenda and its preferential option for the poor precisely in the Judeo-Christian tradition that Marx dismisses? Could it be that at the heart of the religious relationship there is not merely a god we have made in our own image, but an authentic Other who presses in upon us with a purpose and agenda of his own that confronts us and seeks to transform us in a way that, far from making him like us, seeks instead to make us like him?

We have, of course, to put the same searching questions to the bourgeois churches that have often connived with and supported the domination of the rich and the oppression of the poor, in a way that betrays their biblical vocation, and that gives the Marxist dismissal of them its credibility and prophetic power, that has indeed prodded them, in the second half of the twentieth century to rediscover the social implications of their own gospel.

Learning from Feuerbach

Second, if we are not to be mesmerized by the atheist critique, we need also to let ourselves be instructed by it. As orthodox a theologian as Karl Barth can affirm that the projection of the human on to the divine was an all too accurate description of what was going on in the German theology of his own day in which the basis for the knowledge of God was anthropological rather than theological, deriving from human experience rather than divine revelation, our religious insights projected on to God rather than God's being and nature projected down to us (Barth, 1959, pp. 355–61). Feuerbach was, in fact, offering an accurate description of what was going on in much of the Christian theology that was contemporary with him, and, Barth would add, in a great deal of religious thought and practice inside and outside the Christian church long before Feuerbach and long after him as well.

To take a contemporary example, the attack of feminist theologians on the Christian designation of God as Father has often been based on the assumption that, when we so name God, we are, in fact, projecting into the heavens our experience of human fatherhood with all the implications of male domination and paternalistic control that it carries. The center of their argument is not about what Jesus meant when he named God as his Father and invited us to pray to him as such, but rather on what we mean by fatherhood and what the implications are when we project that notion of fatherhood on to God.

Robert W. Jenson exposes the projectionist basis of this kind of thinking as follows:

> ... addressing God as "Father" is said to oppress and exclude women because of the act of metaphorical projection in which it allegedly occurs. All language, it is said, is inadequate to specify God: therefore all language about God must be metaphorical. It is not so much said as supposed without question that *we* coin the metaphors. It is further said that the metaphors which a community then actually comes to use for God project on to eternity the structure of values operative in that community ... Thus "patriarchal" communities will use "Father", "King" and similarly gendered metaphors to their God or gods. Further it is said that a religion constituted by male metaphors both reveals the patriarchal structure of the community whose religion it is and enforces and legitimises that structure.
>
> (Jensen quoted in Kimel, 1992, p. 102)

It is clear that, where that kind of thinking predominates, Feuerbach is alive and well. When we say we are talking about God, we are, in fact, talking about ourselves and the personal and community values that predominate among us; the fatherhood of this god is in the image of the human fatherhood we have either affirmed or rejected; this is a god of our own devising, decked out in the metaphorical garments we have chosen for him.

We will soon go on to contrast this kind of approach in which we project ourselves upward on to God with the authentically Christian approach in which God in Christ projects himself downward to reveal himself to us. But before we abandon Feuerbach and his friends, we can take Barth's advice and learn from them. A great deal of religion in and beyond the Christian tradition can be all too accurately described as a process of self-projection, of constructing a god out of our own ideas and experiences. That process can be seen to be at work in the rarefied realm of the philosophical, in the communal level of the political, and on the intimate level of the pastoral.

Learning from Feuerbach – philosophical projections

At the philosophical level, human existence is characterized by, on the one hand, a great affirmation of and longing for life in all its fullness and, on the other hand, by an awareness of the brief, limited, and imperfect nature of the life we actually live. So it is easy and natural to think of God as the ultimate and perfect expression of the life we long for, which is the basis of the good things in the life we actually enjoy and that he is, hopefully, the champion and defender of all these good things against all that would threaten and destroy them, the guarantee and promise of the completion of that life in a better life to come.

On that basis we can construct our idea of a god who would embody that unlimited life, whose value we affirm, and whose completion we long for. We are finite and bounded by space, time, and powerlessness, but he is above these limitations and so is infinite, eternal in relation to time, and omnipresent in relation to space. We know only a little, but he is omniscient and knows everything; we are the victims of suffering and ultimately of death, but he is impassable – and so incapable of suffering – and immortal – and so exempt from dying. Such a god is ideal, in both senses of that word; he is perfect in his being and his powers, but that being is defined by our ideas that reflect our appreciation of the life we have and our longing to overcome all that threatens and limits it.

The god who is decked out in all these abstract adjectives beginning with "im" and "omni" is the god who features in much of what is called natural theology, that is, theology that has its basis in an awareness of the divine that is allegedly native and natural to human beings as such and does not depend on any source of special historical revelation. That kind of natural theology has played a highly significant if also highly ambiguous role in much Christian thinking.

The role of the god of the "ims" and the "omnis" has been ambiguous because it sits, to put it mildly, in considerable tension with the revealed Christian understanding of the God who became incarnate in Christ, was born as a baby, lived a human life in Galilee, and suffered and died on Calvary. How can the infinite become finite? How can the omnipresent get into a cradle? How can the one who knows everything live within the limitations of the knowledge of a first-century

Jew in Palestine? Above all, how can the one who is incapable of suffering and death suffer so terribly on Good Friday and lie in the garden tomb all Saturday? Theologians have struggled with such questions with varying degrees of success down the centuries, but Christians who are committed to the belief that the real God, indeed the only God there is, is the God who has revealed himself in Christ's saving death and resurrection, may be left with the suspicion that the god of natural theology, in so far as he stands in contrast with and, indeed, in contradiction to the God and Father of our Lord Jesus Christ, is a god of our own constructing, the idealization and projection of our own thoughts and wishes and desires, the very process that Feuerbach and Freud described.

Whether of course all natural theology can be accounted for in this way and written off as human self-projection that involves no authentic contact with objective reality is quite another question, to which we will offer an answer before this chapter is finished. The fact that for the validation and completion of our lives we want the god of the "ims" and the "omnis" says nothing at all, as Freud himself conceded, about whether and how far our wishes are fulfilled in objective reality, and such a God really exists. It does, however, create a suspicion that one powerful factor that shapes and controls our affirmation of such a god is our need and our desire to think that he exists, just as Feuerbach claimed. Whether, as he also claimed, it is the only factor, remains to be explored.

Learning from Marx – political projections

The atheistic dismissal of religion as projection is more obviously applicable on the political level. Ever since

Aaron set up the golden calf at the foot of Mount Sinai where Moses was communing with the living God, human societies have fashioned and propagated religions that were designed to reinforce with divine sanctions the values that predominated in that society and invoke divine protection against all that threatened them. Roman emperors called themselves sons of God because their predecessors and presumably all that they stood for had become divine. Adolph Hitler often invoked "the Almighty", who was in fact the apotheosis of the ruthless and tyrannical power that he himself exercised. In a less extreme but still analogous way, nineteenth-century missionaries found it hard to distinguish between the God of the gospel and the god of the British Empire. For such as David Livingstone, the spread of Christianity and what he called the spread of civilization were part and parcel of the same God-given vocation; in our own day the inauguration of the kingdom of God is easily confused with the inauguration of American capitalist democracy. Dominating powers of all kinds have not been content to rule on earth; they have aspired to rule in heaven also, to claim that their gods were like themselves and approved of what they were doing; all of which is grist to Feuerbach's mill.

Learning from Freud – personal projections

The processes of projection operate personally as well as philosophically and politically. If you talk to people about the fatherhood of God, the way they hear what you are saying will be greatly influenced by the kind of relationships they have had with their own human fathers. If their fathers have spoilt and cosseted them with overindulgence, they will expect the same of God; if their father's love has been conditional upon their achievements, they will worry about whether they have done enough for God to love them; if their fathers have been indifferent or remote, the nearness and the attentiveness of God will be ideas hard to cope with; if their fathers have been threatening or even abusive, the idea of a divine paternity will be a source of revulsion and fear. God's fatherhood is construed in terms of human fatherhood. In contrast, something quite different can be seen to be happening when Paul says that "I bow my knees before the Father, from whom all fatherhood (*pasa patria*) in heaven and on earth takes its name" (Eph. 3:14). Here God's fatherhood is not conformed to ours, but rather ours to his – we are in touch with a process of projection that is moving in exactly the opposite direction, not from us to God, but from God to us.

One is reminded at this point of the remark of the Roman Catholic writer, George Tyrrell, about the nineteenth-century writers of lives of Jesus, like Strauss and those who succeeded him; they looked down the well of history but what they saw at the bottom was simply a reflection of their own faces. We easily see in the gospels what is congenial to us and too easily screen out what we do not want to acknowledge. For example, is the Jesus of the gospels credibly the champion of family values he is nowadays often made out to be? Or is it really legitimate to affirm all that Jesus says about God's love for sinners and to play down the fact that he still judges them as sinners and calls for their repentance? My image of God can be skewed and distorted not only by my positive priorities but also by the deafness to the word I do not want to hear and the blindness to the truth I do not want to see, both of which I have contracted from the cultural context in which I live.

Theologians and preachers, as well as politicians, know how to spin. In short, I am in danger of making God as I want him to be whenever I take it for granted that what matters to me matters also and as much to him, or that what is not important to me is equally unimportant to him. It is a game that, partly consciously and partly unconsciously, we are all well skilled at playing.

On all these levels, it is good to sit, even if only for a moment, in the philosophical schoolroom of Feuerbach, the political workshop of Marx, and the psychological seminar of Freud; the corrosive acid of their skeptical atheism, in its three distinct forms, can eat away at much false religion, even if at the same time it threatens the true.

Modern atheism and biblical prophecy

The third thing to be said about the deconstruction of false religion undertaken by our three modern champions is that it is as not as new as it looks: it was practiced by the biblical writers in both the Old Testament and the New in relation to the false religion that they also sought to expose and destroy. The purpose of the biblical prophets was to attack what they saw as idolatry along the same lines as Feuerbach and his atheistic friends and to expose it as the human invention and the impotent illusion that they knew it to be.

The polemic that Isaiah and his fellow prophets launched against much of the religion that surrounded and threatened pre-exilic Israel bears a considerable resemblance to the attacks of the projectionist atheists on the religion of nineteenth-century Europe.

Whose Image?

That polemic is summed up by a psalmist, denouncing the idolatrous religion that was threatening to infect and corrupt the faith of his people.

> Their idols are silver and gold, the work of human hands. They have mouths, but do not speak, eyes but do not see, noses but do not smell. They have hands but do not feel, feet but do not walk; they make no sound in their throats. Those who make them are like them; so are all who trust in them.
> (Ps. 115:4–8)

To make gods in the image of men is the essence of all idolatry, whether the resultant idols are the physical artifacts of our hands or the cerebral projections of our minds, and the result of both is an impotent religion that imprisons us in its illusions and distracts and distances us from the genuine sources of our liberation. On that negative critique both Feuerbach and Isaiah could agree.

It is, however, one thing to expose the illusion but quite another to discern the reality for whose sake it is swept away. For the nineteenth-century atheists, all religion is false religion; for them and for the secular society that they both reflected and helped to create, the only salvific reality is human reality with all its powers and purposes so that the only answers to the human dilemma are those which we ourselves can provide.

For the psalmist and those he represents, the situation is quite different. The verse before the ones just quoted runs, "Our God is in the heavens, he does whatever he pleases" (Ps. 115:3). The illusory impotent gods of our own creating are rejected in the name of the true God who, far from being the helpless prisoner of our imaginings, is "in heaven", and has a being and a reality that is distinct from ours, so that what he is in himself is something we cannot know unless he chooses to tell us.

Far from depending on what we might think about him, he stands in judgement on all our thinking because "my thoughts are not your thoughts nor are my ways your ways, says Yahweh. For as the heavens are higher than the earth, so are my ways higher than your ways and my thoughts than your thoughts" (Isa. 55:8, 9).

This is a God who "does whatever he pleases," who does not have an illusory existence in the shadowy world of projected ideas, but has a will and a purpose that is his own and a power to exercise them in a way that stands over against our will and our purpose and makes us aware of a living personal and active reality that is quite different from our own.

The divine realm on this showing is not an empty screen at the back of our minds passive to our projections; it is the occupied centre of an ultimate reality that is the creative centre of all other realities including our own. This is a God who may have chosen to make us in his image but will certainly reject all our attempts to make him in ours, simply because, quite apart from us and what we think we can make of him, he is who he is. As God said to Moses, asking for his name at the burning bush, "I am who I am" (Exod. 3:14). In order to know what that image is, we have not to search our own ideas of infinity, eternity and divinity, but to know the original of that image in order then to know what it is in our being, including our thinking, that is an authentic reflection of his.

The poet R. S. Thomas writes of a God who says:

I am the bush burning
at the center of
your existence; you must put
your knowledge off and come
to me with your mind
bare.[1]

From projection to revelation

In other words, we have to turn from the world of projection, where we are dealing with the truth or falsity of ideas, to the world of revelation, where we are dealing with the personal interactions of a living God with his people. Probably the better translation of God's self-designation that we have just quoted from Exodus 3:14 is "I will be what I will be." That implies both a reticence and a promise. God is not an object available of human investigation who can be intruded upon by human speculation; he is Lord both of his life and ours, and of our knowledge of him. If he is going to be known, it will be in a way of his own choosing and by a process of his own controlling. But the future tense implies a promise that in the history of exodus, wilderness, and possession and all that lies beyond, at the start of which Moses stands, God will reveal his name and, in his historical interaction with us, by what he does and says, tell us who he is.

This Old Testament perspective continues and culminates in the New, where God's self-initiated revelation reaches its climax in his own coming in his own Son. "No one has ever seen God. It is God the only Son who is close to the Father's heart, who has made him known" (John 1:18). This is echoed in Jesus's prayer in Matthew.

> I thank you, Father, Lord of heaven and earth that you have hidden these things from the wise and the intelligent and have revealed them to infants: yes, Father, for such was your gracious will. All things have been handed over to me by my Father; and no one knows the Son except the Father and no one knows the Father except the Son and anyone to whom the Son chooses to reveal him.
>
> (Matt. 11:25–27)

These two very different witnesses to the New Testament gospel nevertheless both emphasize God's continued control over his own self-revelation; his rejection of the arrogant human attempts of the wise and the intelligent to master his mystery; that the knowledge of God becomes normatively available when people are enabled to relate to the historical interaction of the heavenly Father and the incarnate Son.

Two contrary projections

All this is in the starkest contrast to the project of Feuerbach. For modern atheism, and indeed the kind of theology that follows its methodological lead, any claim to a knowledge of God is to be understood in terms of an upward projection from us to him; for biblical revelation it is to be understood in terms of a downward projection from him to us. For one we are the reality which he images; for the other he is the reality that we imagine.

As we have already seen, there is no doubt that the process of upward projection is a powerful factor in the genesis of religious ideas. As Calvin put it, the religious imagination is a very productive *factorium idolum*, churning out fresh idols, tailor made for every time and culture. The crucial question is whether God's downward self-projection that we call revelation is also a formative and potentially an even more powerful factor in all, some, or any of our claims to authentic knowledge of and real relationship with God. Is the subjective thrust that drives us to fabricate the gods we want being resisted and challenged by a counter thrust in the opposite direction in which God seeks to rescue us from our addiction to illusory idols and relate us again to his own reality, which is the source from which we come and the hope of salvation to which we are called? Is the God who is the covenant Lord of Israel's history and who has acted decisively and savingly in Jesus Christ in a way that opens up that covenant history to the whole world just another and more magnificent projection of the benevolent and almighty father figure we all need and long for, as Freud alleges? Or, alternatively, do we really encounter in him an authentic Other, who breaks in upon the myth of our human self-containedness and opens us up to the reality that can at last make sense of who we are and where we are going?

That is the decisive question that any meaningful encounter with the claims of the Christian revelation poses, not usually in the abstract way in which we have stated it, but in a much more concrete and personal context, in which, in a rich diversity of ways, we are asked whether we are prepared to commit ourselves to the reality of the God who presents himself to us in Jesus Christ so that we come under a persuasive compulsion to affirm the truth of what he is to us and does for us so that all our thinking depends upon it.

As Bishop Ian Ramsey used to say, there come these moments when the bell rings and the penny drops and we know that what we are affirming is not our own invention but that which is given to us by another than ourselves, indeed by God. Or as Paul puts it to the Corinthians, "What no eye has seen nor ear heard, nor the human heart conceived, what God has prepared for those who love him, these things God has revealed to us through the Spirit, for the Spirit searches everything, even the deep things of God" (2 Cor. 2:9, 10).

God remains in charge of his revelation, not just in the giving of it in Christ, but in the receiving of it in the Spirit, who does not force it upon us from outside, but opens our eyes so that we see it for ourselves, willingly embrace it, and freely commit ourselves to it. To make such a commitment is indeed a conversion, a whole reorientation of our life so that the center of it lies not any more in ourselves but on the one who has revealed himself to us. Furthermore, it is a conversion that has to be affirmed, confirmed, and deepened many times as we encounter, both intellectually and existentially, alternative philosophies and situations of suffering and meaninglessness that again and again whisper, often very convincingly, in our ears that the thing we have built our lives on is, indeed, a man-made illusion, however magnificent, and that Feuerbach was right after all.

But in the face of such doubt there is a stubbornness about the gospel and of the God who as the Father gives it, as the Son incarnates it and as the Spirit engenders our commitment to it. It has a power to hold us to itself when so many other forces around us and within us are pulling us away from it, so that when Jesus asks us as he asked his first disciples, puzzled and confused in their day as we often are in ours, "Do you also wish to go away?" the only answer that we can give is, "Lord, to whom can we go? You have the words of eternal life" (John 6:68).

Post-modern skepticism

In our own day the deconstructing skepticism that Feuerbach applied to religion has in much post-modern thinking been extended to all claims to know the truth about any reality that is objective to us. Not just the gods but the world and our own selves are seen as our own constructions, and all claims to truth can be dismissed as having their source in the same process of subjective projection which is the first cousin to the nineteenth century atheistic critique of religion.

Against such a background the Christian claim to have made contact with the person who incorporates in himself the ultimate truth not just about religion but about the whole of reality seems to be totally naive, so that those who uphold it are more likely to be mocked than crucified.

The contemporary obsession with that kind of skepticism can easily conceal from us that its base is not unassailable insights but an alternative commitment of faith. Hans Küng has put it this way in regard to the nineteenth-century atheist:

> All proofs or arguments of the eminent atheists are certainly adequate to raise doubts about the existence of God but not to make God's non-existence unquestionable. ... Atheism too lives by an indemonstrable faith; whether it is faith in human nature (Feuerbach), or faith in the future socialist society (Marx) or faith in rational science (Freud). The question then can be asked of any form of atheism whether it is not itself an understandable projection of man (Feuerbach), a consolation serving vested interests (Marx) or an infantile illusion (Freud).
>
> (Küng, 1987, p. 229–30)

In other words, atheist faith as well as Christian faith faces its challenges. The post-modern situation that has rejected the possibility of revelation has also rejected the humanistic optimism of Feuerbach and Freud and the political utopianism of Marx as themselves illusions and has offered no new faith to take their place. Their cynicism about religious knowledge has extended its range and now affects the alternatives to religion that they so confidently offered. The beginning of the twenty-first century does not have much faith or hope left in human goodness, political utopianism, or psychiatric salvation and, indeed, in its more sophisticated post-modern expressions, has little faith that there is any possibility of knowing any universally binding truth about objective reality. When a society affirms no common vision of a reality beyond itself and no responsibility to values that are given to it rather than created by it, that society fragments and disintegrates; the evidence multiplies that this is exactly what is happening to our own society in our own day.

Not makers but mirrors

If the idols of our own making that reflect our own image are toppling all around us, it might be time to ask, What vision comes into focus when we see ourselves not as the masters but rather the mirrors of an ultimate reality on which we depend? Is there any word from outside ourselves that could help us to see ourselves as we really are and enable us to become what we were meant to be?

The scriptural doctrine of the image of God offers such an alternative anthropology. It is a phrase that is often thrown about loosely and out of context, but it is the purpose of this book to explore in a quite specific way how it relates to its whole biblical context as part of the revelation of the God who reveals himself in Israel and in Christ. Our ability to discern the image depends on our access to the original; to recognize ourselves as God's image, we have to be in touch with the God that we are reflecting.

The actuality of revelation

All of which brings us back to the question about the actuality and the possibility of such a revelation, something that Feuerbach and his friends ruled out of court *a priori* almost without discussion and for which the kind of post-modern thinking we have been describing has even less room. If there is not a reliable disclosure of anything, there is certainly going to be no place for a reliable disclosure of a living God.

One of Karl Barth's central theological axioms was that when we are talking of God, it is the actuality that determines the possibility and not the other way round. We do not limit our openness to what God has done by prior notions of our own about what he could do; rather, our basis for recognizing what he can do is what he has already done – a principle with massive implications that we cannot explore now.

Accordingly, we do not approach the question of revelation by asking whether this or that theory of knowledge, whether modern or post-modern, allows for its possibility, but by asking whether, where, and how God has actually made himself known, where he has acted and spoken in ways that have opened our eyes and our minds to both his reality, his nature and his purposes toward us.

To that question Christians give what is fundamentally a Trinitarian answer: that God has decisively revealed himself through his incarnate Son and has enabled us to receive that revelation through the work of his Spirit. The only reason for believing that is possible is that it has actually happened and that we have been made aware by God himself that it has actually happened. It is, in other words, a matter of testimony and not a matter of proof; it is an encounter with a personal reality rather than a theory about an impersonal absolute; it is a revelational gift rather than an intellectual achievement. "Flesh and blood have not revealed this to you, but my Father who is in heaven" (Matt. 16:17). It initiates and requires intellectual explication and understanding, the *fides*, the trust, is prior to the *intellectus*, the understanding, as the tradition of Augustine and Anselm would have it. *Credo ut intelligam*, I believe so that then I may go on to understand what it is I believe and how it interacts with and affects everything else that I also know.

That means on the one hand that no one can be argued into Christian faith, but equally on the other hand it means that Christians are not allowed to retreat into a rather smug and private ghetto, congratulating themselves that they have seen what others cannot see. Having claimed the actuality of revelation, we have to establish and indeed defend its possibility. In other words, we have to face the hard questions that arise when we affirm that the Triune God is at the center of reality; we have to cope with the objections of all who deny that possibility and show that on Christian presuppositions we can give an account of the world and of our knowledge of it that is internally coherent and, while never anything like complete, is at least as plausible and can give as comprehensive an account of human experience as its humanistic and atheistic alternatives.

In terms of anthropology, we can see ourselves as the image of God only when we know the God that we image, but in the light of that knowledge we have to show that we can give an account of human life that resonates realistically with what we know about ourselves and offers us perspectives on and hopes for ourselves that are not otherwise available. It is to that task on that basis that this book seeks to make a contribution. When we know the triune God, what does that tell us about what matters most about ourselves?

The world that answers back

In the next chapter we will go on to explore the biblical basis for that kind of anthropology. Before we do, it will be helpful to draw together some more general conclusions that will underpin all that follows. Affirming, therefore, as a matter of Christian testimony, our faith in the God who reveals himself in his Son and by his Spirit and incorporating the salutary lessons that we have leaned from Feuerbach and company, we can claim that, not only in our knowledge of God but in our knowledge of the world as well, there is operating a double process of projection.

A specific example will help to make the point clear: during a stay in Melbourne, we were taken on a visit to a Gallery of Victorian Art, in which the work of the artists of the Australian state of Victoria was exhibited in chronological sequence from the time of the first European settlements down to the present day. Looking at the earliest pictures, we noticed how the Australian landscape was presented in the distinctive colors and tones of the English countryside or sometimes even of the Swiss Alps. European eyes looking at antipodean scenes saw in them what they had been used to seeing, projected on to them what they had brought with them, and so were not able to see what was really there. But thirty or forty years later, all that began to change. Australian reality asserted itself against Pommie imperialism, as it has been doing ever since, and the pictures began to represent more faithfully the landscape of Victoria with its distinctive browns and eucalyptus greens.

The world around us has a toughness that will not let itself be endlessly pushed around and manipulated by our prejudices and preconceptions. It answers back and insists that we take account of it as it really is. It shrugs off what our minds project on to it and instead teaches us to adapt our thinking to its givenness.

It is this ability of reality to answer back and penetrate and reject the presuppositions that we foist upon it which modifies the premature and exaggerated cynicism of those who think that we can know only the world we have made and not the world as it is. To use Kantian language, the thing in itself can give a good account of itself and discriminate between the categories we bring to its understanding by disrupting the inappropriate and affirming the more appropriate among them.

In scientific enquiry, by the concepts we employ and the experiments we make, we set up projects that put the natural world to the test, but what counts in the end are not our questions but their answers; we have to adapt our concepts and modify our experiments to make them more and more adequate to the nature of the reality we encounter. We have to ask the world the right questions in order to receive the right answers. Our projections are the conceptual instruments that we use to probe reality, but we have constantly to devise better and more sophisticated instruments that will do greater justice to the world we are trying to know. Knowledge involves the encounter of the probing and projecting subject with the object of its investigation, but it is true knowledge, not when the object is conformed to the imaginative activity of the subject, but when the imaginative activity of the subject is conformed to the reality of the object, when our thinking becomes, in some sense, the image in which its originating object is more or less faithfully reflected.

The God who answers back

If all knowledge involves this double process of projection that we have been describing, this is because on a Christian showing, it is a world made by a God who himself answers back. This double process is deeply embedded in Paul's account of idolatrous religion in the first chapter of the Letter to the Romans. For Paul the positive root of all religion is the will of the Creator to make himself universally known through his creation. "For what can be known about God is plain to them, because God has shown it to them. Ever since the creation of the world his eternal power and divine nature, invisible though they are, have been understood and seen through the things that he has made" (Rom. 1:19, 20). The knowledge of God described here does not have its source in human argument or speculation, but rather, in God's self-revealing activity, "God has shown it to them." This is not a process of human discovery (natural theology) but rather a process of divine unveiling (general revelation). In a very real sense we can say that the Creator speaks through his creation, that the things that he has made image and reflect the one who made them. For Paul this revelation in nature is much less specific than God's special revelation to Old Testament Israel, to say nothing of his ultimate self-revelation in Christ. Nevertheless, against Feuerbach and his school, for Paul the root of religion is not our projection of ourselves upward on to God but rather his downward projection of himself through his creation to us; it is not created by us but rather given to us.

The contamination of religion

Paul also knows all about our self-projection upward on to God, although for him it is not the factor that creates religion but rather the factor that unmakes and spoils it.

> For though they knew God, they did not honor him as God or give thanks to him, but they became futile in their thinking and their senseless minds were darkened. Claiming to be wise they became fools; and they exchanged the glory of the immortal God for images resembling a mortal human being, or birds or four footed animals or reptiles ... They exchanged the truth about God for a lie and worshipped and served the creature rather than the Creator, who is blessed for ever. Amen.
> (Rom. 1:21–23, 25)

The religion that has its root in the gracious downward projection of God to us, is contaminated and distorted by our upward projection of ourselves and the world on to God – and that is the very heart of the idolatry that Paul is here denouncing. Religion as God gave it is his gracious self-unveiling, religion as the well nigh universal human phenomenon that we experience is what Paul calls a lie.

Notice "a lie," not a baseless fabrication; not, as the atheists would have it, the product of our corporate imaginings that has no counterpart in reality. On the contrary all lies gain their plausibility from the elements of faithfulness to reality that they incorporate, but their deceptiveness stems from the fact that the presentation of that reality is fatally distorted and warped by what we make of it, in a way that is analogous to but more profound than the distortions imposed by British artists on the Australian landscape.

These latter are the distortions of relatively superficial prejudices that quite soon yield to the reality presented to them; but the distortions of human religion go far deeper. Paul speaks of the "ungodliness and wickedness of those who by their wickedness suppress the truth" and of the wrath of God that that incurs (1:18). Human religion as experience reflects in a multitude of different ways a deep alienation of our mind and thinking from God's mind and thinking, that makes us want to be our own gods, the primal human temptation as described in Genesis 3; to become our own arbiters of what is true and false, what is good and what is evil, and which impels us to make our own gods in our own image and turn his revealed truth into our distorting projections.

What Paul is describing here is not so much the personal decisions of individuals, but rather the universal and corporate alienation and rebellion of the whole of humanity, into which individuals are born and by which they are shaped. All our religions, on this showing, give, in their different ways, evidence of our involvement in that rebellion and, at the same time, of our captivity to it and our consequent inability to rescue ourselves from it. As a race, we have chosen to make and to be our own gods; the wrath of the living God against us consists of his ratification of that choice. As C. S. Lewis used to put it, he says to us, "Your will be done." "And since they did not see fit to acknowledge God, God gave them up to a debased mind and to things that should not be done" (1:28).

Revelation that reconciles

But not for ever! We may well ask Paul on what basis he dares to reach an assessment of the human religion of his day that in its very different way is as devastating and negative as anything that Feuerbach produced. For an answer we may look to the verses that immediately precede the passage we have been looking at: "I am not ashamed of the gospel; it is the power of God for salvation to everyone who has faith" (Rom 1:16). What Paul is offering here is an assessment of the religious scene as it looks to someone who has been brought to faith in God's definitive self-revelation in the gospel of Christ.

To be rescued from the distorting influences of our own self-projection which ruin our relationship with God, he gives us not just revelation but reconciliation, so that we can be converted from the self-centeredness that projects ourselves upward to the God-centeredness that is enabled to receive what God projects downward. In Christ, God himself becomes the God-centered man that the rest of us have failed to be, the one who is undistortedly receptive to his Father and is able to convey his Father to us. "He that has seen me has seen the Father" (John 14:9). In the Holy Spirit our humanity is joined to Christ's humanity, his mind becomes our mind, the preoccupation with ourselves that distorts all life and especially religious life is exposed and we become progressively reoriented in mind to God and so more and more enabled to image his being in our being and his life in ours.

The clash between our upward projection of ourselves and God's downward projection of himself in Christ is never in this life completely resolved. Christian history gives ample evidence of how powerful people have sought to reshape the Christian gospel to incorporate their own ideas and further their own interests and – personally, politically, patriarchally – to make it the expression of whatever ideology is current at the time, rather than a prophetic challenge to it.

But just as Australia answers back rebukingly and transformingly to domineering British artistic misrepresentation, so God's Trinitarian self-revelation has the power to answer back to all our tendencies to traduce it; and because it has in Christ and the Spirit an ability to convert and transform, it has at the heart of it a promise of liberation from misrepresentation into progressive approximation to the truth.

This is the gospel of which Paul is not ashamed and it is in the light of that gospel that he offers his diagnosis of human religion in the passage we have been looking at. Human religion in all its forms is in different ways the expression of an idolatry that is parasitical upon a genuine revelation of God. As against the atheism that writes it all off as fantasy Paul recognizes, as at Athens, the activity of the same God that he has encountered in Christ, but at the same time a human self-projection that takes possession of that truth and remolds it in idolatrous ways.

In the light of Christ we cannot say that human religion, and indeed all human thinking about ultimate issues, has nothing in it, because in all sorts of ways it shows that it has God in it. At the same time, in the same light of Christ, we begin to see that it has too much of us in it; far from uniting us with God, it separates us from him, and in order to be rescued from that separation we need to be in constant and receptive relation to what God has done in Christ, so that he can image himself again in us and liberate us from our arrogant desires to image ourselves in him.

To make that specific, instead of imposing our experiences of fatherhood on God, we look at the kind of fatherhood that is revealed in God's relationship to Jesus and let ourselves be told that that is the kind of relationship he wants to have with us, his children, and that we are to reflect in our human relationships with one another, a relationship that has at its heart not patriarchal domination but liberating love.

Summary

In this chapter we have sought to identify in the most general way the processes that operate in human knowing and especially in our knowing of God. We have sat at the feet of the nineteenth-century projectionists and have learned much from them that echoes the scriptural attitude to religion. But we have, over against them, insisted that God is not a passive screen for the projection of our image, but has decisively imaged himself in a human life that has the power to transform other human lives so that they can begin to reflect him also. The great question is whether there is such a reconciling revelation of God or whether to claim that there is simply the rather more sophisticated product of the same old process of wish fulfilment.

To convince us of the reality of that revelation is the work of the Holy Spirit; what we can do is try to spell out, in the light of that conviction, what contribution revelation makes to our anthropology, our understanding of ourselves in relation to God and to others. How much of what we already know about ourselves does it confirm as God-given? How much does it expose as idolatry and sin? How much does it require and offer that our ambiguous way of being human should be transformed to that new way of being human that is incarnate in Christ? If God's revelation in Christ is true, then we should be able to see how it shows us the ultimate truth about ourselves. When we know the original, we will be able to recognize the image. If the original is phony, the image will be a shadow; if the original is glorious, the image will be bright.

To get our bearings on that, we now turn to the biblical story of the living God who has imaged himself in Christ.

2 Biblical Image

When we turn from the philosophical and apologetic issues of the last chapter to what the Bible has to say about the relationship between God and humanity, we find, in the very first chapters of the Old Testament, the source of all our thinking and talking about a divine original and a human imaging. Feuerbach, as much as the Christian orthodoxy he rejects, is dependent for the categories of his thinking on the central affirmation in Genesis 1 that God made men and women in his own image and likeness. He also starts from the claim that someone made someone else in his own image; for him we made God in ours, for Genesis God made us in his. The two are engaged in the same argument on the same terms, however contradictory their conclusions, and that fact leaves open the possibility of a continuing discussion between them.

It has often been noted that, although an approach to anthropology in terms of the *imago Dei* dominates the theological tradition, the biblical basis for it in the Old Testament is entirely confined to the book of Genesis, apart perhaps from Psalm 8, which, while not using image of God language, echoes Genesis 1 in its affirmation of human dignity "whom you have made a little lower than God and crowned them with glory and honor. You have given them dominion over the works of your hands; you have put all things under their feet" (Ps. 8:5, 6).

Gerhard von Rad comments on the small number of texts in which *imago Dei* occurs but insists that the surprising fact is that it should occur at all. "The central point in OT anthropology is that man is dust and ashes before God and that he cannot stand before his holiness. Thus the witness to man's divine likeness plays no predominant role in the OT. It stands as it were on the margin of the whole complex." Nevertheless he finds it "highly significant that OT faith adopted this theologoumenon in dealing with the mystery of man's origin" (von Rad on "eikon" in TDNT, 2:390).

That significance is greatly increased when we see that it is to the Genesis creation narratives that the New Testament writers turn when they are looking for categories that will help them to understand how God and man are related to one another in Jesus, who is presented as the new and ultimate Adam who has been made in the image of God. To see their full meaning we will have to set the Genesis stories in that Christological context.

But even looked at in their own immediate context, these stories raise many of the central questions that a biblical anthropology has to address and give some pointers to the answers as well. That is why they have been much more prominent in subsequent theology than in the biblical material itself. That is why, for example, Ray Anderson can say, "Certainly no attempt at theological anthropology can ignore the superscription which biblical revelation places over the archway leading to the arena of the human. 'Then God said, "Let us make man in our image, after our likeness."'... (Gen 1:26) This is the point of departure for all biblical understanding of the form of the human" (Anderson, 1982, p. 69).

Genesis – cosmology or anthropology

A statement like that shows that, although the narratives of Genesis 1–3 are no longer in mainline Christian thinking, seen in terms of a revealed cosmology in competition with modern science, they are still taken all the more seriously as foundational for anthropology, and, as we will see, it is on their basis that the leading theologians of the second half of the twentieth century – Barth, Brunner, Pannenberg, Moltmann – construct their various understandings of a humanity that has been made to image God but has fallen from that high destiny and needs to be recalled to it and reinstated in it in the incarnation death and resurrection of Christ.

It can indeed be credibly argued that, far from being demoted by the modern dismissal of its account of the world's beginning, the Genesis narratives have in fact been delivered from concerns that were irrelevant to their authors, so that when we have stopped arguing about seven days of creation over against eons of evolution, we are more able to hear what they actually want to say to us.

The theological genius who put Genesis together was not interested in the remote beginnings of everything. He employed the cosmological categories of his day to get his message across, but the message itself was about how the God of Israel is related to the humanity that he has brought into being, how in the light of that relationship they are called to relate to one another and to the world in which they are set, and how, having failed in their relationship to God, they have failed in the other two relationships as well.

The God he shows us is not a God who does our science for us, and, in the areas of cosmology and paleontology, pre-empts human enquiry by divine revelation, but rather a God who commissions and enables us to "fill the earth and subdue it and have dominion over the fish of the sea and the birds of the air and over every living thing that moves upon the earth" (1:28). Of the exercise of that dominion our science is a prominent and important part. But its exercise is a task for us rather than a given from God.

In other words Genesis is not about our origins but about our relationships, to God who made us, to the other people who are with us, and to the environment of the world around us; and its revelational and anthropological authority lies in its exposition of God's purposes for us in these relationships. That purpose, far from being impaired, is enhanced and exposed by its emancipation from functions and concerns that are alien to it. To quote Ray Anderson again,

> It [the concept of the *imago Dei*] is the foundational concept for understanding the biblical teaching concerning the nature and value of human personhood. In taking up the question of what the *imago Dei* means for human personhood, we address an issue that touches virtually every other tenet of Christian belief. The essential nature of human being is determinative for the understanding of the kind of redemption God has wrought for human beings through his Son, Jesus Christ, who is the true image of God.
>
> (Anderson, 1982, p. 70)

On the basis that what Genesis says about humanity is foundational for and affirmed by everything else that the Bible says on the same subject, we can go on to examine the Genesis stories more closely from this perspective.

The two creation stories

Before we do, we have to take account of the fact that we are dealing with two stories and not one. The first story sets humanity in the cosmic setting of the creation of heaven and earth and of all living things; the second sets Adam in the much more domestic context of the Garden of Eden and with much greater precision explores his relationships with God, with other living creatures and with Eve his wife. In setting them side by side the redactor of Genesis offers us not contradictory alternatives, but complementary accounts of what it means to be human and to live in the world with God and other living things.

It is the first more formal and cosmic story that gives us the image of God language that we are exploring. The second story, which does not use that language, can nevertheless be regarded as an indispensable exegetical commentary in which we are invited, as it were, to zoom in from the cosmic dimensions of the first story and watch in some detail the new-made human beings as they come to terms with where they are and the relationships into which they have been introduced by the very fact of being created in the image of God.

Humanity, crown of creation

In the first story, the creation of man and woman is clearly signaled to be the climax toward which the whole process is moving. Light, sun and moon, plants and animals are made by simple divine decree "And God said, let there be ... and there was." By contrast, the creation of humanity is preceded by divine deliberation and resolution, "Then God said, 'Let us make humankind in our image, according to our likeness'" (1:26).

The import of the divine plural in this verse – "Let *us*" – is much discussed in the theological tradition and we will return to it in due course. What we need to note now is that men and women are special because of the unique relationship with God that the words "image" and "likeness" indicate and that, because of that unique relationship to God, they have a unique place and function in creation as the verse goes on to indicate, "let them have dominion over the fish of the sea, and over the birds of the air, and over the cattle ... and over every creeping thing that creeps upon the earth" (Gen. 1:26).

This dominion over the creation is the consequence of the imaging of the Creator; we have authority over the creation in virtue of our likeness to the Creator so that it follows, as Genesis 3 makes clear, that if the relationship to the Creator goes wrong and our being and actions no longer reflect his being and actions, then our authority over the creation will also be distorted and what is wrong in our attitude to God will be manifested in what goes wrong in our dealings with one another and with the created order over which we were set.

The connection between being human and imaging God on the one hand and between imaging God and exercising authority over creation on the other is emphasized again when God's resolution in Genesis 1:26 is executed in God's creative act in verse 27: "So God created humankind in his image, in the image of God he created them; male and female he created them." To make sure that we will not miss it, the verse tells us not once but twice, and therefore three times in two verses, that being made human means being made in God's image, and in doing so uses the Hebrew verb *bara* three times to emphasize that in this making of humanity God's creative activity reaches its goal and its crown.

Male and female

To that he immediately adds the new statement that being human in the image of God involves being male and female, because being male and female in relationship to each other opens up the possibility of becoming the procreators of new human life, and in the conception and bearing of children imaging the creative activity of God. That is, in fact, how the narrative continues, "God blessed them, and God said to them, be fruitful and multiply" (Gen. 1:28). They are to become many, in order that they may express their likeness to God in the different ways in which they exercise the authority over his creation that, as the strategic center of his purposes for his world, he has resolved to give them. "Be fruitful and multiply, and fill the earth and subdue it and have dominion over the fish of the sea and over the birds of the air and over every living thing that moves upon the earth" (1:28).

Image, dominion, gender

So within these three verses (Gen. 1:26–28) we have three leading ideas that are repeated and interwoven: human imaging of God, human dominion over the earth, and gendered human relationships as the expression of the one and the possibility of the other. We therefore need to explore these three ideas first exegetically and only then theologically and into that exegetical enquiry of the first creation narrative we need to incorporate the supplementary insights offered by the second narrative. We can understand better what Adam was made to be when we see what he actually was in Eden.

The key concepts here are image and likeness and to these we now turn. The two Hebrew nouns in 1:26 are *selem* (image) and *demut* (likeness). Scholars have discussed the relationship between the two terms; the consensus seems to be that they are nearly equivalent in meaning but that the emphasis in *selem* is that the image *represents* that from which it derives, whereas the emphasis in *demut* is rather that the image *resembles* that from which it derives.

Image as representation

Selem was used of images of pagan gods and of kings who in their rule on earth represented and acted in the name and power of the god who ruled in heaven, without, of course, necessarily being like that god. Such pagan usages may explain the reticence of the Old Testament beyond Genesis 1 in using image language, since the second commandment (Exod. 20:4) explicitly forbade the making of any image of Yahweh, the God of Israel. Nevertheless, by his use of the word the Genesis writer is insisting that although we may not devise images of God, God is nevertheless free to create us as images of himself.

Furthermore, Genesis takes a word that expressed the divine right of kings to represent and image their gods and applies it not to special people but to human beings as such. Not the king, but Adam, Everyman, is created in the image of God and has the calling and the dignity of being his representative. Gordon Wenham makes the point, "Whereas Egyptian writers often spoke of kings as being in God's image, they never referred to other people in this way. It appears that the OT has democratised this old idea. It affirms that not just the king, but every man and woman bears God's image and is his representative on earth" (Wenham, *Genesis 1—15*, in Stanley J. Grenz. *The Social God and the Relational Self*. Westminster, John Knox: 2001, p. 201).

We might prefer to say that that the *imago* has been universalized rather than democratized, but Wenham has rightly drawn attention to the egalitarian note that has been sounded in this passage, so that it offers the first biblical basis for seeing the *imago* as the affirmation and guarantee of the inalienable dignity of every human person in virtue of their creation. That is confirmed in the covenant with Noah in Genesis 9:6, "Whoever sheds the blood of a human, by a human will that person's blood be shed; *for in his own image God made humankind*" (italics mine), and also in the only passage in the New Testament in which the image of God is used in this universal way, where James is drawing attention to the tongue's potential for sin, "With it we bless the Lord and Father, and with it we curse *those who are made in the likeness of God*" (Jas. 3:9, italics mine). Human beings are to be neither killed nor cursed because, solely in virtue of their humanity they bear the image of God.

Image and dominion

The notion of image as representation coheres well with the notion of men and women as God's representatives in exercising dominion over the rest of creation. God's rule over the world was seen in pagan societies as being represented and exercised by the king, but for Genesis that rule is exercised not exclusively by one man but by Adam, Everyman, the whole of humankind.

Human dominion over the non-human world is nevertheless not an adequate definition of what it means to be in the image of God. As Stanley Grenz reports "Although at one time some scholars linked the *imago Dei* directly with dominion over the creation, the near consensus in recent years has been that in the Genesis text, dominion is not to be viewed as an explanation of the *imago Dei* but as a consequence of creation in the divine image" (Grenz, 2001, p. 197).

Our likeness to God

This conclusion is strengthened when we look at the second term *demut* which is translated as "likeness." As von Rad explains, "The basic word *selem* (image) is more closely explained and made precise by *demut* (similarity) with the simple meaning that this image is to correspond to the original ... that it is to resemble it" (Gerhard von Rad. *Genesis*. London: SCM, 1970, p. 58). It is not just that humankind rules on earth in a way that represents the way that God rules in heaven, but that they do so on the basis of a real resemblance between the divine being that creates and the human being that is created. The massive difference between Creator and created remains, but within that difference there is a similarity which the one bestows on the other in that act of creation. Like the rest of the creation we owe our being entirely to the will and purpose of God, but our distinctness from the rest of creation is that God has mirrored himself in us, made us to be like himself so that he can relate to us and we to him in a way that is unique.

So much we can derive from the cryptic statements of Genesis 1:26, which, with the already noted exception of Psalm 8, are never referred to again, let alone explicated or expanded within the Old Testament. That is why the Christian theological tradition has had free scope to understand what it means to be in God's image in many different ways, some of which are more and some of which are less consonant with the biblical context from which they start. Genesis 1:26 is a tantalizing text begging for further exposition and the theologians have not been slow to oblige. As we will very soon see, that exposition is, in fact, offered in the writings of the New Testament which provide a controlling context to which all theological understandings of the *imago Dei* are answerable and in terms of which they can be assessed.

Continuing for the moment on the exegetical level, we can see how the notion of human dominion, which in the first creation story also remains undefined, is made more explicit in the second story in relation to Adam in Eden. "Then Yahweh took the man and put him in the garden to till it and to tend it" (2:15) on which von Rad comments, "Work was man's sober destiny even in his original state. That man was transferred to the garden to guard it indicates that he was called to a state of service and had to prove himself in a realm that was not his own possession" (von Rad 1972, p. 80).

The prime duty of Adam in relation to the rest of creation is to guard, tend, and develop the world that God has created, so that his action in fostering it reflects God's attitude in making it. Only in the next verse is Adam given permission to "freely eat of every tree of the garden" (2:16). The command to tend has priority over the command to take; Adam's deployment of the rest of creation to meet his own basic needs is not to become exploitative and destructive. The creation belongs to God and the human vocation within is to respect its integrity and the purpose of its Creator. Human stewardship of creation has to image God's affirmation and care for what he has made.

When, however, the narrative goes on to describe Adam's naming of the animals, the creative and fulfilling aspect of his vocation is made more explicit. "The man gave names to all cattle and to the birds of the air, and to every animal of the field" (2:20). Until he does that, the creation is unordered and disorganized. As Jolles puts it, "man attacks the confusion of the world; by probing, restricting and combining he brings together what belongs together. That which lies piled up in the confusion of the world does not at the start possess its own form; but rather what is here distinguished with discrimination receives its own form only as it comes together in the analysis" (Jolles *Einfache Formen* quoted in von Rad pp. 82–83).

Whatever that last sentence may mean, the general point is clear: Adam with his naming, that is, with his language which distinguishes and so identifies the creatures that God has made, is the means by which the intelligibility of the creation can be affirmed and its limitless potentialities that are "piled up in confusion" can be recognized and realized. It is by human language, knowledge and consequent action that the creation can become what God designed it to be. The perfecting and the completing of the creation does not come about apart from human beings whose speaking, knowing and doing are expressions of the fact that they are in the image of God. In other words, Eden without Adam is and will remain a potential paradise; whether or not it becomes a perfected paradise depends on what Adam and his children do with it.

One is reminded of the pious ladies visiting a beautiful garden, being overheard by the head gardener to exclaim at the wonder of a God who had made it all so lovely and muttering under his breath, "You should have seen what it was like when he had it all to himself." That gardener was a good theologian reflecting exactly what we find in Genesis and affirmed in Romans.

> For the creation waits with eager longing for the revealing of the children of God; for the creation was subjected to futility, not of its own will but by the will of the one who subjected it, in hope that the creation itself will be set free from its bondage to decay and will obtain the freedom of the glory of the children of God.
>
> (Rom. 8: 19–21)

Such a verse assumes a New Testament understanding of sin and redemption, to which we will have to return, but its basic point is that without human intervention or with the wrong kind of human intervention the rest of creation remains in unfulfilled futility. What the garden becomes depends on what the gardener does with it and whether, in what he does, he shows himself to be a mirror of God, reflecting the likeness of his Maker.

Adam and Eve

The explication of the human vocation in creation has shown how close its connection with being in the image of God is. Nevertheless, as the second creation story makes clear, human life is not itself fulfilled in that vocation to the non-human creation. The creation will find its fulfilment in Adam but Adam will not find his fulfilment in his work with the non-human creation. He can perfect it, but it cannot perfect him. His work is not his home. His relation to the animals is no adequate answer to his human loneliness. His naming of them is an incident in his search for a relationship that will complement and satisfy him. "Then the Lord Yahweh said 'it is not good that the man should be alone. I will make him a helper as his partner'" (2:18). So as a first but failed attempt to fulfill that program, God makes and Adam names the animals. Yahweh knows but Adam has to discover that "for the man there was not found a helper as his partner" (2:20).

In the first creation story man and woman are made simultaneously and their relationship has a very close connection to their being in the image and likeness of God. The point of that story is that the two belong inseparably together, so that the humanity God wills essentially consists of man and woman in mutual dependence and complementarity. They are equal in the sense that neither has any meaning apart from the other.

Emil Brunner, commenting on this text, wants to make sure that we do not miss its unique significance. The double statement that God made man in his own image and that he made them male and female has about it

> a lapidary significance, so simple indeed that we hardly realise that with it a vast world of myth and Gnostic speculation, of cynicism, and asceticism, of the deification of sexuality and fear of sex completely disappears ... In the whole long history of man's understanding of himself this statement has only been made *once* and at this point. Otherwise in a hundred different ways, man has always said something else that contradicts this statement; sometimes he says too little and sometimes too much ... On account of this statement alone the Bible shines out among all other books of the world as the Word of God.
>
> (Brunner, 1939, p. 346)

We can understand the meaning of both gender equality and human sexuality when we take seriously the fact that men and women are made together in the image of God.

The man and the woman

The second story makes the same point in its own way, by showing us the man without the woman and making it quite clear that he remains fundamentally unviable on his own. In these feminist days, the commentators are quick to point out that there is nothing derogatory to women in describing them as man's helper or help-meet. If we look at the other uses of the Hebrew word 'zer used here, we will find that in its characteristic use, it does not denote the assistance given by a subordinate to a superior but rather the help rendered by one who is strong to one who is weak, and often of the help that God gives to his people (cf. Exod. 18:4; Deut. 33:7, etc.). Thus, without twisting the text in a modern feminist direction, we can say that the relationship envisaged between the man and the woman in the second story is consonant with the equality affirmed in the first story. The man and the woman need each other and cannot be themselves without the help of the other. As Westermann puts it, "The man is created by God in such a way that he needs the help of the partner – hence mutual help is an essential part of human existence" (Westermann, 1984, p. 227).

Another way of saying the same thing is that the one is incomplete without the other and, on this showing, at the root of sexual desire is the search for completeness in an other who shares my humanity and yet has that humanity in a way that I do not have it, just as I have my humanity in a way that she does not, so that for completeness there has to be a donation of a dimension of humanity from the one to the other.

To say that is to stray well beyond our present exegetical concerns; but all that is already implicit in Adam's cry of delight as he wakens from the divine anesthesia and sees Eve. "Then the man said, 'This at last is bone of my bone and flesh of my flesh: this one shall be called woman for out of man this one was taken.'"(2:23) This is followed by the writer's comment "Therefore a man leaves his father and mother and clings to his wife and becomes one flesh" – a verse affirmed in the New Testament as foundational to the understanding and right functioning of human sexuality in the teaching both of Jesus and the apostles. There are three comments to be made here that point to questions that we will have to look at later.

1. *Man and woman – husband and wife*

In the man–woman relationship the relational has priority over the procreational. Eve is created to be Adam's companion before she is commissioned to be the mother of Adam's children. Their life is primarily to be a life together as husband and wife and their sexual relationship is an expression, celebration, and creative consolidation of that togetherness. The togetherness of husband and wife is the basis of their fecundity as father and mother and is therefore prior to it, as it is in this story. The modern wedding liturgies that make the first purpose of marriage the mutual help and comfort that husband and wife ought to have of each other are more in line with this story than the older ones that gave priority to the begetting and bearing of children.

2. *Man and woman – father and mother*

We have, however, immediately to add that although the relationship has the priority, in the plan and purpose of God that relationship is in its very nature creative in a way that images the creativity of God himself. As in his love he creates life out of nothing, so they, out of the life that is constituted by their sharing of love, also produce new life. The second creation story dwells exclusively on the relationality; for the connection between relationality and creativity we have to go back to the first story with God's command to them to be fruitful and multiply (1:28). When that connection between the relationality and creativity of love is for any reason impeded and a couple is childless, while their love remains, there is the sadness that what is between them has been prevented from expressing itself fully outside themselves in their child.

3. Man and woman – male priority?

We need also to take account of the fact that the second creation story, over against the first, affirms a priority of the man over the woman which sets it in very real tension with contemporary sensibilities in this matter. If we take the first two chapters of Genesis together, we have to ask ourselves what we can make of the fact that alongside the equal participation of man and woman in the imaging of God and their need for one another for the completion of their humanity, the man is there before the woman; in contradiction to the order of things for everybody else, she comes from him rather than he comes from her. "This one shall be called Woman for out of Man this one was taken" (Gen. 2:23).

Recognizing that this story has repercussions in the teaching about male headship in the New Testament, we will have to ask ourselves whether this element in it has to be dismissed as an illegitimate intrusion of patriarchy into a narrative that is basically pointing in a more egalitarian direction, or whether it is saying something that is integral to God's will and purpose for a humanity that is created in his image. We will be able to address the question profitably only when we have got much further into our understanding of the meaning of being in the image of God. For now we simply note the question and put it on the agenda for fuller treatment later.

Relationships ruptured

There is a final exegetical consideration that we need to note here because it also opens the door to one of the central areas of theological discussion about the image of God. Genesis 1 and 2 are followed by Genesis 3 which famously recounts that the relationship with God into which and for which the human couple were created was disrupted and distorted by the break with God in which they yielded to the temptation to become their own gods with the result that their God-dependence became self-dependence and they themselves became the autonomous arbiters of what was good and what was evil (3:5). So to speak, the mirror of their lives which was pointed outward at God was turned round, so that it now pointed inward at themselves, with the resulting alienation from God that the rest of the chapter describes.

That raises the question as to whether and in what way sinful humanity can still be said to be in the image of God. That is a question that has been much discussed in the theological tradition and to which diverse and contradictory answers have been given. Whether you think the image of God has been lost or distorted depends on the prior question of how you understand that image; before we can know what sin does to it, we must first know what we think it is. To all these questions we will in due course have to return.

On a purely exegetical level, it is worth noting that in Genesis 9, when God is making his covenant with Noah after the flood and therefore in a context in which the sinfulness of humanity is very much the center of attention, the reason why people are held accountable for murder is that their victims are made in the image of God. "Whoever sheds the blood of a human, by a human shall that person's blood be shed; for in his own image God made humankind" (9:6). The writer of Genesis reckoned that in our sins we are still in God's image.

Genesis – exegetical conclusions

To summarize, we have found that in the Genesis creation stories the affirmation that humankind is created in the image of God is set in a context that is also concerned with our external human relationships with the non-human creation and our internal relationships as men and women and that these three concerns are themselves intimately inter-related.

It is also clear that the key relationship is that of the human creatures to their divine Creator; only when we know how we image God will we be able to see how that imaging expresses itself coherently in the way that we order the world and our relationships. That we are like God, is, as we have seen, strongly affirmed in three verses of Genesis 1, but it is not explained there or anywhere else in the Old Testament. To give content to it we have to turn to the New Testament where the imaging language reappears and is set in a fresh context that helps us greatly to determine what it means.

Anthropology and christology

A quotation from my old Edinburgh teacher Norman W. Porteous will take us straight to the heart of the matter.

> Nothing could make clearer the tremendous impact of the revelation of God in Christ than the fact that it has almost completely obliterated the thought of man as being in the image of God and replaced it with the thought of Christ as being the image of God, that being understood in the sense of perfect correspondence to the divine prototype.
> (Porteous, 1962, p. 684)

We might want to note that what has been obliterated and replaced is not a concern for what it means for human beings to be in the *imago Dei* but rather any attempt to consider that question by itself, as happens in Genesis. The relevant New Testament passages display the massive insistence to which Porteous rightly points, that the question has to be looked at in a christological perspective; we will know what it means for us to be in the image of God when we first know what it means for Christ to be himself the image of God, by which, in which, and for which we were ourselves created.

In that last sentence we have made use of a distinction that was already noted by and significant for some of the patristic writers on this subject. As Anderson explains (Anderson, 1982, pp. 70–71), Adam in Genesis is said to be made *"in"* the image of God, whereas in the New Testament, Christ is said to *"be"* the image of God. So in Colossians "He [Christ] is the image of the invisible God, the first born of all creation, for in him all things in heaven and earth were created, things visible and invisible ... All things have been created through him and for him. He himself is before all things and in him all things hold together" (1:15). This terse statement looks back beyond Adam and indeed the whole enterprise of creation and affirms that it has its origin, its prototype, and its meaning in the invisible world and that origin has become visible, incarnate, and human in the person of Jesus Christ. Adam has dominion over creation because he images the Christ who is the model and source for the whole of creation. He is prior to Adam, to us all, as the prototype that Adam, that is, all of us, images and reflects. That point can be neatly made through the grammatical coincidence that in Colossians Christ is said to *be* the image of God and in Genesis Adam to be *in* the image of God.

God's self-imaging

All this points the way to another essential difference between the two. Adam reflects God as his creature, his imaging is coincident with his creating; Christ, on the other hand, images God as being himself integral to the life and being of the God he images. Commenting on our Colossians passage, Arthur Patzia notes that the use of the Greek term *eikon* here "communicates the idea that Christ participates in and with the nature of God, not merely copying, but visibly manifesting and perfectly revealing God in human form" (Patzia, 1984, p. 16). That view is strengthened when we see that in the immediately following verses of this same passage, it is said that "in him [Christ] all the fullness of God was pleased to dwell" (1:19), and indeed, as 2:9 confirms, to dwell "bodily."

That means that in Christ the imaging of God in God and by God is the basis of a human imaging; to use

Trinitarian terminology, what he is as the uncreated Son of God who images his Father, he is also in his incarnation as the created human being he has become. So in his humanity that reflects what he is in his divinity, he becomes the *eschatos Adam*, the ultimate human being that Adam was made and meant to be.

The stamp of God

That Christ is both the prototypical divine imaging of God in God and by God and also the prototypical refection of that divine image in our humanity is confirmed in Hebrews, where the Son is said to be "the reflection of God's glory and the exact imprint [*charakter*] of God's very being and he sustains all things by his powerful word" (1:3). Here *charakter* takes the place of *eikon* in the Colossians passage. The NRSV translation 'exact imprint' does not quite do justice to the Greek, because *charakter* is used *both* of the die that is stamped on to the wax *and also* of the imprint that the die makes on the wax to which it is applied (Kelber, "*charakter*" in TDNT 9:418). Thus, implicit in this verse is the idea that Christ is both the divine prototype that is stamped on to our humanity and so imparts to it the divine image, and is also the human being who has received that image and is the perfect expression of it. In the rest of us, in our over-flexible human nature, that image has been eroded and distorted but in Christ it is fresh and new, authentic and complete.

The substitution of the metaphor of the image by the metaphor of the stamp underlines the dynamic nature of the impression Christ makes on our humanity. The act of stamping wax makes it clear that Christ does not just display God-reflecting humanity, but he imparts it to us.

As Grenz puts it, "In the context of Hebrews 1:1–3 therefore, to say that Jesus is the *charakter* of God's own nature is to acknowledge that he is the active impress of God, the agent through whom God engages in the creative task – that is the work of imprinting the divine image wherever it is to be found in creation" (Grenz, p. 221), and, we might add, of recreating it as well!

Image, word and wisdom

The notion of Christ as the one who shares the nature and being of God and who can therefore reflect that being and nature first in his own humanity and then in ours, is closely connected with the complementary notions of Christ as the Word of God and the Wisdom of God, which, according to the scholarly consensus, are among the chief resources for New Testament christology. To say with John that the Logos was God and from the beginning with God and that all things were made through him (John 1:1–3) affirms that the Logos is all that God is and yet is "with" God and, as such, distinct from God – all that is an alternative way of saying what is said in image language in Colossians and in sealing language in Hebrews.

Likewise in the Wisdom of Solomon, Wisdom is declared to be "a breath of the power of God and a pure emanation of the glory of the Almighty" (7:25) and "a reflection of eternal light, a spotless mirror of the working of God and an image of his goodness" (7:26). Like Word, Wisdom shares the being of God and images that being in herself, so to say with Paul that Christ is the wisdom of God (1 Cor. 2:24), is to invoke that whole background.

Image and Son

Alongside image, Word, and Wisdom, the New Testament and especially the Johannine literature, develops the Messianic Son of God language till it also refers to one who as Son is, so to speak, of the same stuff as the Father and is therefore in his person and work the exact representation of the Father. So the Prologue to John that starts with Logos language ends with Son language, "No one has ever seen God. It is God the only Son (*monogenes theos*) who is close to the Father's heart who has made him known" (1:18). This Father/Son language came to dominate the theological tradition as it formulated its Trinitarian doctrine of God, and it has the advantage over the others, in that it makes clear, as does the gospel story itself, that the relationships between the two manifestations of divinity that all the languages affirm, are fully and completely personal, like the relationship of a Father to his Son.

Nevertheless, image language, logos language, wisdom language, and Son language illuminate one another and together point to the distinct divine being who shares God's deity and reflects all that God is in himself. As Gerhard Kelber puts it, "As Philo's *logos* and the wisdom of Wis. 7 are the image of God inasmuch as God's nature, his radiant light and glory, is impressed upon them, so Christ as the Son of God is the impress of God's nature ... As the *logos* and wisdom fully represent God and allow him to operate, so does the Son according to Hebrews 1:3" (quoted in Grenz (2001) p. 221).

We have immediately to add that Christ's humanity is the means by which his divine likeness to God is accessible and communicable to the rest of us. We cannot participate directly in God's divine being, but the wonder of the incarnation is that God is able to participate in our human being and so reveal to us what it means in authentically human terms to exist in the image of God. What it means to be in the image of God is revealed to us in Christ, not just as something for us to admire and try to imitate, but rather as something that has a transforming dynamic that can get hold of us and reshape us into the same likeness. As Paul puts it in 1 Corinthians 15, "the first man, Adam became a living being, the last Adam became a life-giving spirit" (15:45). What Christ is, is by the action of his Spirit imparted to us to make us like him.

The eschatological image

That thought is spelled out much more explicitly in 2 Corinthians 3. "And all of us, with unveiled faces, seeing the glory of the Lord as though reflected in a mirror, are being transformed into the same image from one degree of glory to another, from this comes from the Lord, the Spirit" (3:18). Here the thought is that the glory of God, the whole shiningly manifest expression of his being and nature, is so mirrored in the humanity of Jesus, that when we are exposed to it, we are progressively transformed by it, so that we manifest with increasing clarity the same nature that is perfectly revealed in Christ.

The parsing of the verb is important here – "we are being transformed." The tense is present continuous; our transformation is an ongoing process rather than a completed condition. The verb is plural; the reflection of the image of God is a corporate concern; each of us in our small mirrors capture an authentic glimpse of his glory, but it takes the whole circle of those who surround him more adequately to reflect it all. The verb is passive; our transformation is not the achievement of our activity, but rather that which is done to us from beyond ourselves provided that we are looking in the right direction. The agent of that transformation is, in fact, identified as the Holy Spirit – "for this comes from the Lord, the Spirit."

When we turn to Romans 8, all these points are underlined. "For those whom he foreknew he also predestined to be conformed to the image of his Son, in order that he might be the firstborn within a large family. And those whom he predestined he also called and those whom he called he also justified and those whom he justified he also glorified" (8:29, 30). The destiny for which God made us is that we should be transformed into conformity to Christ and that imaging is the way to our glorification which can happen only within the gathered company of his people.

These passages from Corinthians and Romans make it clear that to be remade in the image of God is both present process (Corinthians) and final destiny (Romans). We were made human in our creation in order that we might become fully and authentically human in our re-creation in Christ. Adam is shaped according to the image of God so that he might have the potential for being made like God by Christ. He is situated in the context of his relationships with God, the world, and with Eve, because these are the relationships in which he can reflect the love and holiness of God that will transform him in Jesus.

So the New Testament teaching about the image of God is essentially dynamic and eschatological. According to Grenz:

> This eschatological purpose [that we should be conformed to Christ] is the goal that was already in view in the creation

of humankind in the divine image. In this sense Romans 8:29 delineates the final exegesis of Gen. 1: 26–27. In his risen glory Jesus Christ now radiates the fullness of humanness that constitutes God's design for humankind from the beginning. Yet God's purpose has never been that Christ will merely radiate this human fullness but that, as the Son, he will be pre-eminent among a new humanity who together are stamped with the divine image.

(Grenz, 2001, p. 251)

In that sense, the medieval theologians were right when they declared that *gratia non tollit naturam sed perfecit*, that grace does not abolish or replace nature but perfects it. In Christ we become what we were made to be, the clue to what creation is about is to be found in what it is promised in Christ that it should become; as the original got its name and its order from newly made Adam, so the new creation will get its completion and its re-creation from newly raised Christ and the new humanity that stems from him (Romans 8:19–23).

On the exegetical level that means that we will never understand the Old Testament without the New, and specifically that we will never understand Genesis 1–3 till we understand from the New Testament passages we have been considering how the final revelation of the *imago Dei* is not in Adam but in Christ. In Genesis we see how our humanity is shaped: in the New Testament we see that it is so shaped that it might be filled with Christ.

From exegesis to theology

Throughout this chapter we have seen how the exegesis of the *imago* passages has proposed for us a whole theological agenda that we must now pursue. How will the humanity that is made in God's likeness develop its relationships with the natural environment over which it is set in authority, and with the other human beings with whom it is bound in gendered partnership. Crucially, in our relationship with God, how are we like him and what happens to that likeness when we sin against him? And what happens to all these questions when we set them in the light of Christ?

Similarly the New Testament data which assert that Christ is the image of God, both as the Son who is of the same nature as the Father and as the last Adam who is the same nature as we are, raise Christological questions about the relationship between Christ's divinity and his humanity; and, most of all, properly Trinitarian questions about the relationship of the Father and the Son in which the latter images and represents the former. Further, how does the Holy Spirit integrate us into Christ so that we also image the Father in and through the Son?

We have perhaps said enough in this chapter to show how these theological questions arise out of the biblical material and are not imposed upon it. We will now go on to see how some of these questions have been dealt with in the theological tradition that has engaged with the agenda that the biblical material lays down, and ask if perhaps that tradition can be further developed in ways that are theologically justified and shed fresh light on what it means to live as human beings who have been shaped by God so that they may recognize their calling and fulfil their destiny to become like God. To such tasks we now turn.

3 God's Image

On the wall of my study, near where I say my prayers, there are two icons, the one above the other. The central figure in both is Jesus, God's incarnate Son. In the lower icon he is alone; we are invited, as it were, to zoom in on him and look into the mystery of his person and his presence and expose ourselves to the penetrating eyes that look right into the heart of us with a realism that judges us as we are, with a love that accepts responsibility for us as we are and invites us into the transformation that he can bring about that will change us into what God wants us to be and thus restore us in his image.

By that icon we are called to that concentration on Jesus which is the source and center of all specifically Christian thinking, praying, and living. As we saw in the last chapter, it is in that Christ-ward direction that biblical reflection on the image of God itself moves from Adam who was created in that image to Jesus in whom that image is incarnationally embodied and eschatologically fulfilled.

But above that icon that spotlights Jesus, there is the celebrated Rublev icon of the Holy Trinity in which we zoom out from Jesus and see him not in his solitariness but in his relationships to the Father on the one side of him and the Holy Spirit on the other. Here he is still at the center; it is only by facing him and drinking of the chalice he offers that we can gain access to the Trinitarian circle of which he is a part. But here we can see that, although he is at the center, he is not alone. Here in contrast with the first icon, his gaze is not primarily directed to us; rather his head is inclined in the direction of his Father, from whom he comes, whose word he speaks, whose saving will he seeks in his praying and executes in his living and his dying, from whom he receives the victory and the new life of his resurrection, and to whom in his ascension he returns.

Jesus and the Father

It is impossible to make any sense of the Jesus of the gospels if we treat him as a solitary individual whose significance is in himself. From first to last, from the twelve-year-old boy in the temple who even then knows he is about his Father's business, (Luke 2:49) through the agonized man in Gethsemane wrestling with *Abba's* will and purpose (Mark 14:16) to the dying man on Calvary committing himself and his cause into his Father's hands (Luke 23:46) – from the very beginning to the very end, Jesus is who he is and does what he does entirely on the basis of his relationship to his Father; in Johannine terminology he is the Word whom the Father utters and the Son whom the Father begets and bears (John 1).

Jesus and the Spirit

It is equally true that he is who he is and he does what he does in the power of the Holy Spirit whom he both receives from his Father and gives to us. It is through the creative activity of the Spirit that he is conceived and takes human shape in Mary's womb (Luke 1:35); in his baptism the Holy Spirit is given to him to anoint him for his messianic ministry that is thus inaugurated (Luke 3:22), as he himself confesses in his programmatic statement "The Spirit of the Lord is upon me because he has anointed me ..." (Luke 4:18).

In the witness of John the Baptist, as recorded in John's gospel, Jesus is portrayed as at once the recipient, the residence, and the bestower of the Holy Spirit. "And John testified, 'I saw the Spirit descending from heaven like a dove and it remained on him. I myself did not know him but the one who sent me to baptize with water said to me, "He on whom you see the Spirit descend and remain is the one who baptizes with the Holy Spirit"'" (John 1:32–33). All this is in the context of the evangelist's incarnational christology, as the next verse makes clear. "And I myself have seen and testified that this is the Son of God" (1:34).

In contrast to some contemporary liberal christologies that offer a pneumatological understanding of the divinity of Jesus as a man filled with the Spirit and incarnational christology which sees Jesus as the eternal Son of God made man, John's gospel sees the incarnational and pneumatological dimensions of the person of Jesus as complementary to one another. As the eternal Son of the Father made flesh Jesus is uniquely and prototypically the recipient, the residence, and the bestower of the Spirit by whom he is related to his Father and to us. Any christology, however orthodox, including that of Chalcedon, which omits or plays down that vital pneumatological component, will fall short of a fully biblical understanding of Jesus and will be unable to give an adequate account of how he relates to God the Father and to us.

The Roots of Trinitarianism

It is central to that New Testament witness that Jesus is who he is and does what he does always and everywhere within his relationship to his Father and his Spirit. In saying that, we are at one of the main roots from which the doctrine of the Trinity grew.

The other root, or – perhaps better – the other prong of the single bifurcated root, is the affirmation that the relationship that Jesus has with his Father, and, as later came to be seen, with the Spirit, is unique and defining of God, because Jesus himself shares the being and nature of God. If Jesus is just a man uniquely filled by the Spirit, then the relationship of God to that man is a relation of Creator to creature that is external to the being of God, so that God's being can still be understood in terms of a unitary monotheism.

But if Jesus is in fact the eternal Son, who, as the later creedal statements put it, is "God from God, very God from very God," who is "*homoousios*, of one being with the Father," then God's relationship with him is no longer solely a Creator–creature relationship but rather a God–God relationship which necessitates a whole rethink of our understanding of the being and nature of God, first in a binitarian direction but ultimately in a Trinitarian direction.

It is, in fact, in this direction that the witness of the New Testament decisively points. In Paul, the one who humbled himself and became obedient to death on the cross is the one who "was in the form of God (*en morphe theou)*" (Phil. 2:6). In what is clearly an appeal to already received teaching Paul can set Jesus alongside God as co-creator of the universe: "Yet for us there is one God, the Father, from (*ex*) whom are all things and for (*eis*) whom we exist, and one Lord, Jesus Christ, through (*dia*) whom are all things and through (*dia*) whom we exist" (1 Cor. 8:6).

In that amazing identification of the crucified and risen man from Nazareth as co-partner with the God of Israel in the creation of the world, Paul asserts their unity of being so that the divine name *kurios* can become the personal name of Jesus. Yet at the same time he maintains their distinctness from each other, as the prepositions make clear. Creation is *from* and *for* the Father, but it is *through* the Lord Jesus Christ. The one is the source and destination of the creation, the other is the executive agent through which it comes into being and is set in motion toward that destination.

Equally when he is speaking of reconciliation Paul can quite naturally affirm that the work of Jesus culminating in the cross is the work of God. "All this is *from* (*ek*) God who reconciled us to himself *through* (*dia*) Christ and has given us the ministry of reconciliation; that is *in* (*en*) Christ God was reconciling the world to himself" (2 Cor. 5:18, 19).

Once again the prepositions are important, as the inserted italics emphasize. "In" asserts God's identification with the decisive human action of Jesus on Calvary, but "from" and "through" distinguish the parts of Father and Son in that action, the Father as its authorizing source and the Son as its executing and indeed executed agent. To reconcile the world to himself is not a work for a creature, but a work for God, and both in its willing and in its enactment in the creaturely world, it is God himself who is at work. For this to be so, both the identity in being and the distinct roles and relationships between God and Christ come into prominence; the more developed doctrine of the Trinity attempts to do justice to both these factors and at the same time to affirm the more subtly distinct personal action of the Holy Spirit in the works and being of God.

We have already seen how in Johannine christology the inter-relating of Father, Son, and Holy Spirit form the background of his presentation of the gospel story. Indeed, as I have pointed out elsewhere[2], the discussion of these relationships is conducted with great subtlety and sophistication in the so-called farewell discourses in John 14–16 in a way that is much more sensitive than anything in Paul to the identity and distinction between Son and Spirit and therefore moving toward a more fully Trinitarian rather than binitarian understanding of God's work and nature.

But throughout, these relationships are presented as being between distinct subjects who are equally divine, so that they are relationships that characterize and define the life and being of God. The Word who became flesh in Jesus is the Word who was with God and was God from the beginning and who again was his executant partner in the work of creation. Once again the preposition "through" is in evidence: "All things came into being *through (dia)* him and without him not one thing came into being" (John 1:3). In this relationship he is God's Son who shares his Father's being and nature. The glory we have seen in the Word made flesh is the glory "as of a father's only son" – like Father, like Son. The one who reveals the invisible God, in so doing, reveals himself as participant in the godhead: "No one has ever seen God. It is God the only Son who is close to the Father's heart who has made him known" (1:18).

The christological affirmations of Paul and John are far from identical. Part of the difference between them is that much that is still implicit in Paul becomes explicit in John, but both affirm the equal divinity of Father and Son and at the same time the distinctiveness that emerges in the way that they relate to each other. The same twin affirmations in different degrees of explication can be discerned in Hebrews and Revelation and in Colossians and Ephesians, which are Pauline in theology whether or not they were written by him. All this is evidence that the twin roots of Trinitarian doctrine are firmly planted in the soil of New Testament Christology.

Those who have a concern for Christian/Muslim relationships often object that the doctrine of the Trinity is one of the chief hindrances to mutual understanding between the two faiths and often imply that it is a hindrance that could be removed without much loss, a judgement which itself implies that the doctrine of the Trinity is some kind of metaphysical speculation that is irrelevant to the New Testament gospel.

In contrast to this, we have been claiming that the questions that the doctrine of the Trinity addresses arise directly from the high Christology to which, in different ways, the chief New Testament witnesses affirm, so that the real question that Christians and Muslims have to answer is the question that Jesus addressed to his first disciples at Caesarea Philippi: "Who do you say that I am?" If you answer it with Islam, that he is the second last prophet before the definitive revelation made through Mohammed, then indeed a Trinitarian understanding of God is at best irrelevant and at worst blasphemous. If, however, you answer the question as Peter did, followed and developed as he was by the rest of the New Testament, then the question about how the Son of the living God is related to his Father comes into focus as standing at the center of theological attention.

Developments in the doctrine of the Trinity

We have been seeing that identity of being and distinctiveness of relationship are the two gospel affirmations that generate a Trinitarian doctrine of God, and that remains true when that doctrine comes to formal doctrinal expression in the development that leads to its creedal formulation in the creeds of Nicaea (325) and Constantinople (381).

To affirm the identity of the divine being in its three hypostatic manifestations is to remain true to the Old Testament emphasis on the oneness of God famously expressed in the *Shema* of Israel, the Jewish Confession of faith that begins, "Hear, O Israel, Yahweh our God is one Lord…" (Deut. 6:4) and that captures the fierce insistence on the sole sovereignty of the God of Israel against all competing divinities. This one God had made everything, and everything depends on him; a loving and exclusive loyalty to him is the way to life and salvation and to divert that loyalty to any other is to fall into idolatry and death. What the Old Testament says about the single sovereignty of Yahweh, the Christian gospel says equally strongly about the one God who is Father, Son, and Holy Spirit. The oneness of God is far more than a theory of philosophical monotheism; it is at the heart of living faith and practical obedience.

Unity and differentiation

The insistence on the relationships that differentiate the Trinitarian persons from one another is equally essential to that living faith, because it tells us what kind of unity we are in fact affirming when we say that God is one. It is not the oneness of a single solitary divine subject, remote and aloof in his static perfection and his exalted aloneness with no one to love but himself until he makes a world. When theologians have begun to think of God in that way, typified most perhaps in Muslim thinking, they have been unable to find any room for the sending of God's Son in his incarnation and for the revelation of the nature of God's divinity in the dynamic interchanges between Jesus and his Father in the Spirit that constitute the ministry of Jesus and that can alone give significance to his sacrificial self-offering on the cross. If God is who he shows himself to be in the Father's sending of his Son and in the Son's responsiveness to his Father, then we have to understand the unity in a very different way from the solitary sovereignty we have been describing.

We have in fact to describe it in the way that the Johannine Jesus described it when he said on the one hand, "the Father and I are one" (10:30) and on the other hand, "the Father is greater than I" (14:28). The former verse affirms a oneness that does not abolish but rather embraces and includes a two-ness in the life of God, where the analogy is not with the unity of a solitary individual but rather with the oneness of a family group who have a genetic unity, because, so to speak, they are all made of the same stuff. That results in a personal and moral unity that binds them together in a common loyalty and a common purpose, but that does not exclude a diverse set of relationships between the members of the family that shows how within that unity they differ, the one from the other.

When Jesus says, "The Father and I are one," it is that sort of unity that he is affirming. Father and Son are of the same stuff, of the same being and nature, as the creeds will later affirm when they say that the Son is begotten not made, of the same substance (*homoousios*) with the

Father, so that their relationship is not that of the creator with his creature, but constitutes the one life of the one God.

The same point is often made in the context of the statement in 1 John that God is love (4:8, 16), not just that he shows himself to be loving in relation to his human creatures, but he is so toward us because he is so first antecedently in himself apart from us. The very notion of divine love as it is affirmed in the gospel requires the duality of the one who is the subject of that love, the lover, and the other who is the object of that love, the beloved. Love is the abolition of solitariness, and, at the same time, the creator and the manifestation of unity. Thus the Father and Son in the dynamic of their love eternally give themselves the one to the other in a way that expresses their indivisible oneness and their intrinsic two-ness. It takes two to love but, in loving, these two show that they are one.

This is one of the ways in which Augustine in his *De Trinitate* invites us to understand the triunity of God. The Father is the lover, the Son the beloved, and the Spirit the love that is between them and that unites them. We might want to object that the divine does not flow only in one direction from the Father to the Son, but also responsively from the Son to the Father and that this way of understanding the Spirit fails to do justice to him as himself an active personal subject. Nevertheless, compared to some of the other ways in which Augustine approaches the Trinity, this one comes much closer to seeing the divine life, certainly of the Father and the Son in terms of a relationship between personal subjects who love each other and as such it is faithful to the relationships depicted in the gospel story.

Ontological unity and functional subordination

We have, however, immediately to add that within that unity of being and loving that we have been describing, in which the three persons are equally divine, there is differentiation of order. That is why Jesus says not only "the Father and I are one" but also "the Father is greater than I." Within the life of the one God, there is one who sends and one who is sent, one who commands and one who obeys, one who is exalted in glory and one who dies abandoned on the cross. The ontological unity of being does not preclude the difference of function between Father and Son, so that, in what I have called a functional subordination, the one is first and the other is second and equally the functional subordination does not threaten the ontological unity but indeed presupposes and requires it to attain its true significance.

Karl Barth gives a magisterial exposition of this point, insisting that the humiliation and obedience of the Son is not a temporary and incidental feature of the incarnation but is rather an authentic revelation in history of who God is in his own eternal being. He goes on:

> If God is in Christ, if what the man Jesus does is God's own work, this aspect of the self-emptying and self-humiliation of Jesus Christ as an act of obedience cannot be alien to God. But in this case we have to see here the other side of the mystery of the divine nature of Christ and therefore of the nature of the one true God, that he himself is also able and free to render obedience.
>
> (Barth, 1956b, p. 193)

He summarizes the point in this way:

God's Image

> If in faith in Jesus Christ we are ready to learn, to be told, what Godhead, or the divine nature is, we are confronted with what is and always will be to all other ways of thinking a mystery, and indeed a mystery that offends. The mystery reveals to us that for God it is just as natural to be lowly as it is to be high, to be near as it is to be far, to be little as it is to be great, to be abroad as it is to be at home.
>
> (Barth, 1956b, p. 192)

This understanding of God's divinity has implications for our understanding of our own humanity, to which we will return later. Sufficient at the moment to note that in this understanding of the Trinitarian being of God, the unity and the differentiation, far from being opposed to one another, are each the defining context in which alone we can make sense of the other. That means that our doctrine of the Trinity must be constructed in a way that gives each its proper place.

Trinitarian deviations

Two of the classic Trinitarian heresies can be seen as constructions in which one of these factors begins to crowd out the other. The unity of the Godhead can be threatened either by a tritheism that sees the three divine persons as three independent individuals who have a being and existence apart from their relationships with one another. As far as I know there has never been a theological advocate of such a tritheistic doctrine of God; but certain theologians, both patristic and modern, have been accused of moving too far in a tritheistic direction by overemphasizing the autonomy of the three divine persons over against each other so that their unity and interdependence is allowed to fall into the background.

The other way in which the unity of the godhead can be called into question is by an ontologically subordinationist understanding of the Father/Son/Spirit which, in the theology of Arius, gave rise to the crisis that prompted the Council of Nicaea. For Arius, only God the Father was properly divine; Son and Spirit, though uniquely exalted above all other creatures, still belonged to the created rather than to the divine order of being. The Arian doctrine of God is therefore a unitarian monotheism in which the question of the ontological unity and equality of Father, Son, and Spirit within the one being of God is explicitly denied.

There are lots of Arians around today for whom Jesus is no more than an exalted religious leader, one among several such, rather than God incarnate, and the Spirit is no more than the religious expression of the corporate identity of either a part or the totality of the human community. For those who espouse such an approach, this book will be of little interest; if there is no Trinity, there can, by definition, be no Trinitarian understanding of the image of God. As we will see in due course, a monotheistic theology will produce an individualistic anthropology, and often has, whereas a properly Trinitarian theology, in which God is understood as a community of autonomous but totally interdependent persons in relationship, will yield a very different picture of the humanity which is made to reflect and mirror the life of such a God in its own.

The unity of God can be threatened in two very different ways by a theoretical tritheism and an actual subordinationism. But there is also danger in the opposite direction, whereby an over-concentration on the oneness of God can obscure the distinct personal identities of Father, Son, and Holy Spirit and the uniqueness of the complementary roles and functions that each fulfils in the inner life and outward action of the triune God.

The Trinitarian heresy in which this danger is actualized is known as modalism, in which God's manifestations as Father, Son, and Holy Spirit are seen as contingent, temporary, or penultimate features of his revealing and saving activity, which have no ultimate significance for the eternal being and life of God himself. Either successively or simultaneously he appears in the mode of Father, Son, and Spirit, but these are temporary roles that he plays in order to fulfil his purposes; behind the paternal, filial, and pneumatic masks that he wears, there is the one God in the undifferentiated unity of his eternal being.

This heresy is often identified with the name of Sabellius who taught that in the Old Testament God showed himself as Father, that for the thirty years of the incarnation he showed himself as Son, and that from Pentecost onward he has manifested himself as Spirit. In such a blatant form the modalistic heresy is easy to understand and to refute, but it has appeared and goes on appearing in far more subtle and sophisticated forms, wherever the God of the biblical gospel is subordinated to the god of philosophical speculation, and the rich interpersonal relationships of the three divine participants in that gospel narrative are relativized in favor of what T. F. Torrance has characterized as the god behind God, the single simple infinite source and center of all reality in which diversity is traced back to the ultimate unity from which it comes.

Put differently, a typical modalist, rather than following Sabellius in his fiction about the three successive faces of the one god, would be more likely to say that God is Trinitarian in his revelation, but unitarian in his eternal being, even if we cannot penetrate beyond the Trinitarian revelation to the ultimate reality of the God behind it. He is Trinitarian in relation to us but what he is in himself is beyond our telling. In technical theological language, there is an economic trinity in revelation, but we cannot speak of an eternal trinity which is immanent to the life of God.

All this, of course, is in defiance of the patristic rule, strongly affirmed in our day on the Catholic side by Karl Rahner (Karl Rahner. *The Trinity*. London: Burns and Oates, 1976) and on the Reformed side by Karl Barth (Barth, 1975, p. 479) that as God is in his revelation, so he is in himself, that his action proceeds from and is consonant with his inner being. As Rahner's famous dictum puts it, the economic Trinity is the immanent Trinity (Rahner, 1976, p. 22), that in encountering God as Father, Son, and Spirit, we encounter not the penultimate and the contingent, but the ultimate and the eternal, God as he is from eternity to eternity, that the relationships that constitute the gospel also constitute the eternal life of God.

To summarize, Arianism and Modalism reach much the same destination by different routes: the one abolishes the unity of the Trinity by removing Son and Spirit from the divine realm, the latter by refusing to give ultimate significance to the inter-Trinitarian relationships and affirming behind them a unipersonal or perhaps impersonal or even unknowable god.

Trinitarian orthodoxy – West and East

Against all such aberrations, orthodox Trinitarianism insists on defining the divine life in terms of both unity and diversity; in God there is both oneness and threeness. Under that orthodox umbrella there have nevertheless developed different emphases in the churches of the Greek East and the Latin West; the East says "three" with a louder voice than it says "one," and the West says "one" with a louder voice than it says "three."

To put the same point in another way, for Western Trinitarianism, the oneness is the given and the threeness the problem, which has not always been successfully addressed with the result that, in its failure to do full justice to what Pannenberg calls the self-differentiation of the Trinitarian persons, the West is in danger of modalism. On the creedal level one has only to look at the so-called Athanasian Creed, which is, of course, Western and has nothing to do with the great Athanasius, to see that what it really wants to say more than anything else is "And yet there are not three Gods but one God."

Augustine and the Trinity

That this is the tendency of the West is further evidenced by the Trinitarian doctrine of Augustine at one end of the Western tradition and that of Karl Barth at the other.

Augustine's *De Trinitate* is one of the foundational works of Western Trinitarianism. In it he is concerned to affirm and to build on the foundations of Trinitarian orthodoxy that he has inherited. He is much concerned to repudiate tritheism, subordinationism, and modalism, and to relate and explain the Trinitarian assertions that God is three persons in one God. All in all, it is not too much to claim that Augustine's achievement is such that he has marked out the territory for all who come after him and, if we want to see further than he did, it can only be by standing on his shoulders.

Nevertheless, in the way that Augustine carries these worthy intentions there are very real problems that have haunted Western Trinitarianism ever since. We have already seen that Augustine can speak of the Trinity in terms of the interpersonal relationship of the lover and the beloved, but that is not the predominating analogy that he employs. He thinks rather of the Trinity in terms of individual self-consciousness.

As Colin Gunton puts it, "The crucial analogy for Augustine is between the inner structure of the human mind and the inner being of God, because it is in the former that the latter is made known, this side of eternity at any rate, more really than in the 'outer' economy of grace" (Gunton, 1991, p. 45).

On this showing, when I want to know about the inner life of God, I turn not to the gospel story where God reveals himself, but to my own inner life. There I discover that I know myself and I love myself, so that I can distinguish a self that does the knowing and the loving, a second self that is the object of that knowledge, and a third self which is the object and the expression of that love. So I am, as it were, a created Trinity who can identity my one self as, firstly, the knower and the lover; secondly, the one who is the object of the self's knowing; and thirdly, the one who is the expression and object of the self's own will and love. And, since I am made in the image of God, I can use my knowledge of myself as trinity to clarify my knowledge of God as Trinity. Gunton quotes Augustine himself to this effect. "We might now attempt to raise our thoughts to that supreme and most exalted essence of which the human mind is an image – inadequate indeed but still an image" (Gunton, 1991, p. 47).

Such a summary of Augustine's complex thinking is itself woefully inadequate, but it does perhaps throw light on the central features of an understanding of the relationship between the Trinity and the *imago Dei* which has been hugely influential and indeed predominant in much Western theology. We may assess its outstanding characteristics as follows:

1. Its Basis is inner experience

It bases itself on inner experience rather than on historical revelation, although, of course, Augustine seeks to back up that experience with appropriate biblical quotations that fit in with it. Out of my understanding of who I am, I construct a theory of who God is and, in so doing, attempt to proceed directly from myself to the immanent Trinity, bypassing or at least sidelining God's self-revelation in Christ and the Spirit.

It is not hard to see how such an approach is vulnerable to Feuerbach's criticism from which we started and can with some justification be written off as a human self-projection into the heavens. It is certainly open to the methodological criticism that it interprets our understanding of God on the basis of our understanding of ourselves rather than basing our understanding of ourselves on our understanding of God. It moves from the image to the original, rather than from the original to the image. It seeks to know God in terms of Adam rather than Adam in terms of God. It assumes a natural knowledge of God rather than depending upon God's will to make himself known.

2. It does not do justice to the persons and their relationships

The three divine identities that this model affirms are no more than three aspects of a single self. It is not hard to understand how this kind of Trinitarianism will major on the oneness and be unable to take proper account of the three-ness in God. The relationship between myself as knower and myself as known is a relationship within a single individual identity, and as such it is quite different from the properly inter-personal relationship between a father and a son.

Augustine is aware that the three-ness of the divine persons far exceeds the three aspects of the human mind that he has described, but his basic analogy does not allow him to give a satisfactory account of this personal divine three-ness. After all, aspects of the self have not the kind of autonomy over against each other that can in any way be compared with the freedom in their relationships with one another that distinct human persons enjoy.

It is highly significant that the actual relationships that are the basis of a biblically founded doctrine of the Trinity are expressed in specific inter-personal categories. However close to his Father Jesus shows himself to be, their relationship is always expressed in terms of the love and obedience that one person offers to another, and they are never seen as expressions of the self-consciousness of one divine individual. In terms of Augustine's dominant analogy, it is hard to the point of impossibility to make sense of what went on between Jesus and his Father in the garden of Gethsemane. When you relativize the biblical revelation, you almost inevitably relativize the tripersonal nature of God.

3. It legitimizes an individualistic anthropology
On this showing, God is presented not as a society of self-differentiated yet totally inter-dependent sources of personal action, but as an individual self-consciousness whose selfhood manifests itself in various aspects. Such an individual God mirrors and provides a basis for the understanding of our humanity in individualistic rather than relational terms. The spotlight falls on the interior mental life of the individual and the relationships by which it is constituted rather than the social relationships of people with one another that are enabled and expressed in the bodily being through which they communicate and interact with one another.

This kind of Trinitarianism involves the failure to take full account of the presence of an authentic personal other, both within the life of God and the life of human society. It is significant, as we will see, that when the tradition that stems from Augustine seeks to identify the image of God in men and women, it speaks in terms of the characteristics of individuals and emphasizes rationality rather than relationality as that which makes us like God.

Over against all that, the kingdom of God that is at the center of the proclamation of Jesus is about the establishment of right relationships between parties who are genuinely other, whether the partners are God and us or both human. Our calling is not to retreat into our interiority in order to find the image of God deep within us, but rather to be freed from our self-involvement so that we can move out to give ourselves to God and our neighbors who have an independent personal existence distinct from our own and can therefore give to us and receive from us. God's will in Christ is for the right relationships of distinct persons with him and with others because he himself is constituted by right relationships between the distinct persons of Father, Son, and Holy Spirit.

4. It depreciates the Holy Spirit

The Augustinian model has great difficulty in identifying the distinct personhood of the Holy Spirit – a difficulty that has characterized Western theology down the centuries to our own day. In terms of his individualistic analogy, the best that Augustine can find to say is that the Holy Spirit is love, and, as such, the bond that joins Father and Son in one. As he himself puts it, the Holy Spirit is not a substance but a relationship, the relationship of mutual self-giving love between Father and Son and, as such, the gift of love to us. This model could easily lead to a binitarian doctrine of God in which Father and Son are bound together by their love to each other, and Western Trinitarianism has often been implicitly and occasionally explicitly binitarian.

The bother is that a relationship is not a person, even though persons are constituted by their relationships, and love is self-giving and therefore requires a subject who gives. The Holy Spirit is the giver of love (Rom. 5:3) rather than the love that is given. The New Testament picture of the Spirit as the dynamic personal subject who has his own distinctive hypostatic function and being in perfecting what the Father has initiated and the Son has achieved is hard to accommodate within the Augustinian model of the Spirit who timelessly relates Father and Son. It is not surprising that in the Augustinian tradition the personal work of the Spirit in incorporating us into Christ was soon reinterpreted in the terms of the infusion of impersonal grace and the Spirit was seen mainly in terms of the eternally perfect and therefore static bond of unity between Father and Son within the eternal life of God.

Barth and the Trinity

If Augustine stands at the ancient beginning of Western Trinitarianism Karl Barth stands, with Karl Rahner, on the Catholic side, at the beginning of its twentieth-century revival and renewal after a long period of liberal neglect.

By locating the doctrine of the Trinity at the very beginning of his *Church Dogmatics*, he is making the emphatic statement that the God he is going to be talking about from the start to the finish of his theology is the God who in Jesus Christ has revealed himself as Father,

Son and Holy Spirit. Over against the Augustinian tradition with its natural theology, Barth sees God's action in Christ as the sole norm for our knowledge of God and in the construction of his doctrine of the Trinity he wants to base himself exclusively on the data of revelation. In fact, Barth bases his doctrine of the Trinity on an analysis of what scripture means by revelation. It is, he says, "the same God who in unimpaired unity is the Revealer, the revelation, and the revealedness" (Barth, 1975, p. 299). Barth reaches this position from an analysis of the statement "God reveals himself." When we say *God* reveals himself we think of the sovereign, transcendent Father who initiates his self-revelation. When we say God *reveals* himself we think of the incarnate, crucified, and risen Son in whose coming and action the revelation is made accessible to us. When we say God reveals *himself*, we think of the Holy Spirit whose action opens our eyes to the Father's unveiling in the Son and makes the act of revelation complete. Because God in his act of revelation shows himself to us as he eternally is in his own being, the inherently threefold structure of the one revelation is the basis for our affirming a threefold structure in the life of the one God.

From this point Barth proceeds in a way that, for all the differences between them, shows how he still stands in the tradition of Western and Augustinian Trinitarianism. For him the implication of the doctrine of the Trinity is that God is the one Lord in threefold repetition. For Barth the three Trinitarian "persons" – a term he dislikes – are not three personal subjects but rather one personal subject in three repetitions or, his preferred term, "modes of being." "The name of Father, Son and Holy Spirit means the one God in threefold repetition, and this in such a way that the repetition itself is grounded in His Godhead" (Barth, 1975, p. 350). On all this we may make the following comments:

1. The divine modes of being

Barth is no modalist. Although he speaks of modes of being rather than persons, what he wants to avoid is the notion that Father, Son, and Holy Spirit are three individuals, and to affirm instead that they are the ways in which the one personal God relates to himself and, far from being, as in modalism, temporary manifestations in revelation are, in fact, constitutive of his own being.

In Barth, as against Augustine, the three Trinitarian modes of being are not in danger of being reduced to the different psychological dimensions of the one divine self. The one personal I of the Godhead is present in Father, Son, and Holy Spirit, and relates to itself in an authentically personal way in terms of I–Thou relationships within both the external action and the internal being of God. Barth, because he is so centered in scripture, can see the Trinity as socially constituted by the personal relationships between the three divine "persons" and therefore as the paradigm for an anthropology that can interpret the image of God in social and relational terms, because the God whom we image is himself constituted by these social relationships.

2. God as a single subject in repetition

Nevertheless, Barth's God, like Augustine's, is still a single subject, albeit in threefold repetition, and his relationships are, in the final analysis, relationships with himself. One has to ask again whether this emphasis on the oneness of God makes room for the real otherness that is required to give full significance to the divine interpersonal relationships and to the central biblical assertion that God is love.

Jürgen Moltmann has been very critical of Barth at precisely this point, accusing him of being too much in thrall to an idealist Hegelian understanding of God as the single absolute subject and suggesting that the data of revelation, which Barth claims to be the sole source of his teaching, in fact point in a different direction.

In Moltmann's reading, the gospel story is not about the unfolding of the Lordship of the one God in his three modes of being. Moltmann goes so far as to declare that he is not a monotheist, if monotheism means, as he thinks it means with Barth, the divine Lordship of a single personal subject, albeit exercised in a Trinitarian way. For Barth, again according to Moltmann, the Trinity is the expression of the sole Lordship of a divine individual, who, as the Father, initiates revelation, and, as the Son, embodies that revelation, and who, as the Spirit, makes that revelation known. The whole thing is the work of one dominant individual who fails to acknowledge the freedom of others, so that this God would offer a theological basis for an individualistic anthropology; the dominant divine Lord would be imaged in the man who asserts and fulfils himself in the domination of others (Moltmann, 1981, p. 139ff.).

Such a criticism is perhaps justified in relation to that aspect of Barth's Trinitarian theology against which it is directed. There is no doubt that in his battle against theological liberalism Barth was concerned to assert the sovereign lordship and freedom of the one true God and that he saw the doctrine of the Trinity as one way in which that could be done. But it is central to Barth's doctrine of God that he is defined not simply by his sovereign freedom but by his outgoing and self-giving love and it is the lordship of that love that goes out to affirm the other, which for Barth constitutes the inner life of the Trinity and also his dealings with us in Christ and in the Spirit; his Lordship serves not to dominate but to liberate those toward whom it is exercised, and, as we will see, it is that outgoing love of God for us and our response to it in our loving one another that, in fact, dominates Barth's anthropology in general and his understanding of the *imago Dei* in particular. There is therefore much in Barth which Moltmann's attack fails to take into account.

Nevertheless the question remains whether Barth's insistence that God is not three persons but one person in three modes of being can sit easily with the authentic I-Thou relationships that for Barth constitute the life of God and the life to which we are called in response to God. Does not that love that Barth wants to assert require the personal otherness of the lover and the beloved which the strong assertion of God as the one personal subject in threefold repetition throws into doubt? Are we not, in the end, left wondering whether, despite all the other elements in Barth's exposition that proclaim the opposite, this is a God who loves himself and who models for our imaging an ultimate self-love? In one way in Augustine and in a very different way in Barth, the overriding Western insistence on the oneness of God can be an obstacle to our understanding of the relationships with which the gospel story presents us and can impel us toward a self-affirming individualism that is in blatant contradiction to that gospel. Barth is too biblical for that to dominate his theology, but it is hard to deny its presence as a jarring note in that theology. How Moltmann would remedy that situation we will explore after we have identified another typically Western feature of Barthian Trinitarianism.

3. Barth and the Holy Spirit

Questions have to be asked about the adequacy of Barth's understanding of the distinct personhood of the Holy Spirit. He is quite clear (Barth, 1975, p. 466ff.) that the Holy Spirit is the one Lord God through whom we come to faith in God's self-revelation and as the giver of faith he is distinct from us who are its recipients. But he is also to be distinguished within the life of God from both the Father and the Son from whom he proceeds – Barth is an enthusiastic proponent of the Western *filioque*. The Spirit is distinct from the Father and the Son and yet related to them as their common factor and fellowship. He is "God as the act of love."

This does not take us much beyond Augustine and is vulnerable to the same question as to how a relationship of love between Father and Son can be understood as a third mode of the personal being of God.

Barth never came to write the fifth volume of his *Church Dogmatics*, which would have dealt specifically with the person and work of the Holy Spirit, but he did admit that with his christological focus such a theology would not have been easy for him. In his last years he spoke of his dream that someone else might be able to develop such a theology "that I can only envisage from afar, as Moses once looked at the promised land" (Busch, 1976, p. 494).

We do, however, have evidence from the extant volumes of *Church Dogmatics* of how Barth's pneumatology was developing. In his doctrine of the Trinity, as we have seen, the Spirit is the third mode of being of the triune God, but when he comes to the person and work of Christ in Part Four, there is a growing tendency to understand the Spirit in exclusively christological terms as a way of describing Christ's experiential action in applying the given gospel to believers, in which the acting divine subject is Christ rather than the Spirit.

The affirmation of the *filioque*, with its assertion of a one-way dependence of the Spirit on the Son, has typically led to a playing down of the person and action of the Spirit in which he loses his identity to the Son and, for all his protestations of pneumatological orthodoxy, Barth can be credibly accused of a pneumatological deficit that makes us wonder whether he really needs a third Trinitarian person and could just as well work with a binitarian doctrine of God.

We have now identified some of the consequences of the Western over-emphasis on the oneness of God in both Augustine and Barth, and we can now ask whether the rather different Trinitarianism of the Christian East has anything to teach us about how a right balance between oneness and three-ness can be restored.

The move eastwards – Moltmann

A good transition from one tradition to the other is provided by Moltmann, who, though always a Western theologian, has drunk deeply at Eastern springs and in *The Trinity and the Kingdom of God* tells us where this has led him. As against Barth, Moltmann insists that what is revealed in the gospel is not the Lordship of the one but the free, loving, and open self-giving of the three. "The New Testament talks about God by proclaiming in narrative the relationships of the Father, the Son and the Holy Spirit which are relationships of fellowship and are open to the world" (Moltmann, 1981, p. 64).

The life of God is characterized not by lordly self-assertion but with that kind of self-giving which Moltmann finds depicted in the Rublev icon and which he calls the "tender inclination" of the three persons to one another. Because the life of God consists of the self-giving in which each Trinitarian person gives himself in freedom to another person who is distinct from himself, this God has a basis in himself for going out beyond himself first to create and then to recreate human persons in a free fellowship of outgoing love, other with other, that, on a created level, reflects and mirrors the fellowship of distinct persons-in-relationship that constitutes the life of God.

This is, in effect, the position taken by the Cappadocian theologians of the latter part of the fourth century – Basil of Caesarea, Gregory of Nazianzus, and Gregory of Nyssa. For them, in blatant contrast to Augustine, the three Trinitarian *hypostaseis* are not seen as manifestations or aspects of the one divine self-consciousness, but as three sources of free personal action in rich relationships with one another.

In so doing they redefine the meaning of the word *hypostasis* so that it comes to mean not just a particular existent thing (like a table) but something much more like the modern concept of person. In effect, they redefined the word in order to do justice to the being and action of the God who has revealed himself in the gospel and so presented us with a new concept of personhood with which to interpret the life of humanity. If God is a community of persons, then from our knowledge of him we are able to see that those made in his image are themselves to be understood as persons in community – an approach to the *imago Dei* that leads us in a very different direction than Augustinian individualism.

Our business at the moment is, however, with the Cappadocian doctrine of the Trinity. Colin Gunton quotes Basil of Caesarea as saying in one of his letters that God is "a sort of continuous and indivisible community" whose reality is "a new and paradoxical conception of united separation and separated unity" (Gunton, 1991, p. 96). On this Gunton comments, "the achievement of the Cappadocians, an achievement which Augustine has failed adequately to understand, was to create a new conception of the being of God, in which God's being was seen to consist in personal communion" (Gunton, 1991, p. 53).

Such a doctrine of the Trinity is based on the principle, itself characteristic of the Cappadocians, that as God has revealed himself in Christ, so in himself he is; or, to say the same thing in more technical terms, as he is in the economy, so he is in his inherent ontology. The rich personal interchanges between Father, Son, and Spirit that constitute the gospel story are not to be relativized by an understanding of God's being as a single divine self-relating, but are to be taken utterly serious as the ultimate disclosures of what God is like in his own being eternally. The community of Father, Son, and Spirit that defines the story from Bethlehem to Pentecost is the final disclosure of the being and nature of God. If the story is about "persons in relation", so is the being of God.

The East and the Spirit

With this emphasis on personal distinctness within the life of God, it is not surprising that Cappadocian Trinitarianism is able to come to terms with the distinct personhood of the Holy Spirit much more adequately than the Augustinian West. Basil of Caesarea, in fact, wrote the first sustained treatment of the divinity of the Spirit and in so doing affirms him as a third person over against the Father and the Son. He puts it thus:

> In relation to contingent beings the Spirit is said to be in them "in various measures and in various ways". In relation to Father and Son it is more in keeping with true reverence to say that he is *with* them rather than *in* them ...His eternal pre-existence and his unceasing abiding with Father and Son cannot be thought of without postulating the titles which describe everlasting conjunction ... When we consider the proper dignity of the Spirit we contemplate him as being *with* Father and Son; when we have in mind

the grace that comes from him in its operation on those who participate, then we say that the Spirit is *in* us.

(Basil, *De Spiritu Sancto,* 26,63,64, quoted in Bettenson, 1970, p. 74)

How that explicitly inter-personal "with" is to be understood is a complex question, but on Basil's showing, it is a question which it is both legitimate and indeed necessary to raise. What does the gospel story have to tell us about the specific hypostatic function of the Holy Spirit in distinction from those of the Father and the Son? For the moment we may be content to note how Basil's conceptuality invites us to return to the data of revelation to look for specific Trinitarian answers to such specifically Trinitarian questions.

The East and the unity of God

Before we accept that invitation, we must look at another feature of this kind of Trinitarianism. If the Augustinian West, with its emphasis on the one rather than the three, stands under the threat of individualistic modalism, could it not be said that the Cappadocian paradigm with its emphasis on the three rather than the one stands under the threat of tritheism? Is the oneness of God so conceived that the three Trinitarian persons can be seen as three individual deities who, though they are in the closest relationship with one another, have their being in themselves apart from one another? It is, in fact, the fear that three persons could be understood to mean three individuals that leads Karl Barth to speak of the divine *hypostaseis* as "modes of being" rather than persons.

Basil was aware that his doctrine of God was open to such questioning and this is how he dealt with it:

> We do not scatter our theology into a divided plurality, because the one form, so to speak, is contemplated in God the Father and God the Only-begotten, united by the invariableness of the godhead. For the Son is in the Father, the Father in the Son, since the Father is such as the Son is, the Son such as the Father, and herein is the unity. And so in respect of the individuality of the persons we have one and one; in respect of the community of nature the two are one... The Holy Spirit also is one, and we proclaim him singly attached to the one Father through the one Son, through himself completing the worshipful and blessed Trinity.
>
> (Basil, *De Spiritu Sancto*, 18,44,45, quoted in Bettenson, 1970, p. 76)

Such a dense statement requires a detailed exegesis; we must content ourselves with indicating two complementary ways in which Basil defends himself from the charge of tritheism and affirms the unity of God.

The unity of a shared divine being

Firstly the three Trinitarian persons are one because they all share the same divine nature that, in its unique deity, is so singular that it excludes all plurality. If you have any understanding of who God is you cannot even contemplate the possibility that there could be three gods; and to say that Father, Son, and Holy Spirit each possess that uniquely divine nature is in itself an affirmation of their unity. Here the Cappadocian fathers are expounding the Nicaean *homoousios* with its emphasis on the simplicity and singularity of God that excludes any plurality of an individualistic kind among those who share that nature. Members of a human family may share the same nature and yet be independent of one another because being human is not in any contradiction with being many. But the divine nature differs from the human in many ways, but precisely in this respect, that it does not allow for this plurality, to be God is to be one and therefore to say that Father, Son, and Holy Spirit are each God is by definition to say that they are one God.

Divine unity as perichoresis

If that is so, we must still ask how this oneness accommodates the distinctness of the three persons. For an answer to this the Cappadocians point to the gospel affirmation of the mutual indwelling of the Father and the Son. As Basil puts it in the passage just quoted "For the Son is in the Father and the Father in the Son." That, in turn, echoes the words of Jesus to Philip in John 14.

> Do you not believe that I am in the Father and the Father is in me? The words that I say to you, I do not speak on my own; but the Father who dwells in me does his works. Believe me that I am in the Father and the Father is in me; but if you do not, then believe me because of the works themselves.
>
> (John 14:10–11)

The speaking and the acting of Jesus reveal the special and intimate nature of his relationship with the Father. It is such that to encounter the one is to encounter the other. The Father is not just the remote initiating source of the person and work of the Son. Rather, in the presence of the Son, you are also in the presence of the Father, and equally in the presence of the Father you are also in the presence of the Son. Their self-giving love for one another is of such an intensity that the one mediates the immediate presence of the other.

That means that on the one hand that it is out of the question to think of the Father and the Son as two individuals who could have some independent being outside and apart from their relationship with each other. They are who they are and they do what they do only in the closest possible relationship with each other. That is implicit in the relational character of their names. A Father cannot be a Father without a Son and a Son cannot be a Son without a Father.

And yet, at the same time, the nature of the love that unites them so closely is such that it affirms the distinctness of the one over against the other. It takes two to love and, if we are to be true to the revealed data, there can be no modalistic collapse into an undifferentiated unipersonal godhead. Within the unity of being and presence that they share, the Son is not the Father and the Father is not the Son. Within the being of the one God, the Son does not send, he is sent; it is the Son who is incarnate, crucified and risen, not the Father. It is the Father who initiates and the Son who responds to and obeys that initiation; but the Father's initiation is fruitful only through the Son's response to it, and the Son's response is entirely defined by the Father's initiation.

This combination of unity and diversity among the divine persons is described especially in Trinitarian theology of a Cappadocian type by the technical Greek term *perichoresis,* and it is in virtue of their perichoretic relationships with one another that the three persons are one God.

Miroslav Volf defines the notion as follows:

> Perichoresis refers to the reciprocal interiority of the Trinitarian persons. In every divine person as a subject, the other persons also indwell; all mutually permeate one another, though in so doing they do not cease to be distinct persons. In fact, the distinctions between them are precisely the presupposition of that interiority, since persons who have dissolved into one another cannot exist in one another.

Perichoresis is "co-inherence in one another without any coalescence or commixture." ... Being in one another does not abolish Trinitarian plurality; yet despite the abiding distinction between the persons, their subjectivities do overlap. Each divine person acts as subject, and at the same time the other persons act as subjects in it.

(Volf, 1998, p. 209)

It is to this concept of *perichoresis*, which has a long history in the East from John of Damascus in the eighth century, that Moltmann appeals for his understanding of the unity of God and for the refutation of the charge of tritheism that has been brought against it.

The Father exists in the Son and the Son in the Father and both of them in the Spirit, just as the Spirit exists in both the Father and the Son. By virtue of their eternal love they live in one another to such an extent and dwell in one another to such an extent that they are one ... In their *perichoresis* and because of it, the Trinitarian persons are not to be described as three different individuals who only subsequently enter into relationship with one another (which is the customary reproach under the name of tritheism). But they are not either three modes of being or three repetitions of the one God, as the modalistic interpretation suggests. The doctrine of the *perichoresis* links together in a brilliant way the threeness and the unity without reducing the threeness to the unity or dissolving the unity into the threeness.

(Moltmann, 1981, pp. 174–75)

On this we may make three comments:

1. The Spirit as himself the perichoresis

We have been speaking mainly of the Father–Son relationships, and Moltmann rightly reminds us that the third Trinitarian person is also involved in the *perichoresis* and we may well ask how. The answer is, perhaps, that the Spirit is in himself the *perichoresis* of the Father and the Son. The "fellowship of the Holy Spirit" (2 Cor. 13:14) revealed in God's relating to us reflects that "fellowship" of Father and Son which the Spirit enables and creates within the life of God. Augustine has been justifiably criticized for turning the personal Spirit into a relationship between persons which is not itself a person. But the Spirit can be seen as the person who mediates, sustains, and enables the love between the Father and the Son, so that by his personal action he both unites them in an inexpressibly close way but at the same time constitutes himself as the "space" between them so that they do not collapse into each other but remain in their distinct personal integrity over against each other.

This is what we see happening in the baptism of Jesus, where the Father gives himself to the Son in giving him his Spirit and remains distinct from the incarnate Son in his heavenly glory. He is thus the Spirit who, by simultaneously relating and maintaining the distinct personhood of the other two, is not to be reduced to a relationship but is to be seen as the person who completes and unites the godhead in his relating of the Father to the Son.

Furthermore the immanent function of the Spirit so regarded is consonant with the activity of the Spirit in the gospel as revealed. Just as in the one he mediates and perfects the unity of God, so in the gospel economy he mediates and completes the revealing and the redeeming work of the Father and the Son by integrating us into it, and so images the *perichoresis* within the life of God in bringing us in Christ to a relationship with God in which we are united with him and at the same time are affirmed in our own personhood and freedom over against him.

He shows himself to be himself personal by his doing what only persons can do, namely create personal relationships with and between other persons. In such terms we can begin to understand the distinctive function of the Spirit both in God's life and in ours.

2. The primacy of the Father
Within the Cappadocian Trinitarian tradition, questions arise about the primacy of the Father within the life of God. The Cappadocian theologians were concerned to maintain the sole *monarchia* of the Father within the life of God, reflecting the initiating sovereignty of the Father in the revealed gospel. It was from the Father that the Son was begotten and from the Father, and, as Basil said, through the Son that the Spirit proceeded, which is, of course, in accord with the Nicene Creed in its 381 revision at Constantinople. From that creedal basis, however, they drew the implication that the Father was the *aitia*, the source and cause of the whole godhead. John Zizioulos (Zizioulos, 1985, p. 16ff.) points out the advantage of this position in that it makes the ultimate source of all reality, whether uncreated in God or created in the world, unambiguously personal in the *hypostasis* of the Father, rather than, as in the West, the impersonal divine essence of which the three persons are diverse expressions.

Against this, Alan Torrance argues that to say that the Father is the cause of the Son and the Spirit suggests that he has some existence prior to and apart from them: in other words, that the Father is not himself a person who has his being from and within his relations with other persons but rather a self-subsistent individual who has a being of his own apart from the other Trinitarian persons out of which he originates them. In his debate with Zizioulos, Torrance asks this question "If the Trinity derives from a causal act of the Father, is 'the concept of the Holy Trinity' really being conceived as ontologically primordial? Does *the* exclusively primordial reality not actually become the person of the Father?" (Torrance, 1996, p. 292). Torrance responds to his own question with another, and asks whether "the intra-divine communion is not only a primordial concept but an eternal 'given' that is, ontologically, primitive and original" (Torrance, 1996, p. 293).

The conclusion is that the ultimate reality of the godhead is not the person of the Father viewed in that individualistic way, but the community of the "three persons in relation," who have their distinctive being and function always within and never outside their relations to each other. Ultimate reality from which all other reality takes its origin is not the single person of the Father but the tripersonal community of the whole Trinity. The divine community constitutes the divine persons and the divine persons in their distinctiveness and their freedom constitute the community, so that there are no persons apart from the community and no community apart from the persons.

3. The Trinitarian ordering of God's life

We need, however, immediately to add that within this primordial and given divine community, there is a particular ordering of the three persons that is intrinsic to God's self-revelation and that is therefore intrinsic to the ultimate reality that is God's own being, even if it is beyond the capacity of our language and our thought to explain in any adequate way how this is so.

Within and as a part of the Trinitarian community the Father has a place of originating sovereignty. The dynamic of self-giving that begets the Son and spirates the Spirit has its origin and its destination in the Father, as becomes clear in the sending of the Son in his incarnation and the sending of the Spirit on the day of Pentecost. Nevertheless, this initiating sovereignty of the Father makes sense only within the context of the primordial divine community, because it would have no existence or meaning except in relation to the Son and the Spirit toward whom it is exercised. Son and Spirit are who they are and do what they do only in their "from-ness," their dependence upon the Father, but the Father is who he is and does what he does only in the dynamic of his sovereign self-giving to the Spirit and the Son.

The divine community sustains and is sustained by this ordering of the divine persons, which has to be construed in terms of the way in which it has, in fact, revealed itself and not forced, as sometimes happens, into inappropriate conceptual straitjackets, where it is lauded for its equality or denounced for its hierarchy or patriarchy. The divine inter-relating is to be allowed to interpret itself and not conscripted into other forms of relating that, whether we approve of them or not, are inadequate or alien to it. Hierarchies and patriarchies are dominating and oppressing, but the Father's relation to the Son, although it also is the relation of one who initiates to one who responds, is, in contrast to both these others, one that initiates in self-giving love that has to be responded to in a like love which is not a constrained compulsion but itself an act of willing freedom.

The Father's self-giving to the Son in the Spirit at his baptism can only be responded to by a like self-giving which is offered freely in Gethsemane and consummated in costly sacrifice on Calvary, itself honored and glorified in resurrection. What the Father's love requires, the Son willingly offers, and into that interchange of paternal and filial love that is mediated and enabled by the Spirit, we are integrated by the same Spirit in whom God's love is poured into our hearts.

In these events the love of the divine persons that constitutes the life of the divine Trinity is revealed for our redemption and we are in the image of God in so far as we relate to God and to one another in ways that are ordered so as to reflect the revealed relationships of Father, Son, and Holy Spirit. Because the community of these three is indeed the primordial and ultimate reality, it was by and for that community that we were created and it was by and for it that we are being redeemed. It is to that divine community that we are to look when we think about what it means to be made and remade in the image of God.

4. The incarnate Son as the image of the Trinity
We have already said that Father, Son, and Holy Spirit are who they are and do what they do in a perichoretic relationship in which each remains who he is in his distinctness but each indwells and is indwelt by the others. Now we have to see that it is in virtue of that indwelling by his Father and his Spirit that the Son can be the image of the triune God and can transform us ourselves into that image.

To make all of this a bit more specific, we can recollect that sovereign initiation is distinctive of the Father, attentive responsiveness is distinctive of the Son, and unifying consummation is distinctive of the Spirit. When therefore we speak of the perichoretic participation of the Son in the distinctive identities of the Father and the Spirit, we have to show how in the attentive obedience of his living and his dying he manifests both the sovereign initiating power of the love of the Father and the unifying consummating power of the love of the Spirit.

To explicate this we may turn from the difficult abstractions in which we have been dealing to the story of the healing of the Roman centurion's batman in Luke 7. What the centurion, with a discernment that takes him right to the center of the dynamic of Jesus's ministry, sees in Jesus is a man who has authority because he is first and foremost a man who is under authority.

> Lord, do not trouble yourself, for I am not worthy to have you come under my roof. ... But only speak the word and let my servant be healed. For I also am a man set under authority with soldiers under me; and I say to one "Go" and he goes and to another "Come" and he comes and to my slave "Do this" and the slave does it. When Jesus heard this he was amazed at him and turning to the crowd that followed him he said, "I tell you, not even in Israel have I found such faith."
>
> (Luke 7:6–9)

What that Gentile faith grasps is that, through the exercise of what is proper to his Sonship, namely his obedience to the Father, in which he is a man *under* authority, he participates in what is proper to his Father – the power to utter a sovereign word that can take the initiative to break savingly into a situation – and becomes a man *with* authority to issue orders to illnesses.

Further, it is implicit in this story, and indeed to the whole gospel, that throughout his messianic mission Jesus is the one who is anointed, indwelt by the Holy Spirit. All that he does is the living out of the program that he is able to undertake because "the Spirit of the Lord is upon me" (Luke 4:18). The Son, in obedience to the Father, utters the word that has the Father's own power in it and the Spirit makes that word effective in the life of the man to whom it is spoken, by realizing its potential in a fresh situation that has been closed to it and by integrating that man into the Father-Son-Spirit force field through which that power flows. It is in the Son that

God is presented to us in a human life, but through his Trinitarian *perichoresis* that human life images both the Father and the Spirit so that the specificities of their functions and their relationships come into focus. As we look at him we see not just him but the Father who has sent him and the Spirit who fills him, so that in him *imago Dei* is *imago Trinitatis*.

Concluding summary

In this chapter, starting from the New Testament insistence that Jesus is himself the image of God so that it in relation to him that that image has to be understood, we have seen that Jesus cannot be understood as an isolated individual but only in his unique Trinitarian relatedness to the Father and the Spirit.

We have looked at how these Trinitarian relationships have been interpreted in the Trinitarian theologies of the Western and Eastern churches and have seen that for all its riches the former, from its start in Augustine to its modern expression in Barth, has to different degrees been prone to a modalistic temptation to major on the unity of the divine essence and to play down the distinctiveness of the Trinitarian persons and the distinctiveness of the relationships between them and, in particular, to fail to do justice to the person and characteristic work of the Holy Spirit.

Following much recent theology, we have tried to see how the characteristic emphases of the Cappadocian East can give a needed correction to that Western tradition, by seeing the Trinity as persons who share the divine nature but are bound together as "persons in community" connected in a perichoretic union in which they are inseparably one but in which each retains his distinctness and personal freedom over against the others.

We have affirmed this approach, not mainly or merely because, as we will see, it grounds and affirms the current relational understanding of personal reality, but chiefly because it is a good hermeneutic tool for understanding the revealed relationships of Father, Son, and Spirit as they are presented in the gospel narrative, in which the Father sovereignly initiates, the Son obediently executes, and the Spirit consummates and fulfils.

On the basis of that Trinitarian paradigm, we have now to go on to ask, how this God is in fact imaged in human life as created, fallen, and redeemed. If God is "persons in relationship", what does that say about us, and if God is initiating Father, responsive Son, and consummating Spirit, what does that say about the kind of people that in his image we were made to be?

4 Human Image

While I was still writing this book, the publishers asked for the photograph that you can see on its cover – the image of the author who is the source of what you are reading. But to understand in any depth what shaped the book, you have also to understand what shaped the author, and the critics of the book will rightly look not just at the individual strengths and weaknesses that the work is bound to reflect, but at the general cultural and particular theological tradition in which he stands.

They will ask to what extent the spectacles I wear give me a good focus on the material I am attempting to describe and evaluate: where they make me blind and where they help me to see.

I am not an isolated individual who can be assessed in and for himself without reference to context and background, but a white British male who is now in his seventies, who has a very specific historical context, in nature and in nurture, in home and in family, whose thinking and writing shows the influence of the theology of reformed Scotland, of the experience of charismatic renewal of the sixties and seventies, and of wrestling with at least some of the social, theological, ethical, and ecclesiological issues that have been thrown up in the Anglican situation over the last quarter century. It is in both positive and negative relation and reaction to all these that I write what I write and in relation to a much vaster and more complex set of relationships that I am what I am.

Individuality and relationality

I have started this chapter in this very personal way simply to underline the practical and personal implications of all that we will be discussing in it. The issues raised by the relationship between our individuality and our relationality – between what we are in ourselves and what we have been made by the people with whom we have lived and the world in which we have grown up – are in no sense merely abstract and theoretical but have to be reckoned with in all our specific attempts to understand and interpret human life and behavior – including mine in this book.

If we think that individuals are ultimate and relationships subsequent, we will understand ourselves and all that we do in one way; if we think that it is relationships that shape individuals, we will understand it in another way, and if, following the clue of the last chapter, we see ourselves as persons in relationship, we will understand it in a third way, which, as I will be trying to argue, refuses the alternatives of the other two and does justice to what is of value in each of them.

We started the last chapter by insisting in a christological context that Jesus could not be understood in and for himself but only in terms of his Trinitarian relationships with his Father and his Spirit; in this chapter we are asking the same question about ourselves in an anthropological context, namely whether we can be described individualistically in and for ourselves or, if not, what are the sets of relationships that make us what we are?

The same issues that arise with regard to God in the realm of theology arise also in regard to ourselves in the realm of anthropology. This is exactly what we should expect if to be human is to be in the image of God and it invites us to look to what God has revealed about himself to give us vital clues to our human self-understanding, since, in Jesus Christ, God has already imaged himself fully and perfectly in a human life.

The Self that Controls the World

In Augustinian Trinitarianism, we have already seen how the self-conscious human individual who knows and loves himself is the main analogy for his understanding of the Trinitarian life of God, and it is not hard to see how that came to be the basis for the tradition of anthropological individualism in the Christian West: the affirmation, namely that the individual, was the ultimate expression of what it meant to be human and that all the relational networks of society were the creation of the individuals who constructed and comprised them and were therefore ontologically prior to them.

Such individualism was given formal expression in the definition of the Christian philosopher Boethius (ca. 480–ca. 542), for whom a human being is "an individual substance of a rational nature." This concatenation of individuality and rationality in defining what is uniquely human has characterized much Western philosophical and theological anthropology from his day to our own. We are human because, as thinking individuals, we can go out from our sure base in ourselves, in which we know ourselves, to know that which is other than ourselves, to relate to, to assess, and ultimately to master and control the natural and human environment in which we are set.

In our objective and dispassionate knowledge resides our humanity, so that the body is played down in favor of the mind, and emotion, with its impulses and intuitions seen as the impediment to and the enemy of the cool and clear thinking, that makes us human beings, and, when such thinking is applied to the question of the *imago Dei*, makes us most like God because, on this showing, God is himself by his eternal rationality and detachment from all emotion in his imperturbable impassability, in which he can neither suffer nor be moved.

Such thinking is famously developed in the Renaissance thinking of René Descartes (1596–1650), whose well-known formula *cogito ergo sum*, "I think, therefore I am", is offered as the primal basis on which all the rest of our thinking, including our thinking about God, depends. Thus, it affirms the closest possible connection between our individual existence and our rationality. Not in what I think about but in the very fact of my thinking I gain unassailable knowledge of my own existence, in separation and abstraction from the other people and the objects around me. If I do know God, the world, and other people, it is because, first and foremost and as the basis for all other knowledge, I know myself.

In the age of the enlightenment human rationality began to change roles. Instead of being regarded as the faculty by which we know realities that have their being apart from us, it came to be seen as that which itself constructs that reality. The human mind begins to occupy something very like the role of cosmic creator and thus takes the place of God in imposing order on a chaos that, without the activity of reason, is "without form and void."

That is exactly what happens in the philosophy of Immanuel Kant (1724–1804) in which we have an intelligible and ordered world only because our reason takes the unorganized data delivered by our senses and organizes them within the frameworks of space and time, which are regarded as part of the perceptive apparatus that we bring to raw experience rather than attributes of external reality. Similarly the mind imposes upon that reality explanatory categories such as substance and cause and effect that enable us to make sense of them.

In short we have a world and not a chaos because our minds have worked on what is given to us and made out of it something we can understand and control. What God did for us according to Genesis, our minds do for ourselves according to Kant. Rationality achieves not just cognition of an independent world, but the construction and organization of a world that is intelligible to it.

For Kant, the same reason that has creative primacy in relation to our knowledge of the world, has ultimate authority in relation to our morality. The reason that constructs the world that actually exists is also the norm and measure of the world that ought to be. The voice that speaks in the categorical imperative of conscience is not the voice of a God who is above us but the voice of our own reason that is within us. To be moral is to be rational; in knowledge and in action, reason rules.

It is not hard to see how, in such a scenario of human autonomy and creativity, it was quite natural for Feuerbach to draw the obvious conclusion that Kant did not himself draw: that the human reason that makes a world for us to know and tells us how to live in it also makes for us a God who is congenial to us, because we have made him in our own image. All the possibilities from monotheism to atheism are open to us; we may project whatever kind of God we choose.

The so-called age of reason reached its culmination in the philosophy of Hegel in which the whole universe – God, the world, and human beings – was seen in terms of the unfolding of a rational cosmic self moving to its ultimate fulfilment in all the evolutions and convolutions of history. The human self, knowing itself and loving itself, that in Augustine was the paradigm for God, has become in Hegel the paradigm for everything that is.

Such a philosophy was challenged in its heyday by such as Schleiermacher, protesting against what he saw as the imperialistic arrogance of Kant's man of reason and appealing instead to the innate sense of dependence on God that is the root of all religion.

It remains a question to what extent Schleiermacher's man of religion is any more open than Kant's man of reason to a God who exists beyond him and apart from him, and whether the liberal Christianity that Schleiermacher fathered has indeed broken out of the enclosed circle of human autonomy. There are very real questions about whether its center and its norm are still located more in ourselves and in our experience of God than outside ourselves in the God we experience, more concerned with what our religious experience says about him than with what his revelation says about us.

Human autonomy today

However that may be, and although the grand philosophical systems of Kant and Hegel are long superseded, their emphasis on autonomous human beings as the controllers and masters of the world they live in and the source of the values by which they live in it, is very much with us today. We see ourselves in relation to the world as free with our technological know-how to exploit its resources for our own benefit, without proper respect for its own needs and nature, and are discovering in the prospect of climatic and environmental disaster that the world is not our oyster, that it is not endlessly plastic to the demands we make upon it, that we are more dependent upon it than we have been willing to acknowledge, and that it will go its own way in spite of us and take its revenge for our self-regarding disregard for it.

It is in our relationships to other people that the deep-seated individualism of our attitudes becomes most apparent. Covenantal relationships that once bound people to one another in marriage and family life in ties of mutual loyalty and obligation have lost that bindingness and have become secondary to what are conceived to be the needs of human happiness and self-fulfilment.

The rush to possess and to enjoy leaves less time and energy to volunteer, to help, and to care. The function of law is increasingly seen as the means of arbitrating between competitive individuals, each pursuing their own ends and ambitions to make sure that they do not hurt one another, or, if they do, to make sure that they are properly compensated for it. Interest in and responsibility for the wider concerns of the national community is at a low ebb, so that fewer and fewer people bother to vote in elections and can be roused to protest only when their personal interests are seen to be under threat.

The downside of the culture of human rights, which in its positive aspect can protect and rescue people from domination and exploitation, is the ersatz moralizing of individual needs and desires, so that I assert against other people a right to whatever I happen to want. If I want children, I have a right to have them, irrespective or whether I can provide a family set-up that will enable them to grow and prosper; if I do not want children, then I have a right to have an abortion, even if it means that a viable human life will be destroyed.

A culture of deference to authority has given way to a culture of the veneration of so-called celebrities in the worlds of sport and entertainment, simply because they provide the pleasure and the thrills that people value. Footballers and pop singers are idolized, whereas leaders in national life, politicians, academics, and scientific experts, religious leaders among them, are regarded with a cynicism and suspicion that at every turn questions their motives and their competence and delights to expose their weaknesses. Anyone who is seen to have power over me and to be in a position to inhibit or distract me from getting on with my own self-set aims and purposes is seen as a threat that can be removed by undermining the authority that such people exercise.

All in all, the base in the self that was evident even in the orthodox and powerfully Christian theological constructions of Augustine and in the philosophical systems in which such as Descartes and Kant sought to interpret the whole of reality, has been secularized and vulgarized in the individualistic preoccupations of contemporary Western society. No doubt both Augustine and Kant would have been horrified by the way Western society has developed, but much of what is open and dominating in our lifestyle was already latent and secretly but powerfully at work in their thinking.

The persistence of relationality

Of course, the whole picture is not as bleak and black as I have been painting it. The consequences of seeing ourselves as autonomous individuals in charge of our world and our values are undeniably and obviously present in contemporary Western culture, but there is still lots of self-giving love around as well. People are still moved to respond with generosity and sacrifice to the needs of others, to protest against injustices of which they themselves are not the victims, to care for the needs of neighbors, and to respond to international disasters. There are countless teachers dedicated to their pupils, doctors and nurses committed to the care of their patients far beyond the bounds of professional obligation, people in public life who are there to improve and build up society and not simply for power, prestige, and personal gain.

In the world I know best, I had the greatest respect and admiration for people in their thirties and forties in the midst of successful and moderately lucrative careers, who, at the perceived call of God, were ready to disrupt and abandon a whole comfortable lifestyle in order to minister Christ's gospel for much less money and in a society in which they were more likely to experience scorn than respect.

Equally, there can be much love where there is little religion. People who are cut off from their Christian roots still know how to look after their neighbors; human kindness and compassion manifest themselves in places where the gospel of Jesus Christ is not confessed or has indeed never been known.

And as we gladly give to others, so we gratefully receive from them. Very seldom do people regard others solely as the potential obstructers of our self-fulfilment. Alongside our assertion of our rights against others, is our gratitude to the others who have made us what we are in very fundamental ways that we will later explore. For one who resents the shortcomings of parents, there will be nine who recognize their debt to them and to the teachers, mentors, and heroes who in their persons and their writings formed our personalities, shaped our perceptions, motivated our activities, and developed our abilities. Just by being human we are continually winkled out of our self-preoccupation in gratitude to others for what we have received from them and in a genuine care for others that is itself self-giving.

You do not need to be Christian to be human; you do not fall outside the power of Jesus Christ because you have not heard or responded to the gospel of the incarnation. His rule is not confined to the realm of redemption. We have already taken note of the New Testament claim in Colossians and the gospel of John that he is the agent not just of salvation but of creation itself. In that perspective there is no escaping him, because it was through him and for him that we were made. "All things were made through him and without him was not anything made that was made" (John 1:3). The light that comes into the world when he is born is the "light that lightens every man."

Our humanity is made in his image and in so far as that image is defaced and destroyed, so far we cease to be human and are on the way to becoming nothing. On the horizontal level he is, in John Robinson's memorable phrase, the man for others and therefore to be in his image is to be a human being that is orientated outwardly to affirm others, to receive from them and to give to them, and to sin is to distort that orientation so the relationship to others is in different ways subordinated and subjugated to the affirmation of self.[3]

But in so far as sinners have not yet ceased to be human, that basic human impulse and need to go out from oneself to cooperate with and care for others is still operative in them and it is entirely consonant with the affirmations of Christian theology of the christological orientation of the whole of creation to expect to recognize in all people a reflection of the love that made them, however relativized, threatened, and attacked by sin it may be. That recognition is the sign that, whether they know it or not, people are made in the image of God. Rahner spoke of people outside the believing community as anonymous Christians and was much and rightly criticized for so doing, since to be a Christian is by definition to confess Jesus Christ and to look to him for life and salvation. Nevertheless we might more justifiably talk about anonymous image-bearers, because that is the clear implication of the claim that Jesus Christ is involved in the creation of the whole human race.

In these last paragraphs we have gone ahead of ourselves and indicated positions that have yet to be explicated and defended. We have done so because the parameters of the society in which we live, are, on the one hand, the self-affirmation that is enshrined in its intellectual inheritance and in its current state and, on the other hand, the outgoing to others which makes us human. Our task is to reach an understanding of the image of God that takes account of both – to use the technical language of theology – original righteousness and original sin, of our humanity as having its origin in the relatedness of the triune God and its actuality in its rebellion against that relatedness.

The inescapability of God

To say that, whether we know it or not, we are in the image of God is to say that we are related not only horizontally to one another but vertically to God. To reflect an image the mirror must be pointed in the direction of the original; if our humanity is indeed constituted by its relation to the God who created it, it must have built into it not only an altruistic but also a religious dimension. To be human is to be unable to escape the question of God.

A look at contemporary culture would suggest that many of us are managing to escape that question rather successfully. All across Western Europe the churches are left to small ageing minorities and people wonder what will happen to them when the last of the gray heads moves from the church to the churchyard. France takes pride in its secularity, banishes religious symbols from its schools, and proclaims, not without some credibility, that what holds society together is the cement of its secularity, which protects it from the divisiveness of competing religions. Bonhoeffer's dictum is much quoted, "humanity has come of age and has no further need for God to fill the gaps."

People may still give signs of *being* in the image of God, but they show little sign of *knowing* that they are. In fact, the whole idea of a humanity that is constituted in dependence of a Creator without whom it cannot exist, be maintained, or flourish, is fundamentally at odds with the culture of human autonomy and trust in human rationality that we have been describing.

If I see myself and my freedom threatened by the relative power of human authorities so that I refuse them my deference and am suspicious and resentful when their power is exercised, how much more will I be threatened by the absolute authority of an omnipotent creator, refuse him my worship and assure myself that I do not need to worry about his reactions to me or judgements on me because the likelihood is that he does not exist.

The culture of the autonomous humanity that aspires to be the measure of all things is profoundly unsympathetic to the claim that its life is not its own, that it is dependent upon and accountable to a God who made it and is calling it to be like him.

However, that God is not so easily disposed of as the secularists imagine. Many who reject theology embrace spirituality, claiming often as they do so that the spiritual they are exploring is simply a dimension of their own humanity but yet betraying a longing for something that will take them out of themselves and beyond themselves to a reality, however conceived, that will tell them what they cannot tell themselves and give them what they cannot give themselves. That reality can be located in naive superstitions about the stars that control and reveal their future or, with much greater sophistication, in the great world religions in which the God question is recognized and faced, and answers, however diverse and contradictory, are offered to it.

There has never existed a society without a religion, and in the life of even the most secular and militant atheist the God question will somewhere and often unbidden raise its head. Friedrich Nietzsche, often seen as the ultimate atheist and rubbisher of Christianity, in his last year of sanity before he collapsed into madness, wrote in a final frenzy of creativity a series of poems in which he cried out to the God whose existence it had been a major theme of his life's work to deny.

"No, come back, with all your torments !
All the streams of my tears run their course to you.
And the last frame of my heart – it burns up to you!
Oh come back, my unknown God! My pain! My last ... happiness"

(quoted in Küng, 1980, p. 3950).

We can, of course, write off these words as the meaningless aberrations of a man losing his grip and descending into madness, but we may equally well see it as the surfacing of the long oppressed and denied longing of the man's deep heart, to be heard with respect and awe. God is not easily escaped even by Nietzsche! On a lighter note, that other militant atheist philosopher, Bertrand Russell, once confessed that standing facing a magnificent Welsh countryside, he had to hang hard to the top of a farm gate to stop himself having a religious experience!

Wolfhart Pannenberg, in his magisterial work *Anthropology in Theological Perspective*, insists that such a concern with the ultimate is a defining characteristic of our humanity and is, indeed, implicit in everything that we know and do. When we know anything, it is always in the context of everything; there is always a desire to understand how the "anything" we know relates to the "everything" of which it is a part and what significance "anything" as part of "everything" has in the context of ultimate reality. Pannenberg summarizes the point as follows, "the so-called openness of the human being to the world signifies ultimately an openness to what is beyond the world, so that the real meaning of this openness to the world might be better described as an openness to God" (Pannenberg, 1985, p. 69).

If I understand this rather dense statement aright, what Pannenberg is saying is something like this: If the table on which my computer stands exists, it exists only in the context of this room, of this house, of this part of London, of this country, this planet, this solar system, this universe, whose own existence, according to the current theory originates in the big bang from which it all started. But where was that inaugurating exploding itself inaugurated? How far back do I have to go till I come to some ultimate factor that is not dependent on what is before it and around it but is indeed ultimate and gives the whole thing meaning and purpose? These questions are by no means always posed explicitly, but they are implicit in every statement we make.

This is a modern version of the old cosmological argument for the existence of God, but its significance here is that it is introduced in an anthropological context, not as an attempt to validate the existence of God or any conclusions about his nature but to insist that the God question is one that human beings are constituted to ask and pursue.

I have a good friend whose relationship to organized religion is at best marginal, but who is intensely interested in cosmological questions about the origins of the universe, and it is quite obvious from the way he addresses these questions that his interest is driven not just by intellectual curiosity, but by a religious quest for an ultimate that will give significance and meaning to the world he lives in and the life he lives in it. Whether he is looking in the right place is, for our present purposes, beside the point; what matters is not the answers he reaches but the fact that, in virtue not of his spirituality but of his humanity, he is asking these questions and that for all human beings these questions will not go away, despite all attempts to dismiss or suppress them.

The human mirror cannot but point toward the divine original that it was made to image. Our question about the *imago Dei* is not just a Christian question or even a religious question, it is a human question. When people encounter and are involved in the dark mysteries of suffering, when we mourn the death of other people or are brave enough to face the prospect of our own, when we see great beauty in nature or in art or hear great music, we become aware of our relationship to what is ultimate and cannot help inquiring what that relationship might be.

There are many answers to such a question, some of them religious, some of them agnostic, some of them secular, and there are many diverse and complicated factors that decide what answer any human being will give. Among these answers is the Christian claim that the ultimate has revealed himself in all his ultimacy and also in all his human accessibility in the incarnation, death, and resurrection of Jesus Christ, that the ultimate is in fact the triune and tripersonal God whose being and nature we were describing in the last chapter. The virtue of Pannenberg is that he insists that that Christian claim must be made and defended not in the closed ghettos of faith but in the public forum, where believers and unbelievers alike ask the ultimate questions about the life of the world and their own.

Human exocentricity

We may now take stock: what we have been expounding in this whole section is what Pannenberg helpfully calls the "exocentricity" of our humanity – that human persons are not isolated individuals who have their being apart from and prior to their relationships with other people, with the world, and with God. We have looked at idealist philosophies which have set up human self-conscious rationality as a paradigm for the understanding of self, world, and God and have seen how in the idealism of Kant and Hegel rationality has been seen not just as the means of knowing but as the means of constructing and creating an intelligible and moral world.

We have also seen how what was developed in a sophisticated and philosophical way has also been worked out in a culture where the self-fulfilment of individuals and their assertion of their real and imagined rights has been seen as normative for the life of society.

We have, however, also seen how the exocentricity that constitutes our humanity continually breaks through the egocentricity that defies and denies it. This can be seen in the outgoing to other people, in the committed giving to them and receiving from them that characterizes human relationships, in the thrust toward the ultimate that gives evidence of our often covert concern about our relationship with God.

To put these things together, what we discern is a challenged exocentricity, a human life constituted by relationships with God and with others that are often distorted and contradicted by the egocentricity in which we claim that we ourselves are the makers and masters of our life and of our world, but that can be successfully suppressed only by our ceasing to be human and our cutting ourselves off from all the sources from which our life stems, so that ultimately we would cease to exist and die. Jean Paul Sartre makes one of his characters in the play *Huis Clos* say that hell is other people; to the contrary, hell is ultimate solitariness, the final triumph of our egocentricity and therefore our self-inflicted death. This human relatedness to the other is at least open to being interpreted in terms of that personal relatedness to the other that constitutes the life of God as revealed in the gospel.

The world that controls the self

Every coin has two sides; the culture that challenges our dependence on the world in its assertion of our autonomy also challenges our freedom over against the world in its assertion of our heteronomy – of our being determined and programmed by forces external to ourselves that mold and shape us in ways beyond our control.

Kant, as we have already seen, thought of causality as one of the categories that human reason uses to make the world intelligible to it, but much modern science has seen the forces of cause and effect not as the means by which our minds control the world but rather as the means by which the world controls us.

Varieties of determinism

The idealistic philosophy of Hegel was the seedbed for the economic determinism of Karl Marx according to which we are fundamentally shaped outwardly and inwardly by the place in society into which we are born, a society that is itself determined by the class structures that the prevalent processes of production require and create. It is these economic forces – for Marx the oppressive structures of bourgeois capitalism – and not any decisions of our own that determine what and who we are.

At least as powerful in our society is the psychological determinism of Freud, in which the sources of our attitudes and behavior are located in the deep and mysterious forces that influence us on a subconscious level, so that our common sense claim to be in charge of ourselves and responsible for ourselves is undermined and made to look superficial and illusory.

We have lived with Marx and Freud for a long time now, but in power and in fashion at the moment is the biological determinism represented theoretically in the work of such as Richard Dawkins, in which we are seen as the end products of a long and complicated process of biological evolution built in to the genetic inheritance that informs every cell of our body and that programs not just our physical development but our thinking and our behavior as well. In the long-standing debate about whether we are what we are by nature or by nurture, scientific work on the human genetic chain has ensured that the emphasis at present falls heavily on the side of nature and the sense of social and personal responsibility is further diminished and eroded, to the regret of some and the relief of others, because it enables us to argue, as is often done for example in the homosexuality debate, that I am not accountable for my genetic inheritance over which I had no control; it is not my doing but my fate, or even my vocation.

The power of all these deterministic agendas is that they point to forces that are, in fact, powerfully influential in all our lives and that do indeed delimit our freedom. On the personal level, the economic circumstances of the society and the family into which I am born will have a powerful effect on the opportunities that are available to me, and to give me freedom you have to change the society. My psychological and genetic make up are, indeed, given starting points which I will have to take account of at every stage of my life, and which, at different points, will enable and disable, enlarge and delimit my freedom.

It is the awareness of the reality of such external determinants that gives rise to the contemporary perception of ourselves as the passive victims of irresistible compulsions from outside ourselves that absolve us from personal responsibility for what we do and what we are. Moral and criminal aberrations are to be explained in terms of the pressures that social deprivation or parental failure exert on people. My psychological problems are to be accounted for in terms of the kind of mother or sometimes even in terms of the kind of birth I had. People do or fail to do things because that is the way they were programmed and not as a result of the choices or identifications they have made. Sympathy for helpless victims replaces disapprobation for responsible evil doers. To understand all is to pardon all; the only remaining sin is a judgementalism that presumes to allocate blame.

All this demonstrates an admirable tolerance that tries to understand rather than reject and a commendable kindness that wants to help rather than to accuse. But such benefits are too dearly bought if they blur or deny the dignity and freedom of the human person and the ability of that person to yield to or resist the pressures that are exerted upon them. If we are indeed the helpless victims of the forces that shape us, not only do we lose the freedom that makes us human, but we become eligible for the no doubt well meaning techniques and manipulations of all the experts who want to improve us by designing us according to their specifications before we are born or shaping us in their own image afterward.

The line between treating people as objects to be manipulated by psychologically sophisticated advertising or journalism and treating them as responsible agents with minds to be persuaded and wills to respond to what is presented to them is increasingly hard to draw. To cross to the wrong side of that line is to attack the integrity of our personhood that belongs to our being created in the image of God, our reflecting, in the freedom of our humanity, the initiating, responding, and creative sovereignty that makes God God and constitutes the free and personal self-giving in which the Trinitarian persons relate to one another.

The persistence of personal freedom

Just as when in our theorizing our relatedness is denied or relativized, the fact of it thrusts itself upon us, so it is with our personal agency. Even when we are most aware of the faceless forces that determine us, we never entirely lose the awareness that we are not passive objects at their mercy but active subjects with minds to comprehend what is happening to us and to determine our responses to it and with wills to intervene at some point in the causal chain of events and take action to move them in the direction we intend.

Marxism was not just a theory of economic determinism; it drew deeply from the very different roots of Jewish eschatology, and sponsored a secularized and apocalyptic humanism that saw revolutionary action by the proletariat as a way to the classless society that would break the hold of capitalistic oppression. The men and women who started as the victims had the power to act in a way that would break their chains and enable them to emerge as the victors.

The whole point of Freudian psychoanalysis was not simply to recognize the determining influence of the unconscious that inhibited and controlled our freedom, but to devise techniques that would liberate people from these inhibitions and move them toward psychological wholeness.

The biological determinists who most emphasize the shaping power of evolutionary process and genetic inheritance, yet insist that with the emergence of humanity, evolution has entered into a new phase of self-awareness and self-understanding, so that human beings can comprehend what is going on and this opens the possibility of their taking action to control it and turn it in directions that are beneficial to them.

In penal theory, alongside the appreciation of social forces that incline people to criminality, there is an insistence that most people are rightly held responsible for what they have done; their bad behavior is willed behavior; their actions show that they have endorsed with their consent the destructive and antisocial influences that have been exerted upon them and it is in acknowledgement of that personal responsibility that society has the right and the duty to punish them. They may be the victims of evil but they are also evil-doers.

All this stems from the conviction that is deep in all of us, that there is enough distance between human persons and the external forces that bear down upon them to leave room for meaningful and responsible choices about where they will resist and where they will yield, what they will further and what they will oppose, where they will say yes and where they will say no. That is why we feel guilt when we have made the wrong choices and an enhancement of our humanity when we have made the right ones. Where that responsibility is denied and that guilt is no longer acknowledged, we are in the realm of psychopathy, which is on the way to losing the dignity that makes us human.

All this goes to show that even when we maximize the powers and forces that condition and control us, there keeps emerging in all kinds of ways a basic apprehension of human beings as centers of voluntary and responsible decision and action. The relationship between self and world is never one-way but always one of mutual interaction between the world's powers and our freedom.

The post-modern fragmentation of the self

But the attack on the integrity of the self has another and even more threatening dimension. When we move from modernity to post-modernity, the challenge to the human person becomes even more extreme. When we were looking at the idealist tradition, we saw how the self moves from controlling the world to absorbing it in a self that has become cosmic; so here, on the other side of the coin, but in a parallel development, the world whose forces are seen in modernity to control the self, are in post-modernity seen rather to deconstruct and destroy it.

Stanley Grenz concludes his study of post-modern interpretations of self-hood with the following summary:

> The post-modern condition entails the loss of the disengaged isolated observer who as a self-existent autonomous individual forms the primary building block for the purely contractual social order. Rather the post-modern self is constituted by social relationships. The socially formed self, however, is highly decentred and fluid, for a person can have as many selves as social groups in which he or she participates. Consequently, the self is a bundle of fluctuating relationships and momentary preferences. In a fast-changing world however, this leads to a highly unstable, impermanent self.
>
> (Grenz, 2001, p. 136)

That is an interesting statement through which we have to pick our way very carefully. Measured by our diagnostic model of a triune God who is three persons in free and binding personal relationships, there are

Human Image

elements in the post-modern picture with which we must sympathize and other elements that we have to question. We also want to affirm that the self is not the disengaged self-existent autonomous individual of modernity who has a being of its own apart from its relationships. We also want to maintain that self is "constituted by social relationships," but our crucial difference from the post-modern understanding is our inclusion in that web of relationships a dominant abiding relationship with the God who has made us in his image. Our contention will therefore be that, when that relationship with God is taken into account, we have a scenario that offers a richer and fuller understanding of personhood than either the self-existent self that has existence outside and prior to its relationships, and the fragmentary impermanent self that has no abiding life of its own within the web of relationships in which it stands. In due course we will interrogate the biblical anthropology and its Trinitarian base to see what light it can shed on the perplexing juxtaposition of dependence and freedom with which we have been faced by all the material we have surveyed in this chapter.

In the meantime, we have to register how well this post-modern portrayal of selfhood resonates with the existential self-understanding of many people today. Perhaps self-understanding is precisely the wrong word here, because that is exactly what is lacking; people do not understand themselves; they do not know who they are. One remembers again the haunting questions that Dietrich Bonhoeffer asked himself in prison and that sixty years later many more people are asking today.

"Who am I? This or the other?
Am I one person today and another tomorrow?
Am I both at once? A hypocrite before others

and before myself a contemptibly woebegone weakling?
... Who am I? They mock me, these lonely questions of mine.
Whoever I am, thou knowest, O God, I am thine"
(Bonhoeffer, 1967, p. 348).

What Bonhoeffer felt about himself under the pressures of his imprisonment and threatening death, many people also feel about themselves under the pressures of a fragmented society that lacks a coherent center of value and purpose that can hold their lives together. What I am at work with my colleagues seems to have little in common with what I am at home with my spouse and my children; and, if I go to church, what happens there seems to belong to a Sunday world that is personally comforting, stimulating, and even spiritually challenging, but has little carry-over to the world and the community to which I return when the service is over, where the gospel that is proclaimed in the church and the lifestyle it implies is unacknowledged and largely unknown. There are many people who have been in churches all their lives and who have made the faith of the church their own in very genuine and personal ways who are yet unable to come to terms with the fact that that faith has something to say about the attitudes, priorities, and obligations that they bring to the rest of their lives.

The question "What would Jesus do about money, sex, war, the environment?" may be naive, but it is alarming that there are many Christian people who have never begun to ask it in any serious way so that they live in a state of unhealthy schizophrenia with a demoralizing suspicion that in their failure to get it all together, they themselves are in danger of falling apart. The truth is that when I cannot coordinate the various disconnected networks in which I live, I also fail to coordinate myself. It is that failure of coordination, that multiple schizophrenia which is the existential reality on which the post-modern theory of the self is based and from which it gains its credibility.

The survival of the self

The human person, as we have already seen, is, however, much more robust than such theories allow. Despite all attempts to fragment and disrupt it, most people have a real, even if incomplete, perception of a single identity that persists through all the diverse experiences they encounter and the disjointed networks and communities to which they relate. In fact, our very awareness of the disjointedness of our world presupposes the reality of a single subject who operates in all these separate areas. If I were totally schizophrenic, I could never know it; if my divided self distresses me, then there must somehow be a single self on both sides of the divide to know and bear the pain. Even so, we still need to ask about the nature of that presupposed and perceived identity and how it is constituted.

Biblical resources

For this we may most helpfully turn to the resources offered by the biblical gospel, noting first that what we find there will agree with the post-modern diagnosis in that both speak of personhood in terms of relationality rather than individuality. Our selfhood has its source not in ourselves but in our relationship to that which is beyond ourselves. For post-modern thinking, all such relationships are temporary and incoherent, so that the self that has its being in relation to them is also temporary and incoherent. For the biblical model, however, there is a relationship that is constant, faithful, and reliable that therefore can be the source of coherent and continuing personhood, namely our covenant relationship with God.

In the Old Testament, what holds Israel together and gives it a meaningful identity in all the vicissitudes of its history, in exodus, in wilderness, in possession of the land, in exile from it and in return to it, is its continuing relationship with Yahweh, its God. The central reality that holds all these historical experiences in relation to itself and to one another is Yahweh's election of Israel and his covenant with it that is echoed and reaffirmed at every point in its life: "I will be your God and you will be my people."

The promise implied in the first half of that verse and the demand that is implied by the second is what makes Israel Israel. What patriarchs and prophets, kings and priests have in common down the years and in spite of the different perspectives and positions out of which they operate, what enables them to belong together and to communicate with one another is the fact that they live in the good of Yahweh's choice of them and are accountable to his requirements upon them.

His covenant grace and faithfulness in the past has to be remembered and celebrated because it is the basis of the way in which they will cope with the present and of their hope for the future. That he should desert them or they desert him is the end of them, that he should remember them and call them back to himself is the remaking of them. In relation to him is their life; away from him is their dissolution and their death. That is what is implied in the verse from Habakkuk that becomes, with a different resonance, so central for Paul.

"The righteous shall live by their faith" (2:4). The source of the people's life when they are in right relationship with Yahweh, is their faithfulness to him, which is the response to and image of his faithfulness to them. In that, amidst all changes and disruptions, their national life finds its consistent identity and significance.

Further, what gave identity to the nation also gave identity to the individual people who led that nation. One thinks of the procession of men and women of faith celebrated in Hebrews 11 and of the specific Old Testament stories of which that chapter is a summary. Abraham, Moses, Isaiah, Jeremiah, and David were who they were and did what they did because the corporate vocation became personal for them, and the thing that held their lives together and enabled them to cope with the things around them and within them that could have torn them apart, was Yahweh's call to them with its gracious promises and their response to it with its binding obligations.

Leading that procession for Hebrews and for all Christians is Jesus "the pioneer and perfecter of faith" whose human life from start to finish was centered in his relationship to his Father and to the messianic vocation it involved. The twelve-year-old boy in the temple knows he must be about his Father's business; the tortured man in Gethsemane struggles with the horrifying demands that his faithfulness to that vocation imposes upon him. The dying man on the cross, who has been totally faithful to the Father, entrusts his spirit to the Father's faithfulness to him, knowing that his whole life and future depends on it. All the way from beginning boyhood to resurrected manhood, the whole identity of Jesus is constituted by the Father's faithfulness to the Son and the Son's faithfulness to the Father – and it is within that matrix that our salvation, our continuing life and identity, is achieved by Jesus and in the Spirit given to us.

Covenant and creation

To understand how all this impacts on our present discussion, we have to remember that the story of Israel's dealing with its God and of the Church's dealing with its Savior is not just a special story shut up in a religious ghetto and of significance only to the Jews and the Christians who make their home there. It is at the heart of Israel's faith that Yahweh is not just a tribal deity but the creator of the heavens and the earth, the God who relates not just to Abraham, the man of faith, but to Adam, the representative of universal humanity far beyond Israel and that the vocation of Israel is not that it should itself experience the blessings of a covenant relationship with Yahweh, but that through that relationship all the families of the earth should also be blessed.

So also the identity of Jesus in his relationship to his Father has significance far beyond the circle of those who believe in him, because he is the eternal Son through whom all things were and are made. Thus, what happens in Israel and culminates in Jesus is the clue and the key to what Adam was made for and what it means that he was made in the image of God.

The difference between Israel and the rest of the world is not that it has an ontologically different relationship to God than the rest of humanity. If it had, its life would have no universal significance. The difference is that in the election of Israel the universal relationship comes to knowledge and definition – "You only have I known of all the families of the earth" (Amos 3:2). Israel is the place where what constitutes universal humanity is specially and specifically revealed. Jesus the Messiah of Israel is the revelation and the realization of what Adam – Everyman – was made to be. If we believe in the God of Israel who is the God and Father of our Lord Jesus Christ, then we have a basis for understanding universal human identity. Where that revelation is unknown, unacknowledged, or rejected, there will be a whole host of different and incompatible anthropologies to choose from, but if the relationship to the God of Israel is, indeed, ontologically universal, however it may be interpreted, there should be running through all these anthropological options, a common factor that we all recognize and acknowledge in ourselves and in one another, whatever our cultural and religious traditions, that constitutes our shared human identity and that echoes and mirrors, even if from afar, the covenant relationships of Yahweh and Israel.

Obligated responsiveness

Let me try to define what that common factor is in a formula that is as compact and as general as I can make it. What constitutes our human identity is an obligated responsiveness to realities distinct from ourselves from which, on the one hand, we receive the affirmations that give us our identity and which, on the other, make demands upon us that enable us to find ourselves in our response to them. We can explicate that summary and rather abstract statement in a series of points.

The range of responsiveness

It is a statement that covers the whole range of human experience and behavior. In every relationship into which we enter we are dealing with realities that both give to us and demand from us, and it is in the receiving and the giving that we come to know ourselves.

If I am a gardener, my engagement with soil and plants intrigues, enriches, and satisfies me and imposes upon me an obligation to tend and protect what has been put into my care, so that if I neglect it I have failed in my obligation of responsiveness toward it. If I am a scientist, my concentrated commitment to my discipline will shape me, develop me, and give me confidence in my competence to cope with my material and pose upon me an obligation to find and employ categories of thinking and practical techniques that will enable me to do justice to that material and to cooperate with others in so doing.

When we come to interpersonal relationships, the obligated responsiveness of giving and receiving becomes even more obvious. Pannenberg in a masterly interaction with developmental psychology digs deep into the process by which human persons are formed from babyhood onward. For him the process of our personal formation depends on our exocentric relationship to our environment that begins at birth and is completed only at the *eschaton*. Personhood is as much ultimate destiny as present reality. But all the way, it depends on other persons and imposes obligations toward them.

A baby starts with a completely undifferentiated awareness of its environment and is guided mainly by an instinct of self-preservation to its mother's breast. But as the baby begins to mature he begins to become aware, through the signals of love that his mother offers, that she is distinct from him and he from her, she as the loving supplier and he as the needy recipient of all that she gives. Yet in their distinctness these two are bound together in a relationship of love which she initiates and to which he increasingly learns to respond. Thus, the relationship to the other is the condition for the emergence of the self. It is not that I am first a self who subsequently becomes aware of others. I am born into a set of relationships, and because I am loved and affirmed in the central relationship I can identify myself as the one who is the distinct object of that love, who is secure because of it and is invited and, indeed, obligated to respond to it. Where that love is refused or withdrawn, personhood will be threatened and selfhood will fail to develop.

These insights are almost exactly replicated in the indigenous African understanding of the essence of humanity in terms of *ubuntu*, which Archbishop Tutu expounded as follows in a recent lecture:

> We say that a person is a person through other persons. We are made for togetherness, to live in a delicate network of interdependence. The totally self-sufficient person is sub-human, for none of us comes fully formed into the world. I need other human beings in order to be human myself. I would not know how to walk, talk, think, behave as a human person except by learning it all from other human beings. For *ubuntu* the *summum bonum* is communal harmony. Anger, hatred, resentment – all are corrosive of this good. If one person is dehumanized, then inexorably we are all diminished and dehumanized in our turn.
>
> (Tutu, 2004, p. 14)

Such a vision of humanity is very different from the Western individualism with which we have been struggling in this chapter. It is an insight that was formulated long before the culture in which it developed was exposed to Christianity, and yet echoing as it does a view of humanity that coheres with the Christian gospel, it is a powerful witness to the claim that human life in its inter-relatedness itself bears the marks of the tripersonal God who made it.

To resume our argument, the gifts of a good mother are many. Through my relationship with her I will be introduced into a set of other relationships, first within the family and then within the wider society, that will give me much more than she could give and engage me in interests and obligations beyond her control or indeed her ken.

Chief among these gifts and the key that opens the door to many others is the gift of language. Key moments in a child's life are when she can speak and when she can read or write. It is through words that we enter into all that our culture has to offer us and it is through language that a still implicit awareness of others and of oneself as over against these others can be formulated in explicit and conscious thought. Kevin Vanhoozer points out that language has what he calls a "presumption of covenantal relation" which he says "stands for the obligation we have toward our neighbour, as good citizens of language to understand what that person is saying and what that person is doing in her saying. Interlocutors always share one common goal, that of understanding and being understood" (Vanhoozer, 2002, p. 201).

In other words, the very act of speaking falls within the matrix of obligated responsiveness that we have been describing as the essential relatedness of our humanity. To speak and require a hearing implies a promise to speak the truth, and to hear implies an obligation to attend to what is said with understanding and to make an appropriate response to it. It is within that covenantal interaction of promise and attentiveness that we relate to our world and the people in it.

It is when that interaction becomes most personal, and therefore most like the interaction that constitutes the life of God, that it has the power to affirm and maintain our own personhood. It is the covenantal relationship of commitments of being loved and of loving in response to that love in the areas of our lives in which we are most intimately involved that create and maintain a solid basis on which we can build a stable sense of identity. In a good family, in a good friendship, in a good marriage, within the love that both unites me to the people who offer that love and both obligates and frees me to return that love, in the bonds of that kind of mutual commitment, the faithfulness of the love offered is the anchor for the stability and continuity of the self that receives it; *Amor ergo sum*, I am because I am loved.

In all these ways in different areas of my life, in working with things, in belonging to a society that has stable commitments to a set of cherished values and to communities and groups within it that espouse particular causes, in being loved by and loving people around me, in the different degrees of giving and receiving that all these different interactions involve, I can identify myself as the one who receives what is given and who is stimulated and enabled to make a free and personal response to it. In all these commitments I find the meaning and purpose of who I am and what I am for.

Identity, affirmed and threatened

But we cannot forget that these apprehensions of meaning and purpose are, as post-modernism insists, fragmentary unless we can identify some ultimate relationship that will hold them all together. If the different aspects of life on which I depend for my identity – work and home, public and private, church and world, past and present – remain separate from one another, then at best I will be unable to adjudicate the different claims that each makes upon me and will be torn apart by them. At worst I will collapse into the depersonalizing schizophrenia we have already described where I can no longer make an adequate response to these claims because I have no confidence in who I am and no conviction about where I am going.

Alongside that fragmentation that post-modern approaches identify, there are also powerful forces that, unlike the benign influences we have been describing, relate to me in ways that are not liberating of my personhood but rather threaten and oppress it. The fear that the self might be controlled and overwhelmed by forces that are hostile to it, which we have already discussed, is far from being without substance. To grow up is to discover that not everybody is as affirming of me as the parents, teachers, and friends who have been the agents of my growth. There are people, social structures, and institutions that will ride roughshod over my personal integrity in order to use me and subjugate me to their own purposes.

I may have bad parents who will not give me what I need. I may be born into a situation of economic deprivation that will stop my potentialities from being realized. I may be seduced and deceived by media that spin the truth in ways that deny me access to reality. I may be isolated, rejected, and even persecuted because by race, color, or religion I am different from the predominant culture. I may be limited and disabled physically or mentally by genetic inheritance over which I have no control. I may be the victim of the cussedness of circumstances that by accident, illness, earthquake, or flood make the things I was living for inaccessible to me and leave me in despair.

In life as actually encountered there is that which affirms and draws me into these covenantal relationships of giving and receiving in which we find ourselves, but there is also that which fragments, frustrates, and threatens our personhood; it is that ambiguity between what makes us and what unmakes us with which we have to live, and it comes into final focus in the fear and prospect of death, the unavoidable threat that the last word will not be with what affirms us but with what abolishes us. That prospect, for all our attempts to suppress it, consciously or unconsciously haunts us with the threat that all our little islands where we enjoy the relationships that make us flourish will be engulfed in a dark sea of nothingness that will make an end of us all. We are in the words of Hebrews "those who all our lives are held in slavery by the fear of death" (2:15).

The ultimate obligation

It is that ambiguity that drives us to the ultimate question, the God question, which, as we have already seen, arises in every human culture. Which side of the ambiguity we have been describing does ultimate reality affirm and which does it deny? Is that ultimate reality itself the source of the covenantal relationships in which persons are created and nourished, because that reality is itself constituted by the perfect giving and receiving of free persons? Or is it itself finally impersonal so that it relativizes our personhood and requires us to lose our personal distinctness in some cosmic whole? Are the gods themselves ambiguous and arbitrary, are there contrary divine forces working for our making or our unmaking so that the ultimate outcome is eternally unresolved, or is the experienced ambiguity itself the ultimate reality with no divine force behind it to direct it, so that we are the victims of a directionless world that will end in human death and cosmic entropy?

All these questions are raised by the nature of human experience; each culture has formed its own responses to them, and all the various answers that we have suggested in the last paragraph have in different combinations and permutations been formulated and are being given in contemporary human communities and mediated by the processes we have described to the people who are born into these communities.

Until our own day, these communities, with their different answers to these ultimate questions, have lived in geographical isolation so that the differences and contradictions between them have been noted and discussed rather than existentially encountered. Increased immigration and advances in communication have changed all that, with the result that the clash of cultures has become an experienced reality which is itself destabilizing in the way each answer is challenged and potentially relativized by the other answers that are incompatible with it. How can the vision of ultimate reality that I have inherited go on giving purpose and significance to my life if I begin to regard it as only one among many ways of understanding that reality, and on what grounds can I offer it to others, who have been shaped by quite different religious traditions, as in some way better than their own?

The thing to note here is that amidst all their diversity there is a factor that all the cultures and the religions share, that brings them into relation with and respect toward each other. It is precisely that structure of obligated and committed responsiveness that has kept emerging throughout this chapter as the constituting factor of human personhood. The convictions and values that come to us from our cultural and religious traditions present themselves to us with different degrees of authority to which we respond by entering into binding commitments to them in which we recognize their truth and pledge ourselves to live in the light of it.[4] The ultimate commitment is to the ultimate reality which for most cultures is known as God, even though his being and nature are understood in many differing and, indeed, contradictory ways.

Nevertheless, across the cultural and religious divides, people recognize and respect in one another the same structure of commitment to that which has first been given to them and has then been internalized by them in the response that it has won from them. That is why Christians have defended the rights of Muslim women in France to dress in a way that their religion requires. We recognize the covenantal nature of the obligation and defend the right and the freedom of those who seek to fulfil it, even when we do not share the content of that obligation.

It is that sense of being bound in the same kind of commitment to diverse and contradictory religious understanding and practices that makes interfaith dialogue at once so compelling and so difficult, because we have to relate to other people in a paradoxical combination of respectful recognition of their commitments and yet a contesting of much of what these commitments lead them to affirm out of our own ultimate loyalty to the Lord Jesus Christ and the universal truth claims of his gospel.

Our business as believing Christians in this situation is to make good the claim that this structure of receiving and responding that constitutes human personhood can be understood coherently, credibly, and cogently as the reflection in universal human experience of that relationship with God that is revealed and clarified in his covenantal relationships with Israel, culminating in his relationship with the Messiah Jesus, which is itself the incarnational expression of the interpersonal life of the triune God. We become human in the way that we do through our receiving from others. It is in our relationships with them that we become aware of ourselves as persons capable of and obligated to committed responses to other people and to God, who is the ultimate source of the giving and receiving that structures our life – all that is the reality and the sign that we are created in the image of God.

When what it means to be in that image is expounded in the christological context toward which, as we have seen, the biblical witness clearly points, it will lead to understandings of humanity and of the receiving and giving into which it is called, which are different from and indeed challenging of the anthropological understandings of other faiths and cultures.

Our business in all this is to bear intelligent but above all gracious witness to what we have learned from Christ about human nature and destiny, in the hope that the Holy Spirit will speak convincingly and convertingly through that witness to those who approach these questions starting from different cultural and religious presuppositions and therefore make different emphases and reach different conclusions. In the end of the day the answer to the question "Who do you say you are?" will depend on the answer we give to the question of Jesus, "Who do you say that I am," and, as Matthew reminds us, the answer to the latter question is given not by flesh and blood but my Father and the Spirit he gives.

Conclusions

It is now time to summarize the conclusions toward which this chapter has been moving. We have seen that the attempt to see individual human beings and the world to which they are related as dualistic alternatives in conflict with each other, is inadequate to the reality that we are seeking to address. On the one hand, the rational self has no independent being over against its environment that enables it to exercise an imperialistic control over that environment, but is at every point dependent on that environment to make it what it is. Our personhood and its attributes are not our possessions but the gifts that reach us through our relationships with others that mediate our ultimate relationship with God. On the other hand, although that environment has in it natural, personal and institutional forces that can oppress our personhood and inhibit its freedom, as the creation of an affirming and loving God it has in it a basic beneficence that affirms and enables our personhood, that sets us in a covenantal structure that establishes, affirms, and maintains our freedom and our obligation to make responsible choices about how we will respond to what is offered for our apprehending knowledge, for our appropriate action, for our committed love.

It is this structure of responsible obligation which holds across the whole range of our human experience and which, in an unending series of relationships with things and people, gives a consistent and abiding sense of our identity as those whose response has been, is being, and will be required yesterday, today, and tomorrow and who remain ultimately accountable to God for the responses that we have made. All the partial relationships that constitute our lives in different ways and to different degrees are designed to reflect and introduce us to the ultimate relationship to God whose affirming grace is mirrored in and conveyed through the things and people among whom he sets us and whose absolute claim upon us is reflected in the relative claims they make on us.

Personalizing postscript

In this chapter we have perforce been dealing in sweeping surveys, massive generalizations, and abstract arguments. It is good therefore to end by looking at one example of how all this worked out concretely, personally, specifically, and rather movingly in the life of one man.

In his little book, *Invitation to Pilgrimage*, John Baillie speaks of his childhood in a Highland Manse and of its shaping influence on the rest of his life.

> I cannot remember a time when my life seemed to me to be my own to do with as I pleased. From the very beginning its center was not in itself or in me, but outside itself and me. I was of course, in the first instance, under the authority of the elder members of the household ... I was under orders and it was from my father or my mother or my nurse that the orders came. Yet my earliest memories clearly contain the knowledge that these elders did but transmit and administer an authority of which they were not themselves the ultimate source ... I understood that my parents were under the same constraint that they were so diligent in transmitting to me ... What then was the ultimate source of the authority which my parents were thus doing their fallible best to administer and under which they stood no less than I? What was this constraint that was laid on us? Whose was this greater will that we were called upon to obey? Whom were my parents pleasing, since they were not pleasing themselves, and whom did they want me to please in pleasing them? Once again, I have no memory of a time when I did not know the answer. From the beginning I knew that it was God.
>
> (Baillie, 1942, pp. 37–39)

The passage was worth quoting at some length because it matches point by point the understanding of human personhood that we have been expounding.

Firstly, it is a description of what we might call a covenantal childhood. The young John comes into self-awareness in a developing consciousness that he is encountering a gracious authority that requires of him and wins from him a response of willing obedience and in that encounter he discovers an identity that will grow into the adult and the theologian that he will become but will be the constant factor that will hold his life together and give it meaning and purpose. For that very reason, to be thus addressed in imperative terms is itself an act of great grace because in that address, the freedom and integrity of the boy and the man from whom the response is required is established and consolidated.

Secondly, the relationship with God into which Baillie enters is not an innate possession that he holds in the inner recesses of his individual soul; it is not adjectival to him so that he only has to search deep within to find it. It is relational, it comes to him as an undeserved gift from outside himself in the first place through the mediation of his parents who introduce him into the community of the Christian church in all the particularity of its expression in the Highland Presbyterianism of the end of the nineteenth century, so that home and church become the bases from which his encounter with God and his understanding of it can expand and develop. His parents, in the exercise of their loving authority, are to him the authentic reflection of the ultimate authority of God. In the Pauline phrase, he sees as in a mirror the glory of the Lord and that starts him on a long journey in which he himself can be changed into God's likeness (2 Cor. 3). so that his father's God whom he would not have known apart from his father becomes his own God who reflects himself in his own life in ways that are different from his father.

In a phrase that is important for Baillie's later theology we are here in the presence of a "mediated immediacy"; through the God imaged in his parents, Baillie comes to a knowledge of God that no longer depends on his parents in which he, like them, genuinely, even if always partially and fallibly, mirrors the same God. It is within the dynamics and interactions of all these relationships that persons have their being, and people come into a free responsiveness to other people and to God that mirrors the interpersonal Trinitarian relationships that constitute the three persons freely giving themselves to one another within the life of God.

Thirdly, from the Christian perspective which has been our controlling point of reference throughout this chapter, John Baillie, like many of us who are cradle Christians, was born into a highly privileged context into which the light of Jesus Christ shone from the very beginning, so that the whole dynamic of our relationships with God and with one another, which in different contexts would have remained implicit or been understood in quite different ways, for him and for us became explicit from the start. We do well to remember that much is required from those to whom so undeservedly and generously so much is given.

For all that, we do well to remember that even on those who have been born into cultural contexts where he is unknown or even rejected, the light of Christ shines because it is the true light that lightens everyone (John 1:9). That is why, because we are in the sphere of Christ in virtue of our creation even when we do not share in his redemption, we can have a measure of human identity apart from any Christian identity. We are made human beings because, in the basic structure of things, we enter into the beginnings of personhood though being loved and liberated by other people and by them inducted into an obligated responsiveness to ultimate reality, however conceived. To be so made and so related is to be created in and for the image of God.

Body, soul, and spirit?

Before we close this chapter we should ask how the understanding of human life in terms of its external relationships with God and with other people itself relates to the traditional understanding that sees the human individual as made up of body and soul, according to a bipartite analysis, or body, mind, and spirit according to an alternative tripartite analysis. Jesus himself speaks in these terms when, for example, he warns his disciples not to fear "those who kill the body but cannot kill the soul" (Matt. 10:28), making a clear distinction between them and contemplating a possible separation of the one from the other. We need therefore to ask how this way of looking at things relates to the relentlessly relational approach we have been adopting.

N. T. Wright is very helpful at this point. Speaking of Paul's understanding of the different components of our humanity, he says,

> Just as, for Paul *soma* [body] is the whole person seen in terms of public, space-time presence and *sarx* [flesh] is the whole person seen in terms of corruptibility and perhaps rebellion, so *psyche* [soul] is the whole person seen in terms of, and from the perspective of what we loosely call the "inner" life ... Paul can use the word *pneuma* [spirit] to refer to the human "spirit" by which he seems to mean ... the very center of the personality and the point where one stands on the threshold of encounter with the true god.
> (Wright, 2003, p. 283)

On such a showing body, soul, and spirit are not separable components of a complex individual self, but are descriptions of the one self in the different sets of relationships in which it stands to the world (body), to itself (soul), and to God (spirit).

We have to recognize that the word *psyche* plays a different part in Paul's tripartite description of our humanity than it does in the bipartite approach implied in our Matthew quotation from Jesus, where body stands for our relationships with the world and this present age and soul for our relationship with God and the age to come, and the point is that we can lose the former without losing the latter.

Such differences in linguistic usage reflect variations in the same basic approach to our humanity that sees that its being is constituted not in the isolation of its individuality but in the different relationships in which it stands. And that is so, whether we distinguish body and soul with Jesus, or body, soul, and spirit with Paul.

In other words, the terms body, soul, and spirit are meaningless apart from the relationships to the world, other people, and God in which the self stands. That we should be body, soul, and spirit is not simply part of ourselves but comes to us in virtue of the relationships to that which is outside ourselves and on which we depend. We are body, soul, and spirit as persons and not as individuals, because, as we have been insisting throughout this chapter, we image the God whose own being is not that of a solitary individual, still less of three such individuals, but of Father, Son, and Holy Spirit in inextricable relationships with one another, three persons, and one God.

5 Triune Image

In the last chapter we located the image in the relationality in which human persons have both their being and their freedom. For all the great gulf between Creator and his creatures, the basic structure of human life reflects the basic structure of the Trinitarian life of God. To say that is not to say anything new or original but simply to echo the central anthropological insight of much mainline contemporary theology. My proposal, however, is that we should move beyond such generalities to a much more specifically Trinitarian understanding of our humanity.

We are in the image of God, not just because our personhood is dependent upon our relationality, but because, by virtue of our creation by the triune God, we mirror the Father, we mirror the Son, and we mirror the Holy Spirit. To be authentically human means to reflect in our relationships, first, the specific relationship that the Father has with the Son, second, the specific relationship that the Son has with the Father, and third, the specific relationship that the Spirit has with the Father and the Son.

Further, if that is what constitutes the *imago Dei*, it is marred and defaced when, in our relationships with one another, we fail to reflect that which makes the Father Father, that which makes the Son Son, and that which makes the Spirit Spirit. In other words this proposal has hamartiological[5] as well as anthropological implications; it tells us about both our personhood and our sin. To clarify this we need to ask in a more specific way than we have till now what it is that the three divine persons share and also what it is that distinguishes them from one another.

The God who is free to love

We can start by asking what the three Trinitarian persons have in common, in traditional terms: what is the divine *physis*, nature, that they all share. To clarify this we cannot do better than turn to Karl Barth's famous description of the character of the God who has revealed himself to us in Christ and who is eternally what he has thus shown himself to be in history.

At the center of Barth's doctrine of God is his exposition of the thesis that the God who comes to us in Christ is the "One who Loves in Freedom" (Barth, 1957, p. 257ff.). We know this God because, freely and under no constraint but that of his own love for us, he gives himself for us in Christ and to us in the Spirit, in order that he may redeem us into that fellowship with himself that is our salvation and our life.

But he can love us freely because, prior to us and apart from us, he is love; his own being is characterized by the love with which the Father in the Spirit loves the Son and the Son in the Spirit loves the Father. He does not need us in order to have an object for his love. He is in his own life both the loving Father and the beloved Son who fulfil their love for each other in the loving Spirit who mediates and perfects their love. Because God is love in himself, his love for us is not a necessity of his being, but a free act of his grace.

That love and that freedom are not two attributes of God that are in any kind of open or latent competition with each other. His freedom is not an arbitrary omnipotence, an infinite freedom of choice that human beings vainly imagine is the peak of self-fulfilment. God's freedom is not the freedom to do anything, perhaps to love and perhaps not to love. His freedom is the freedom to be true to himself, and therefore to be true to the love that constitutes his own being. As Barth puts it:

> Freedom is of course more than the absence of limits, restrictions or conditions. That is only its negative and to that extent improper aspect ... But freedom in its positive and proper qualities means to be grounded in one's own being, to be determined and moved by oneself. This is the freedom of the divine life and love. In this positive freedom of his, God is also unlimited, unrestricted and unconditioned from without. He is the free Creator, the free Reconciler, the free Redeemer.
>
> (Barth, 1957, p. 301)

God's freedom can never be understood apart from his love. When he creates us, it is in love and for love; when he judges us and rejects us in our sinfulness, it is because we are living and acting in contradiction to that love; when he redeems us it is because that love cannot in the end let us go and gives itself utterly to bring us back to itself. In all his dealings with us his free acts confirm and express his free love.

His freedom is in fact integral to his love, because if it were not free it could not be love. Love that is not the spontaneous act of the lover but is compelled by something else is not love, or at any rate not the kind of love that God has for us. Love that does not affirm the personal integrity and respect the freedom of the one it loves to make a spontaneous and free response to it, will become violent or manipulative of its object and so cease to be love.

That is why perhaps John Donne's prayer, "Ravish my heart, three-personed God," cannot be answered in the terms in which it is made. God's love does not rape or ravish; it has a very different and even more powerful causality of its own that works always within its respect for our human integrity; it attracts and it persuades, it woos, it allures, and it wins the only response that could be appropriate and acceptable to its own nature: the free personal response of a converted heart.

That is why God cannot save the world by an act of imposed omnipotence, but only by an act of the self-giving love of Christ received in free personal acts of faith which, by his work of regeneration the Holy Spirit inspires and enables, but which are authentically our own.

It is in this love and the personal freedom that is integral to it that the Trinitarian persons have their being within the one life of the one God. Because each is equally God, each loves with God's love and is free with God's freedom, and that is what makes possible the personal relationships between them that come to incarnate expression in the gospel and that constitute the dynamic of mutual self-giving in which God lives and by which we are saved.

The distinctness of the divine persons

Nevertheless, within that life and in the accomplishment of that salvation, the freedom of the one divine love is expressed in three different ways which define the hypostatic distinctness of Father, Son, and Holy Spirit over against each other. When we were surveying the biblical material as developed in Trinitarian theology, we identified these distinctions. In the Father we identify the initiating sovereignty of the divine love; in the Son we identify the obedient responsiveness of the same divine love, and in the Spirit we identify the perfecting creativity of the same divine love. It is in the initiating of the Father, in the responsiveness of the Son, and in the creativity of the Holy Spirit that God's life is lived and God's work is done. In the unimaginable but always personal union of their self-giving to one another, each has a perichoretic participation in the others, so that as he obeys the Father, the Son participates in the authority of the Father; as he sends the Son, the Father participates in his self-offering on the cross; as he applies and perfects what the initiating of the Father and the responsiveness of the Son have accomplished, the Spirit shares in the creativity of the one and the responsiveness of the other.

The Trinitarian image

If the freedom of the divine love is expressed within the life of God in initiation, obedience, and consummation, then to image the life of that God is to mirror in our humanity the initiation of the Father, the obedience of the Son, and the creativity of the Spirit as the harmonious but distinct expressions of the free love of God within a human life and a human community. As human beings made in the image of God, we are so fashioned that in our relationships with other people, we also initiate, respond, and fulfil, and so mirror the distinctive functioning of the divine persons. In that way *imago Dei* is, indeed, *imago Trinitatis;* the undefined likeness of Genesis becomes explicit and specific in the light of the whole divine revelation of which Genesis is a part. In this way we can see and begin to test the anthropological implications and insights of this kind of Trinitarian theology.

Image and sin

This approach also has hamartiological implications; as well as telling us about the constitution of our humanity it tells us also about the nature and consequences of our sin. If to be in the image of God is to reflect the divine love and freedom in a human life, to sin is to reject the exocentricity of that love in favor of a self-affirming egocentricity as the motivating factor in our own actions and relationships and as a result to limit, restrict, and deny the freedom of other people to reflect the image of God in and for which they also were created. Just as love and freedom are two integrated aspects of God's being, so the refusal of love and the denial of freedom are connected aspects of human sinning. We sin when we refuse to love and when we refuse the responsibilities of our freedom and, in either case, imprison ourselves in many different bondages. We are sinned against when others withdraw from us the affirmation, respect, and care that express love. We sin actively when we oppress others, personally or socially, so that they are deprived of the freedom to be what God made them to be. Furthermore, just as the love and freedom of God take specific and distinctive forms in the three Trinitarian persons, so there are distinctive denials of love and freedom, rebellions and oppressions that relate in distinct ways to the initiating love of the Father, the responsive love of the Son, and the fulfilling love of the Spirit.

The image restored

Further, this model has implications and insights into the nature of our regeneration and sanctification, which consists in the recovery of our lost freedom in relation to what the Father has done through the Son and in the Spirit and in a reorientation toward and a new acceptance of the divine love, so that we initiate in ways more like the Father, respond in ways more like the Son, and come to a fulfilment that expresses and conforms to the work of the Holy Spirit. In this way, human initiating, responding, and fulfilling are in a balanced interpenetration that itself reflects the perichoretic unity of Father, Son, and Holy Spirit. Thus we have a model that can yield new perspectives on our creation, on our fall, and on our restoration.

In the sections that follow, leaving the restoration for a chapter of its own, we will look positively at what it means to mirror the free love of each of the divine persons and negatively at the specific ways by which in each case that expression of the divine love can be contradicted and denied.

The image of the initiating Father

The distinctive function of the Father which emerges in his Trinitarian self-revelation in Christ is that he is the sovereign initiating source who, in the unconstrained freedom of his love, intervenes in the human situation and gives it out of the resources of his life-saving possibilities and realities that it could not produce out of its own.

The Father is the God who throughout Israel's history does new things for his people that they could not do for themselves and at the climax of the biblical story, in a time and way of his own choosing, intervenes decisively in the life of the world in the incarnation of his Son. It is the Father who so loved the world that he gave his only begotten Son (John 3:16). The coming of the Son depends on the sending of the Father. The words that Jesus speaks are not his own but the words that he hears from the Father; the works that he does are the works he sees the Father doing (John 5:19). Jesus commits himself to the cross in Gethsemane because he has come to see that his death is at the heart of the saving purpose and will of *Abba*. It is the Father who had initiated the creation of the cosmos and who also initiates the recreation of the cosmos by raising his Son from the dead. It is the Father who will inaugurate the fulfilment of all things in a parousia at a time that it is for him alone to know and to fix.

All in all, there is what we have called a "from-ness" that defines the distinctive place of the Father within the Trinitarian ordering of the divine action in history, which faithfully reveals the divine being in eternity. That is what is involved in speaking of his purposeful initiation of all the works of God.

Reflecting the Father

It follows, therefore, that to be in the image and likeness of the Father on the human level means that in our life in general and in our dealings with other people in particular, there are to be areas in which we are graciously enabled and bindingly called to be proactive[6] and not simply reactive, where over against other people and our environment we are given both the obligation and the ability to intervene in situations and accept responsibility for turning them round into directions which they would not otherwise take. It belongs to the dignity and worth of our humanity that we should have the opportunity and be under moral constraint to think through what needs to be done in the specific occasions in which we are involved and to take active steps to recruit and enthuse others so that we can cope with the hindrances and the people that stand in our way.

The mandate to lead

God the Father is the prototype of leadership, and to be made in his image means that initiating leadership is constitutive of our humanity as such and is not confined to the talented and self-confident elites with which we often associate it. In Genesis it is Adam, the representative of all the rest of us who, in the immediate context of his being created in the image of God, is given the dignity and the duty to "have dominion" over the rest of creation and "to fill the earth and subdue it" (1:26, 28). The modern complaint that this mandate to initiating intervention has often been exercised in an exploitative and ultimately destructive way with little respect for the created world is a sign that we are sinners who do not relate to God's world in the way that he himself relates to it. He looks at what he has made and affirms it as good, so that the same love that created it is the love that conserves and develops it to its fulfilment. When our dealings with the world do not reflect that respect and care for the conservation of the world, then we are no longer mirroring the love of the Father for what he has made.

Nevertheless, the misuse of the mandate does not abolish it. That mandate provides a theological basis for modern science in which human initiatives have exposed and actualized the hidden potential of the created world in ways that have transformed the whole life of the whole world. The idea that natural process has some kind of privileged inviolability over the human harnessing of these processes in the service of the wellbeing of human beings and their fellow creatures appears in all sorts of contemporary contexts, for example the debate about birth control and the possibilities of the genetic modification of crops and of the human genome.

In a biblical perspective the rule of God is not to be identified with the rule of nature. The purposes of God are fulfilled not by leaving things as they are, but by the identification of these purposes by human minds and their furtherance by human intervention in a world that by itself will never become what it was made to be. The Old Testament mandate of Genesis is reaffirmed in the New Testament mandate of Romans 8, where we are told that the creation which, left to itself, will relapse into futility and decay without appropriate human intervention is groaning and travailing and is waiting for the children of God to be revealed; its freedom and glory is derived from and dependent upon theirs (8:20–22).

Shall we play God?

We are often told that to intervene in the processes of nature and especially in matters of life and death is to play God. But if we are made in the image of God, then to play God is exactly what we are invited to do and there are, in principle, no no-go areas from which our interventions are excluded.

The problems arise when the god that we image in our interventions is a god of our own making, who is ultimately ourselves. Adam is made free in the whole garden, with the exception of the one tree whose fruit would turn him into his own master, who deals havoc to the created order by ruling it in terms of what seems good and what seems evil to his own egocentricity rather than as the steward and servant of God the Creator and the reflector of his love for all he has made.

To insist on that human vocation to align the creation with the Creator's purposes is not, of course, to legitimize any specific human initiative. To say that there is no area from which our initiatives are excluded does not, by itself, determine which of these initiatives are justified and which are not, and there have been many such initiatives whose destructive potential is enormous, as environmentalists rightly point out.

To say, for example, that the realms of life and death – our being born and our dying – are areas where the will of God has to be discerned and done by us and not areas where nature is left to take its course, does not by itself determine what an appropriate initiative should be, still less provide a basis for abortion or euthanasia. What it does do is, on the one hand, emphasize the covenant responsibility of human beings for what they do with the world and, on the other, insist that God's ways for his world have to be discerned not in terms of some so-called laws of nature, but in terms of what God has revealed of his purposes for the world and our part in them in the incarnation of his Son.

God reflects himself not in natural process but in historic self-revelation. Our clues to God's plans for his world are not in nature itself, which is often red in tooth and bloody in claw and where everything lives by eating everything else, but in the Word made flesh who is the ultimate expression of God's love for the created world and knew well how to intervene in it by healing diseases and calming storms. His were, from first to last, the initiatives that sprang from a prior obedience, a love for the world that reflected his Father's love for the world, and it is to that kind of obedient intervention in the life of the world to which we ourselves are called.

Such leadership is to be exercised not only by humanity corporately in its dealings with the environment, but by particular men and women in their dealings with one another in the society of which they are part and in the personal and domestic spheres that are our immediate and daily concerns. It is in our vocation to live in the image of the Father that the political slogans about equal opportunities for everyone find their theological basis. A central aim of any educational system that incorporates Christian priorities is that it should equip people to take initiatives that will contribute to the wellbeing of the community in whatever spheres of activity are appropriate to them and their gifts, some large and public, some small and private.

The Father's image flawed

From this perspective the image of the Father, who takes initiatives in the freedom of his love, is inhibited and distorted when people are oppressed or themselves become oppressors of others. To be oppressed is precisely to be deprived of the opportunities to take the initiatives to which one is called and for which one is gifted; to be an oppressor is to be in a position to do things that affect others but to exploit that position in ways that are far from caring and affirming of others but are driven by a self-assertion that represses, dominates, and controls others and deprives them of their freedom in order to exercise its own.

In both cases the fact that the oppressed and their oppressors live and act within the structures of the *imago Dei* will become evident even when that image is warped and distorted. The oppressed will sooner or later react to their oppressors in resistance and rebellion against those who have deprived them of their God-given freedom. Even when the oppressors exercise their freedom in ways that are in contradiction to the loving purposes of the Father, their freedom to do that is still a misused gift of God.

The Father's image exemplified – negative

The operation of these dynamics in the personal and social situations that make up everyday experience confirms that what we are dealing with are not theoretical theological constructs but illuminating descriptions of what actually takes place as people relate to one another.

In one of the Church of Scotland parishes where I was minister, there was a leading elder who on a personal level illustrated the typical relational dialectic in which the oppressed in one context become the oppressors in another. In his working life he was the chauffeur of the manager of a local business. He went where he was told, waited till he was wanted, and had no say at all in the way his working day was structured. But when he came on to church territory and into the Kirk Session, a place where he could exert influence and power, he turned into something of a tyrant, who, to restore the balance, wanted to rule the roost, who knew how to make trouble if he was not consulted and was, indeed, given a veto over every issue that arose.

It was not hard to see, even if as a green young minister I was a target of the attempted tyranny, that in the church he was striving for a freedom of initiative of which he was almost totally deprived at work, but the way he used his freedom limited and threatened the freedom of others, so that it never quite managed to image the sovereign but liberating love of the Father. All that he did confirmed that his life was structured by the freedom that he longed for and the love that his longing for freedom inhibited, so that it was indeed life in the image of God but in it that image was marred and defaced.

In another of my Scottish parishes, the operation of the same dynamic could be clearly discerned in a more corporate context. In a town whose life revolved around heavy industries of steel and coal, life was deeply affected by the distinctions of class and status that working life imposed. There was a great gulf fixed between those who worked as laborers at the bottom of the pile and did the repetitive dogs-body jobs that required no initiative and the skilled tradesmen and foremen who had a vitality and self-worth that stemmed from the responsibility for things and people that they carried in the steel works.

At home and in social exchanges the laborers could easily become sullen and uncooperative, shrugging off on to their wives the responsibility for the handling of money, the rearing of children, and the reception of visitors, while they themselves hid behind their newspapers and could be winkled out only with the offer of a cigarette. The deprivation of responsibility in one area resulted in a refusal of responsibility in another and as a consequence a restriction in the ability to show love and care to wife and family. Such men often turned into alert, caring, and responsible human beings only when they kept greyhounds or pigeons or ran a boys' football club, where they could set the agenda and take the decisions and become, at last, people on whom others, be they animals or people, depended.

The industrial revolution, to fulfil its needs for unskilled labor, created generations of people who were treated as factory fodder and molded into a lifestyle in which it was difficult to grow into the fullness of life which only the freedom to receive love from and to give love to others can bring. It is a tribute to the robustness of our humanity made in the image of God that in such an adverse environment there were still marriages and parents who provided the basis for a love and affirmation that enabled people to emerge from all that could have dehumanized them into open, giving, and fulfilling lives.

The Father's image exemplified – positive

On the positive side, it is significant that great movements of human liberation keep on arising in societies that have been shaped by the Judeo-Christian tradition with the gospel of the triune God at its heart. Sometimes these movements have had explicit Christian leadership. Even when that is not so and societies that were once confessedly Christian have become openly secular, the understanding of human beings as those made in love and for liberty which has its roots in the God of the Bible has so far survived its loosening from its religious moorings and continues to inspire movements of protest against oppression that demand and work for the liberation of the oppressed. The more we know of the oppressions that remain firmly seated in parts of the world which have been shaped by very different religious traditions, the more we realize the biblical roots out of which the Western respect for human freedom still lives. One thinks of course of the classic struggle against slavery, for prison reform, and for humanitarian factory conditions in the nineteenth century, of Martin Luther King, Nelson Mandela, and Desmond Tutu and the fight against apartheid, as well as the women's movements and current calls for the canceling of third-world debt in our own day.

In all such movements we can recognize the mirroring of the Father's liberating love, in so far as they do genuinely set people free and do not simply replace one ideological oppression with another. The motivation to liberation is strongest where the Father's love is known and itself is able to shape people into its likeness, but it is never totally absent, because even if they do not know it, people are made in the Father's image and in that love that is his gift and his call to them, however marred that gift may become in their hands and however faintly that call may ring in their ears, there is something in people which will resist oppression and strive for freedom and in their created exocentricity will turn them in genuine concern for others to help to set them free.

Such is the recurring evidence that we are made in and for the image of the Father. That is to be set beside the other evidence that our created exocentricity is always under threat of being negated by our fallen egocentricity. Our love of self can become so absorbing that we cease to respond to the needs of others to be cared for and to be free. In our manipulations and misuse of others we can ourselves become, either personally or by our conformity to social structures that are advantageous to us and oppressive to them, obstructions to their ability to fulfil God's purposes for them or his call to them. Or we ourselves, like some of the laboring men we have been describing, can be so enslaved by internal addictions or social oppressions that we lose the motivation to assert our own freedom.

If we could escape from our engagement with the love and freedom of the God who made us, we would cease to be human, and yet in the light of the lives that we in fact live that engagement is very often a source of shame, reproach, and judgement on the love we have failed to show and the freedom we have lost for ourselves and denied to others. The inescapability of the *imago Patris* and, at the same time, our inability to give a true reflection of it is the human dilemma from which most of all we need to be set free. It is to address that dilemma that God takes a new sovereign initiative of love in the sending of his Son.

The obedience of the Son

If purposeful sovereign initiation is the *proprium*, the defining hypostatic characteristic, of the Father, willing responsiveness is the *proprium* of the Son. Here we see the same love and freedom that we see in the Father in the mode of sovereignty, given a distinctive personal expression in the mode of obedience by the Son. The Son does not send, he is sent; he is not, on his own insistence, the ultimate source of his own living, speaking, and acting; his words and deed are his responses to what he has seen and heard in his unbroken attentiveness to the Father. As D. M. McKinnon puts it, "At the heart of that ministry we find realised a final, haunting receptivity. Yet that receptivity never rots away into a passive acceptance" (D. M. McKinnon. *Themes in Theology.* London: SCM, 1987, p. 154).

In another passage in the same book McKinnon quotes approvingly the statement of an Italian friar that "obedience is the most insidious of all the temptations" (McKinnon, 1987, p. 152), meaning that to obey another passively and compliantly without enquiring about the rightness and justness of what is commanded and the status of the one who is commanding, can be an abrogation of personal responsibility in which one surrenders oneself to be the unchallenging tool of another's will.

To vow to one's country or any other earthly claimant of our loyalty the love that asks no questions, as the patriotic hymn enjoins, is to be in danger of taking one's place among the manipulated masses that cried Crucify on Good Friday and that in the course of history have cheered unthinkingly in support of all the tyrants who have imposed themselves upon them. It was that kind of passive obedience that led thousands of German civil servants to the efficient organization of the transportation of the Jews of Europe to Auschwitz and Buchenwald. In all these ways obedience can indeed become the most insidious of temptations.

The freedom of the Son's obedience

The obedience required of Jesus and offered by him is of a quite different order. The God who in giving his commandment to the first Adam in the garden gave him also the responsibility and the freedom to obey it and restores that freedom – lost in sin – to the second Adam, so that he responds to the Father with an active affirmation that says his own Yes to the Father's purposes and so images in his response the freedom of God's love, not, in his case, the sovereign freedom of the Father to command but, as we saw in the last chapter, the equally divine responsive freedom of the Son to obey.

The testimony to that freedom is the forty days of temptation in the wilderness, in which Jesus faces and makes real decisions about how he will execute the Messianic vocation that his Father has entrusted to him. It is in being left alone to face the wrong ways of being Messiah that it becomes clear that his Father has, indeed, entrusted his saving purposes to his Son and that the Son has accepted that responsibility and spoken his own No to the ways suggested to him by the Tempter and his own Yes to the way into which his Father has called him. The proposing will of the Father and the assenting will of the Son are aligned in commitment to the way of bringing in the kingdom that will ultimately lead to the suffering of the cross.

The testimony to the agony of that freedom is the struggle in Gethsemane for the final affirmation of the Father's purpose when the shadow of the cross is no longer in the distance but looms in its immediate proximity. It is equally important that the prayer that is decisive in that situation, "Thy will not mine be done," should be both an expression of the Son's surrender to the Father but also the expression of the Son's own homologation of the Father's will for him.

The saving efficacy of the passion requires not just that the Son should suffer but that he should suffer in a willing obedience which he offers vicariously on behalf of all of us, that in the very place where we are executing upon him the No of our rebellious unfreedom, he should, in the very fact of his hanging there, utter the great Yes of the love that offers himself with heart and soul and mind and strength to his Father in the ultimate fulfilment of the first great commandment and to us in fulfilment of the second. As the Johannine Jesus himself puts it, "For this reason the Father loves me, because I lay down my life in order to take it up again. No one takes it from me, *but I lay it down of my own accord*. I have power to lay it down and I have power to take it up again. I have received this command from my Father" (John 10:17, 18). A compelled cross and an imposed suffering could have no saving efficacy; they could not be the authentic response either of the Son to the Father or of the man reflecting the free love of the God who made him.

And yet, precisely as the deed Jesus does of his own accord, it is not an act of his own proposing and devising but his response to the command of his Father, the obedience of the one who is second to the one who is first, of the one who is sent to the one who sends him. Both the freedom and the obedience are defining of all that he does for us; it is in that obedient freedom that he identifies with us and acts in a way that is relevant to and transformative of the human situation, and it is in participation in the free obedience that we will image the ultimate Adam, who himself perfectly images the Son of God. The Letter to the Hebrews reflects the dynamic of the free obedience that makes Jesus our great high priest and sums up all that we have been saying.

> In the days of his flesh Jesus offered up prayers and supplications to the one who was able to save him from death and he was heard because of his reverent submission. Although he was a Son, he learned obedience through what he suffered and, having been made perfect, he became the source of eternal salvation to all who obey him.
> (Heb. 5:7–9)

He has this freedom not adjectivally but relationally, not as the defining characteristic of an individuality that he possesses prior to and apart from his relationship to the Father, but as the gift of the Father who within that relationship entrusts his purposes to his Son in such a way as to leave room for him to assent to them and thus to make them his own. Only as the one who loves in freedom could he be God, but the Son's way of loving in freedom is his attentive obedience to the Father.

Reflecting the Son's obedience

If that is so, then for us to be in the image of God the Son means that a constituting factor in our lives will be relationships with others, where we are not first but second, not leading but following, where we are not in command, but have to conform ourselves to conditions and demands that are shaped and set by others and by the society to which we belong, where the main concern is not with our rights that others are bound to respect, but with our duties to others that we are bound to fulfil. This is a not a message which it is easily heard in a culture that idolizes human autonomy. Contemporary society on the positive side exalts and seeks to maximize the unfettered freedom of choice of the human individual to the extent of determining who will be born and when we will die, and, on the negative side, resents and subjects to a hermeneutic of suspicion all the structures of authority that used to command our deference. The monarchy and the political, educational, scientific, and law-enforcing establishments have been subjected to almost gleefully scathing criticism, initiated by the media that reflect, albeit in exaggerated ways, our common preoccupations. From that process none of them has emerged with their authority intact, so that what used to be seen as almost unchallengeable is now seen as vulnerable and fundamentally untrustworthy, so that we are more and more thrown back on ourselves and our choices to determine the values by which we live. All this adds up to a situation in which we are more than happy to be told that being human involves being as initiating as the Father, but much less so to be told that it also involves being as obedient as the Son. The Sinatra syndrome, "I did it my way," afflicts us all.

Attentive responsiveness

For all that, it remains true that attentive responsiveness is not just an ethical imperative, but is, in fact, constitutive of our humanity. Our freedom is not an attribute of an independent individuality that enables us to choose whether and how much we will attend to the claims of others. The freedom is not prior to the claims; rather the claims are the foundation of our freedom.

Remembering Pannenberg's account of the genesis of our personhood in the child's relationship with the mother, we can see that it is in being loved by others that we become aware of what it means to respond to others; it is in their responsiveness to us that we come to know how to respond to them. Our selfhood with its freedom is their gift to us, that enables us to assess and to respond to their claims upon us; it is through our responsiveness to the people and the society that precede and surround us that the whole content of our selfhood is received, and through the relative claims of others the ultimate claim of God is mediated, a claim that does not overwhelm our freedom in a coerced heteronomy, but in its very claiming requires an authentic personal response to it. Colin Gunton puts it like this:

> Freedom is a relational concept in the sense that it cannot be understood merely individualistically. If we are free it is in large measure because others enable and empower us to be free. Freedom may be something that we exercise or fail to exercise as particular beings, but our particularity is at the same time something that comes to us from the other beings with whom we are related.
> (Gunton, 1995, p. 122)

That fundamental dependence on others works on many different levels. If the police put me in prison, I lose one kind of freedom. The legal framework of the society in which I live determines to what extent I am able to say what I think and do what I choose. The genetic inheritance that is bequeathed to me will determine that there are some things I can do well and others that I will never do at all. The relationships, values, and economics of the family in which I grow up will open up some external possibilities to me and close off others, and will shape me in a way that makes some personal responses natural to me and others very difficult. The kind of education I receive will open some doors and close others. It is within that whole network of an inevitable exocentricity, with its giving and its receiving, its enriching and its restricting, its exercise of responsibility toward me and its requiring of responsibility from me, that I become a free person who is both dependent upon and accountable to the impersonal and personal environment which has made me what I am.

The accountability derives from the dependence: I owe my world my attentiveness to its claims because I have received from my world all that I have, and that relationship to my world images my ultimate relationship to my Creator who has the final claim upon me because he is the ultimate source of all my life and freedom. My dependence on him is the basis of my responsibility to him and that ultimate obligation to the creator relativizes my obligation to the created world. "We must obey God rather than men."

But the God on whom we depend is the God who has made us in his image, and to be in his image is to receive from him the freedom to respond to him. In him, love and freedom are so closely bound together that freedom is freedom to love and love therefore enables freedom. When Jesus in Gethsemane is considering his ultimate response to his Father's loving purpose, he is not battered with exhortations, enticed with promises or threatened with consequences. On his knees before his Father he is given room to make his decision, so that when it is made, it is the response of his own love to the love that has summoned him to his sacrifice and allows him space to say his own Yes to that summons.

So, authentic human action that images the Father does not bully or coerce but, in respect for others, seeks to persuade and to win so that they make their own free responses to what is offered to them. Equally, authentic human action in the image of the Son does not let itself be determined by the pressures of the powerful, the seductions of the advertisers, and the manipulations of the exploiters, but takes responsibility for its own actions and its own opinions and can give a reason not only for the hopes that it has but for the choices that it makes.

The space to respond

A good teacher rejoices not when her class learns by rote and can accurately reproduce what she has instilled into them but when her pupils catch her enthusiasm for her subject and go on to develop it in ways she never thought of and to depths that are beyond her capacity.

A good parent rejoices when the child who in teenage rebellion has for a time distanced himself from the standards and the precepts of his home in order to find room to be himself, eventually shows that he has appropriated and made their values his own not in slavish imitation of his parents lifestyle but by developing a lifestyle of his own in which what his parents offered him is critically but creatively expressed in ways that are appropriate not to his parents' generation but to his own.

A good minister of the gospel soon learns that what he imposes on a congregation by authoritarian imposition will not long survive his departure, but what they have freely embraced and made their own from his teaching, leading and pastoring will become part of the living tradition of that parish that will continue to exercise influence in it long after he has gone.

What we have been saying has important implications for Christian evangelism and the proclamation of the gospel both inside and outside the believing community. It will be readily agreed all round today, even if it was not always so, that compelled conversions are against the whole genius of the gospel and of the nature of God himself as we have been expounding it. But what is not so easy to discern is the point at which legitimate persuasion which leaves room for personal response becomes psychological manipulation that denies the respondent that room and seeks to dominate rather than liberate his will.

I have attended a service at a world famous evangelical church in which, before we sang a hymn or said a prayer, we were told what our attitude and our reaction to it ought to be and, after a very full sermon, another minister took several minutes to tell us how we were to respond to it. My reaction to that was to cry inwardly, "For any favor leave me alone, trust the word to do its own work, let the Spirit lead us to a response that is, for each of us, appropriate to what we have heard!"

In contrast to this, the word as it was spoken and enacted by Jesus left space for people to make their own response to it; he did not dictate to his disciples what they were to believe about him. He presented the evidence of his words and actions and then at Caesarea Philippi sought their verdict on them, "Who do you say that I am?" (Matt. 16:15) and when Peter responded to that with a confession of his Messiahship and implicitly of his divinity, he recognized that the ability to make that confession was itself the work of his Father's Spirit in him. "Flesh and blood have not revealed this to you, but my Father who is in heaven" (16:17). That confession Peter could not have made *by* himself without the liberating insight that came from the Spirit, but Jesus left him room to make that confession *for* himself as something that had not been thrust upon him, but that he had discerned with his own mind and embraced with his own heart.

Defenders of freedom

A false zeal that seeks to force a premature response to the gospel and to exhort us into a manipulated conformity to it can deny us the respect and freedom which is God's gift to those who are made in his image and, as follow-ups on evangelistic campaigns confirm, can produce temporary and superficial responses that do not survive the pressures that compelled them. Preachers and evangelists need to entrust the outcome of their endeavors not to their fervent exhortations but to the gracious work of the Holy Spirit, who is himself the space that God gives us for our responsiveness and so the giver and the guarantee of the personal authenticity and depth of the responses he produces. "Where the Spirit of the Lord is, there is freedom" (2 Cor 3:17).

Christians who understand the vital connection between love and freedom at the heart of the gospel will be the defenders of that freedom across the whole field of human relationships. That is not to deny that in a fallen world there is the need for the kind of controlled and purposeful coercion that the police forces and armed services offer. Those who invade the freedom of others by attacking their persons, their property, their proper political self-determination need themselves to be restrained and punished not in the denial of freedom but in its defense.

However, it is notorious how the legitimate use of coercion which is justified by its claim to defend the freedom of individuals and communities can be corrupted into an illegitimate misuse which deprives communities and individuals of their freedom. Furthermore, the use of that coercion will temporarily restrain the evil that threatens a society, but unless it is underpinned and accompanied by positive action to create an atmosphere in which respect for people is expressed in institutions that enable them to make responsible choices about their own life and responsible contributions to the life of society, coercive violence will simply provoke a downward spiral of retaliatory violence, as the recent history of the Middle East makes quite clear.

While it is utopian to renounce the use of coercive restraint in any circumstance, its use is, in practice, highly ambiguous, and Christians should be prominent among those who are constantly vigilant to identify and challenge its corruptions, not on the secular basis of individualistic autonomy but on the theological basis that seeks to build societies where people are free to make accountable responses to the claims that are made upon them.

Restorative justice

The same point has to be made in relation to the penal sanctions that society rightly imposes on those who disrupt its life. The notorious slogan "Prison works" may be proximately true in the sense that it temporarily deprives criminals of their ability to offend, but it is ultimately profoundly misleading, since shutting people up together will not itself reform them and does, in fact, often consolidate and confirm them in their career of wrongdoing.

A system that defines itself in terms of either retribution or deterrence will not give a proper priority to the penal strategies that will promote what has come to be known as restorative justice. Here the aim is to bring people back into the kind of relationships with both their victims and society in general, in which they acknowledge their wrongdoing and are motivated to make what restitution they can for it; to enter into a new relationship with the world around them in which they are offered the care and help of which they have usually, been deprived, and are thus motivated to respond to that world and its claims not with frustration and resentment, but with a positive and responsible will to play their part in it.

That such an agenda will often fail against the engrained and deep seated resistance of the hardened criminal is obvious, but the results that it can achieve have been highlighted by the work of the Truth and Reconciliation Commission in South Africa, and Archbishop Tutu has the authority of these results behind him when he claims that its philosophy of restorative justice offers a new and promising approach to society's reactions to those who offend against it.

From the perspective of this book, such an emphasis on restorative justice resonates with the way God acts toward us in Christ, where the whole self-giving of his atoning love is directed toward a restoration of right relationships with himself and with others expressed in his forgiveness and our repentance in relationship to the past, and his remaking and our conversion in regard to the future, so that in Christ we begin to respond to God and to others with the same attentive and affirming responsiveness in which he related to the Father and dealt with those he met. That is the saving justice that is directed to our restoration in the image of God.

Responsible obedience

Furthermore, if we are committed to the kind of theological anthropology we have been describing, we need to become the constantly vigilant protectors of the free responsiveness that reflects the Son's willing obedience to the Father. In a society in which all deference is suspect, except perhaps that offered to successful footballers or pop stars, we have to learn to distinguish between those authorities that have a claim to our respect and regard because, amidst all sorts of human weaknesses they nevertheless represent and continue to seek what is good for us, and those whose claims are bogus because they are founded on nothing but hereditary status or economic power and wealth.

Amidst the media bombardment to which we are all subject, in which information can easily decline into spin and become disinformation and ideological manipulation, we have to see that broadcasters and journalists retain as much objectivity as is humanly possible and present a range of opinions and policies that enable us to formulate well resourced judgements and make choices that are firmly based on the evidence that is presented to us.

That such may be a counsel of perfection means that we should be all the more concerned to get as near to it as we can, and to expose those who tell one-sided stories to promote their own interests. The covenantal nature of language, in which by speaking we implicitly claim to be speaking a truth that can be trusted, is always in danger of being corrupted, with the result that the mutual trust that holds society together can easily be destroyed. Behind the free responsiveness of Jesus to the Father is the Father's trust in him and his own trust in the Father, and if, on the human level, there is to be the mutual respect and responsiveness that makes social living possible, it is of first importance that we should be basically trustworthy in our dealings with one another.

Whether and for how long that can happen when the biblical covenantal model is unregarded and, indeed, unknown by many people is a moot point, but those who do know it have a responsibility to do what we can to order our society in the light of it, and to show that, without it, human relating becomes increasingly difficult because we are in danger of ceasing to understand one another as those who have been made in the image of God.

We are made in the image of the Son, which means that our life works as it was meant to when we live in a mutual submission to one another in which we accept our responsibility for one another and enable and affirm one another's freedom. In other words, the Son expresses the freedom of the divine love in his willing service of his Father's purposes for human liberation, and we are so made in his likeness that it is when, at least in some measure, we live as he lived that we are able to live well together, and all this is a matter not primarily of morality and religion but of our ontological constitution as human beings. Jesus does not show us how to be moral or religious, but rather how to be human.

This kind of humanity of which he is the prototype and the enabler is under constant attack from two directions. It can be corrupted by the autonomous individualistic self-assertion that seeks to relativize our response to others in favor of our relentless pursuit of what we perceive to be our own good, which in its ultimate terms is the denial of love. Equally it can be corrupted by the coercive suppression that seeks to fit us into molds that the powerful make for us that deprive us of our ability to make an authentic response, which is the denial of freedom.

In Jesus we see that love and that freedom in perfect equilibrium, so that he models for us and imparts to us a new kind of obedience which is not the response of weakness to power, nor even of duty to law, but rather of the freely offered active self-giving of responsive love to initiating love, of the Son to the Father.

The creativity of the Spirit

If it is true that *Imago Dei* is *Imago Trinitatis*, then we are made in such a way that we mirror in our humanity not only what the Father does and what the Son does, but also what the Holy Spirit does. If the distinguishing characteristic of the Father is sovereign and initiating love and if the distinguishing characteristic of the Son is freely obedient love, then the distinguishing characteristic of the Spirit – hard to capture in a single phrase – is what we might call perfecting creativity. As a biblical base for this, we can look to the teaching of Jesus in the so called Farewell Discourses of John 14 – 16, and especially to that passage in John 16 in which Jesus says of the Spirit three things that point toward the sort of understanding that we are seeking.

1. "He will not speak on his own ... All that the Father has is mine. For this reason I said that he will take what is mine and declare it to you." (16:13, 15) The Spirit does not add any new content of his own to what has been accomplished in the life, death, and resurrection of Jesus by the mutual self-giving of the initiating Father and the responsive Son. The

material, so to speak, on which the Spirit operates in relation to us is that which has been given in the work of the incarnate Son, in which, of course, the Spirit also had an integral part, because the Son himself is conceived by the Spirit, receives the Messianic anointing of the Spirit in his baptism, and, on own confession, is able to carry out his Messianic agenda because, "The Spirit of the Lord is upon me." When, however, the Father gives the Spirit to us through the Son, it is not that he should do a new work that somehow supersedes or complements that of the Son, but rather that he should explore, expose, and apply all that is latent in what the Son has already done.

2. "He will glorify me because he will take what is mine and declare it to you" (16:15). Pannenberg has fastened on this verse as a basis for understanding the Holy Spirit as a source of personal action distinct from the Son. The Spirit brings to the Son, from outside his own person, a new glory that he does not have within himself. Nevertheless, in the work of the Spirit it is the Son who is glorified. The focus of the work of the Spirit is the work of Jesus, not some work of his own that he accomplishes apart from or beyond Jesus. The Spirit is the one who unfolds all that is implicit in the work of the Son, applies it creatively and transformingly in the mission of the Church across the continents and down the centuries in an endlessly enthralling kaleidoscope of new creation in the men and women who, in the Spirit, are brought into the power of the love of the Father as it is savingly incarnate in the love of the Son. He paints new portraits of Jesus in all the personal and cultural contexts of the people and societies that the gospel penetrates, so that Jesus is glorified in what the Spirit does in one way in the Church and in another in the

societies that have been touched by the gospel that the Church proclaims.

3. "I have many things to say to you. But you cannot bear them now. When the Spirit of truth comes, he will guide you into all the truth; for he will not speak on his own but will speak whatever he hears and he will declare to you the things that are to come" (16:12, 13). The Spirit has a basic orientation toward the future. His arrival, as Luke makes clear in Acts 2, is the sign that the period of eschatological fulfilment has at last begun. He remains in all his speaking and leading faithful to his single source in Christ but he releases and applies the mighty love of Christ relevantly and transformingly to people and situations as they emerge in history and leads the Church into the truth on issues that could not be addressed within the confines and culture of Christ's earthly life. What we have now is what Paul calls the first fruits or the first installment (*aparche* and *arrhabon*) of the Spirit. The day when the earth will be filled with the glory of God as the waters cover the sea has not yet come, but the creative Spirit in his sanctifying activity and in his charismatic endowing gives authentic evidence that the new age has begun, and the power that will reshape creation is already at work in those who in the Spirit are related to the Father and the Son. Where the Spirit is at work, the human imaging of the Father and the Son begins to be restored.

If we put these three insights together we see that the Spirit is the one who mediates our reception of the redeeming love of the Father as it is given to us in the incarnate Son and does so in ways that make it relevant and creative beyond the context in which it was first revealed, progressively and continually till it reaches all the life of the world. That is why the Spirit is closely connected with the mission of the Church and the taking of the gospel into all the world as Jesus commanded.

Reflecting the Spirit

The Holy Spirit is the artist of the Trinity who takes the mutual love of Father and Son as his given starting point and expresses it in a vast number of new contexts that show how endlessly relevant and redeeming it can be. It is no accident that it is the Spirit who is associated with artistic inspiration of all kinds, where sculptors, musicians, poets take the givens of creation – stone, sound, words – and find in them unrealized possibilities which their art enables them to realize. The inspiration that empowers them in the realm of creation is in close correspondence with what the Spirit does in the realm of redemption and those who know his work in redemption will recognize the marks of his handiwork in the creation as it is now, as well as the new creation which is coming into being among us.

The perfecting creativity of the Spirit is to be distinguished from the initiating creativity of the Father. Where the action of the Father is characteristically protological, the action of the Spirit is characteristically eschatological. In other words, what the Father starts, the Spirit perfects. Through the Father's initiating creativity, things that otherwise would not exist come into being; through the Spirit's perfecting creativity, things that already exist become what they were made and meant to be. The Father creates life at the beginning and the Spirit from that beginning sets that life into a dynamic which will lead to its fullness at the end.

The Father in creation, incarnation, and resurrection makes new beginnings that bring to being, first the created universe, then the word made flesh, and ultimately the new creation incorporated in the risen Jesus, and in each of these realms the Spirit imparts the dynamic that makes the world alive, that anoints and empowers the incarnate Son, that shares his new humanity with all who believe in him.

It follows that to be in the image of God means that we also in a multitude of different ways are caught up into what we might call a developmental dynamic in which, instead of taking new initiatives, we explore what has been given to us and see how it can be the starting point from where things take at least a few steps toward the way we think things ought to be.

The Spirit and the resurrection

This may become clearer if we look at how the Father and the Spirit are both involved in the quintessentially Trinitarian event of the resurrection of Jesus. Throughout the New Testament the resurrection is seen as the Father's vindication of his crucified Son by a revolutionary intervention that rejects what the crucifying regimes of Israel and Rome have done to Jesus. What the Father does is the contradiction and the reversal of what they did. They rejected him, his Father received him; they banished him to the depths of shame, his Father exalted him to the heights of glory; they said "he shall die," his Father said, "No, he shall live". The character of the Father's action as revolutionary reversal is eloquently underlined in the "But God" of Acts 2:24, where Peter speaks of "this man handed over to you according to the definite plan and foreknowledge of God, you crucified and killed by the hands of those outside the law. *But God raised him up, having freed him from death"* (2: 23, 24).

In unity with and distinction from the Father, revolutionary action is the Spirit's transformative action. So in Romans Paul promises that "If the Spirit of him who raised Jesus from the dead dwells in you, he who raised Christ from the dead will give life to your mortal bodies through his Spirit that dwells in you" (8:11). The reversing action of the Father has to be followed and completed by the transforming action of the Spirit, because revolutions fail unless they lead to radical reconstructions. The old crucifying humanity that has been rejected is not simply replaced by a totally different humanity that has no connection with it; the body that rose, for all its risen glory, is in continuity with the body that was buried; it is the same Jesus with the same wounds but now all transformed in the new creation that he inaugurates. The resurrection of Jesus is a radical revolution in human life inaugurated by the Father in discontinuity with what went before, but it is also a fulfilment of human life in which what is old is transformed into what is new and that transformation is the work proper to the Spirit.

So conversion implies the condemnation and rejection of the old humanity in its alienation from God and its radical replacement by a new humanity that is in right relationship with God, and that happens by the initiation that is proper to the Father. This is the side of things emphasized in traditional Protestant teaching on the subject.

But conversion also involves the long process of a sanctifying transformation of our humanity in which the Spirit grapples with us as we are now and finds ways in which we can at least begin to be changed into an Easter people who have in them something of the new life of the risen Lord. This is the aspect of the matter emphasized in the more Catholic traditions of the Church.

But the revolution of Easter has to be followed by the transformation of Pentecost so that what is disjoined from the old can be progressively conformed to the new. The revolutionary action of the Father and the transformative action of the Spirit are to be distinguished from each other but belong together in the saving action of the one God.

Revolution and renewal

So, if our life is to image God's life, both on the large social scale and the small personal scale, there will be in it moments of revolution, times when it is right for a nation to make a radical break with a past that was unreformably repressive, abolish the old regime and install a new one, repeal the old laws and enact new ones, break the chains of those who have been oppressed and deprived and do what needs to be done to set them free. The contemporary example of this is the overthrow of apartheid in South Africa with all the revolutionary changes that has involved.

On the personal level, the paradigm of such revolutions is Jesus's calling of his disciples with the domestic disruption, the change of career from fishermen and tax collectors to economically risky dependence on charity that it involved. There are times when it is right not to stay but to go; when a young person leaves home for single independence or marriage, when there is a mid-career change of occupation, when people emigrate from situations in search of basic liberty or just a better future, when a friendship or, more debatably, a marriage, has become destructive, when, for those who are open to it, God's call bursts into the continuities of a settled life and summons us to personal revolutions that are both challenging and threatening. And above all there is that revolution of conversion to Christ whose prototype is what happened to Saul on the road to Damascus, where the basic relationship to God is reversed from rebellion to obedience, from rejection to faith, which has to be followed by a long process in which the Spirit works out in the converted life the implications which that new relationship implies. These are all ways in which the initiating love of the Father can be reflected in large and small ways in a personal *curriculum vitae*.

But in all this, renewal is as much on God's agenda as revolution. In South Africa the old that has been rejected cannot simply be abandoned and left behind, it has to be engaged with, the wounds it has left have to be healed in justice and reconciliation, its legacy has to be taken on board and creatively transformed.

In our personal living, sometimes we have to recognize and respond to the call to go and start again elsewhere, and sometimes we have to recognize the call to stay and become involved in creative and transforming engagement with the given circumstances and people who are the context of our lives. To some people Jesus said, "Leave all and follow me," to others he said, "Go home and discover what it means to live as my healed disciple there among your own people." Undoubtedly that is what he says to most of us most of the time. That is the point at which we have to rely on the activity of the Spirit of renewal, whose characteristic concern is not that we should be born, but that we should be born again, not that we should start a new life that has jettisoned its past, but that in the midst of our lives we should be so transformed that we see and enter the kingdom of God, that we allow the life that we already have to be opened to and changed by the operation of God's power within it.

It is the Spirit who offers a positive answer to the question of the skeptical Nicodemus: "Can a man be born again when he is old?" Yes he can, because the givens of his life in which he has grown old, his internal character and his external relations, are plastic to the Spirit who can expose our given lives to the given love of the Father and the Son, in which he himself is inextricably involved, and can make them new.

The initiating love of the Father incarnated in the responsive love of the Son and followed through in the transforming love of the Spirit are mutually interdependent, so that the one can be effective only in its coordination with the others, because in their eternal being Father, Son, and Holy Spirit are constituted in their unity by their inseparable perichoresis with one another.

Nevertheless, just as we have distinguished relationships which reflect what is characteristic of the Father and of the Son, so also we can identify relationships in which our created lives reflect the distinctive work of the Holy Spirit.

The image of the Spirit

To speak of being in the image of the Spirit is more difficult than to speak of being in the image of the Father and the Son. That may be because image language is visual language, and visual language can be used of the incarnate Son, because by the very fact of his incarnation he made himself visible to us: "We declare to you what was from the beginning, what we have heard, what we have seen with our eyes, what we have looked at and touched with our hands, concerning the word of life" (1

John 1:1). Jesus can also speak of his own identification with the Father as the basis of a seeing of the Father: "He who has seen me has seen the Father." Like Son, like Father; the one is such a perfect representation of the other that from the seeing of the Son, we can, as it were, visualize the person of the Father.

Such a visualization of the Spirit is much more problematic. It is attempted symbolically in the dove who descends on Jesus in his Jordan baptism, but the main biblical emphasis is on the elusiveness and sovereign uncapturability of the Spirit. "The wind blows where it chooses and you hear the sound of it, but you do not know where it comes from or whether it goes" (John 3:8).

Just as you cannot make a visible image of invisible wind, so you cannot visualize the elusive and invisible Spirit of God. But just as the invisible wind gives evidence of its presence and its reality in its visible effects on sky and trees and people, so the invisible Spirit gives visible signs that reveal his presence and the nature of his person. As Peter puts it, referring to the signs and wonders of the day of Pentecost, "He has poured out this which you both see and hear" (Acts 2:33). The presence of the Spirit is known, not like that of the Son and through him the Father, in a visible human person, but in his works of powerful transformation and renewal. Thus, although image language is less appropriate to the Holy Spirit, we can nevertheless speak of human acts that correspond to and reflect the distinctive activity of the Holy Spirit, audible and visible things that happen in human life that show that it is a life given by the Spirit, life in which he continues to give evidence of his presence and his power, where he takes on persons and situations, brings them into what Pannenberg has memorably called the force field of his love (Pannenberg,

1991, p. 382ff.), where they are remade and moved on to the end for which they were created.

Reflecting the Spirit's work

So, in our relationships with the creation we mirror what the Spirit shows of himself in the perfecting of the new creation when we interact with the material, personal and social relationships that are the given context of our daily lives, in a way that is designed to move the people and situations we encounter step by step nearer to the realization of the goals that God has for them which are brought into focus in Christ. If we are Christians we know the ultimate goal of all creation is the kingdom of God and we will therefore be all the more accountable for the way we relate to it.

But the Spirit, although his ultimate purpose is to bring people into the knowledge of the Father and the Son, blows where he wills and operates in people and cultures where the Father and the Son are not confessed. Movements of liberation do not always have their origins within communities of faith; they often start not in the church but in the world and indeed have often been resisted by Christian people more interested in perpetuating a *status quo* in which they have vested interests than in discerning what God is doing in the world around them.

To balance that, it needs also to be said that it is those parts of the world that have been exposed to the gospel that these movements have begun, which makes us wonder if the Spirit has sometimes a better footing in societies whose secular cultures have been shaped by the gospel than in churches which explicitly confess the gospel.

However that may be, it is often on the much smaller scale of the everyday activities of ordinary living that we show that our life is constituted in a way that reflects the dynamic of the Spirit engaging with a given situation and moving it toward a creative fulfilment.

We have already shown how that is precisely what artists do when starting with stones and sounds and words, they fashion them into sculptures, music, and poetry that transform the raw materials into things of beauty and significance that become the means by which people communicate deeply with one another and even point transcendently in the direction of God. To do that is indeed to do what the Spirit does.

But much more universally, we do what the Spirit does in the nurture of our children. We start from the raw material of a naked human baby with a genetic inheritance and a pre-natal history that will be basic given factors in her life from its beginning to its end, and we place her in the arms of her mother, into a loving relationship that over a long period will provide the motivation and the means by which that child can grow into the woman who will discover the place and calling in the world in which her life can in very specific ways of receiving from and giving to other people, find at least some measure of freedom and fulfilment.

In that development, home and family are central, and anything that disables and divides home and family will inhibit that process of development and growth. But in the fulfilment of its nurturing calling, families are dependent on the whole apparatus of education, healthcare, and, where needed, the ambulances of social services, to promote that process and perhaps rescue it if it is threatened. To live in a developed society, even allowing for all its faults and failings, is one of the great privileges that can easily be taken for granted but is the envy of the rest of the world. From those of us who all our lives have enjoyed such privileges that lead to such freedom and such fulfilment, much will be required.

More generally still, we do what the Spirit does, when we engage with intractable situations and destructive relationships and look for and expect to find ways in which they can be moved toward positive outcomes. We tackle what is given to us in our human context and which in human terms is intransigent and threatening and expose it to what is given to us in our relationship with God in the hope and expectation that the one will break in transformingly on the other.

This happens consciously and explicitly in relation to the Christian gospel, where in Christ people are open to the Spirit and all the resources of power and love that he brings to us. This should not, however, lead us to play down the fact that, simply as created human beings, our life is still the gift and action of the same Spirit who came in all his fullness at Pentecost, so that to be healthily human is to address the people and situations that we meet with at least something of the resilience, creativity, and hope which are characteristic of the Spirit, and which still appear in people who have no acknowledged relationship to the Christian gospel but whose humanity is nevertheless shaped by their ontological relationship to the triune God.

Culture and controversy

Within the Christian community, we do what the Spirit does when we seek together to relate what is given to us in the Christian gospel with its given authority for all who believe it, to what is given to us in our current culture with its massive influence on all who belong to it, in a way that is faithful to the one and adequately and relevantly addresses the issues raised by the other. All the great controversies that have shaken the Church down the centuries can be traced back to clashes between given gospel and prevailing culture, and the controversies that distress us today, notably about human sexuality, are the latest manifestations of the same clash.

In such contexts there are always those who will distance themselves from the culture in the name of faithfulness to the gospel and also those who will claim that the culture itself offers us new insights that enable us to reinterpret the gospel in a way that affirms rather than subverts it. From such opposing perspectives, come the arguments, the disagreements and, sadly, the bitter divisions that have marked every period of the Church's past.

But in every period and in every controversy the creative Spirit has been at work and has led the Church to an outcome in which the gospel is indeed reinterpreted in a way that enables it to address the concerns of the culture but that is faithful to its origin in Christ. In him all human cultures are judged with the penetrating truth and the immeasurable mercy that define God's relationship to his people, and point them to those transformations that will lead them toward a fulfilment that they cannot find immanently in themselves.

In the midst of the battle a positive resolution seems impossible, but in longer perspective we become aware of a process of sifting and discernment in which the Spirit is the hidden participant in the debate, sorting out what is valid and what is invalid in seemingly irreconcilable opinions and leading toward an ultimate solution in which the mind of God in a particular area of faith and practice can be more faithfully and relevantly apprehended and obeyed.

That has happened in the controversies over Trinity and Christology in the patristic period, over the doctrine of justification in the Reformation period. From all of which bitter controversies that in their day created bitter conflicts and anguished confusion, there have emerged in the leading of the Spirit a mainline Christian consensus that can unite what used to be divided and give the Church something more like a single voice with which to address the world. We have thus, out of our own gospel and our own history, good reason to hope that in contemporary conflicts also the Spirit is at work and will in his time through our listening to him and to one another lead us, as Jesus promised, further into all the truth.

In all these ways the Spirit whose being is characterized by the sovereign divine love expressing itself in terms of transforming creativity, reflects himself in the human activity that stems from the human life which is his gift (Gen. 2:7).

Creativity stifled in sloth

We fail to reflect what the Spirit does in what we do when our actions are not characterized either by creative freedom or transforming love, when we have neither the courage nor the imagination to engage with the *status quo* in hope of moving it toward God's purpose for it.

This is the deadly sin which the medieval spiritual writers called *accedie*, sloth: the abject surrender to things as they are, the cowardly distancing of ourselves from all that is novel or challenging, the clinging to what is familiar and habitual because we lack the energy to cope with what is different and new, the relapse into a geriatric spirituality whose only concern is preservation and is threatened by any attempt at transformation.

It is equally manifest in the cynical middle-aged spirituality that has lost its vision and is inveterately cynical about the visions of others, and in the juvenile spirituality that withdraws from facing reality into the fantasy world of drugs, and of endless entertainment – sometimes even in Church.

All that culminates in what Jesus himself describes as *the* sin against the Holy Spirit (Matt. 12:31, 32), where the creative healing love of God that can transform lives which Jesus incarnates, is seen not as the supreme good to be sought but rather as the supreme evil to be opposed. When God's saving love, which is the source of all hope of salvation, is rejected as itself demonic, then the result is indeed an ultimate hopelessness for which there is no cure because it has thrown away the one thing that could cure it.

It belongs to the fullness of our humanity to respond purposefully, dynamically, hopefully to whatever life throws at us. In the world as it is, that ability will often be attacked and shaken by poverty, adversity, oppression, bereavement, and illnesses that break our spirit and leave us depressed and hopeless. But because our humanity is the work of the triune God and the life breathed into us is the life of the Holy Spirit, there is an amazing resilience about human nature that has a capacity for recovery of hope and commitment. That, to take just one example, can be seen in these people who have suffered a tragic loss of a child or a partner through the criminal actions of others or by incurable sickness, who have not withdrawn into self-pity or collapsed into bitterness and resentment but have been stirred up by what has happened to them to organize action to ensure that what has happened to them will not happen to others. That is, indeed, to do what the Spirit does. The more open we are to the Spirit, the greater the strength of that resilience will become. As

Paul puts it, "We are afflicted in every way, but not crushed, perplexed but not driven to despair, persecuted but not forsaken, struck down but not destroyed" (2 Cor. 4:8, 9).

Creativity corrupted into destructiveness

We can cease to reflect the Spirit in another way, not this time by collapsing into *accedie* but by exercising our imaginative creativity in a way that divorces it from the self-giving love to which it is inextricably joined in the life of God and therefore in creatures who image the life of God, so that it becomes what paradoxically can be called a destructive creativity that uses to the full all the forces of human imagination and skill to undermine and destroy other people. Examples abound.

Theoretical physics, which, with an ingenuity and complexity that puts it beyond the reach of the minds of most ordinary mortals, penetrates the hidden secrets of the material world, is the basis for the technology that launches onto the world the threat and the reality of nuclear weaponry, just as sophisticated biological research opens the door to biological warfare as well as to lifesaving antibiotic drugs. Terrorism has become a global threat because of the ingenious weapons of communication and destruction that sophisticated human creativity has made available.

In the realm of personal relationships, the gifts and abilities that are given to express our exocentricity are turned against people to assert our egocentric interests in a way that marginalizes and rejects them[7]. Where creativity is exercised in the interests of self-love, societies are divided and people are set into all sorts of conflicts with each other within and beyond national boundaries, and, to the extent that such self-love prevails, these societies lose their cohesion and their unity and are threatened by ultimate dissolution.

Conclusion

The picture that emerges from this chapter is that human life as we know it is possible at all only in so far as it images the triune God who made it, when it is free to be initiating in the image of the Father, when it is free to be responsive to the claims of others in the image of the Son, and when it works on what it inherits with a dynamic creativity that reflects the Holy Spirit. Such imaging and the life it makes possible is continually threatened by a loss of freedom and a loss of love in ways that we have indicated, that stem from a broken relationship with God, so that the Christian theological tradition has always had to ask whether and in what sense Adam, who is made in the image of God in Genesis 1, can still be said to be in the image of God after the primeval rebellion of Genesis 3. If sin breaks our relationship to God does it also break, warp, destroy the mirrors of our humanity that were made to reflect God? Our own answer to that question is perhaps already implicit in what we have said so far, but we need to go on to make it explicit in discussion with the different answers that the tradition offers.

6 Marred Image

Our glory is that we are made to be like God; our shame is that, as we are, we are very unlike him. We are like God in the exocentricity in which we open ourselves to receive from and give to other people and so mirror the Trinitarian self-giving that constitutes God's own life. We are quite unlike him in the egocentricity in which we seek to dominate others and exploit and manipulate them in the violent or subtle struggle to get our own way through them or against them, so that what we in fact image is not divine self-giving but human self-assertion.

One of our concerns in this chapter will be what happens to the image of God when those who were made to reflect his life in theirs, begin to center themselves in themselves rather than in him. In other words, what happens when the Adam of Genesis 1 who is made in God's image and likeness becomes the Adam of Genesis 3 who has succumbed to the primal temptation to autonomy and independence that the snake in the garden sets before Eve, "You shall become like God knowing good and evil" (3:5).

The irony is that the human beings who were made to be like God by reflecting him, now, in a quite different way, become like God by replacing him! The authority to determine good and evil that was located in the Creator is now located in the creature, so that good now means good for me and bad now means bad for me, so that I no longer center my life in him and find my good in obeying him, but rather center my life in myself and find my good in seeking my own self-fulfilment.

Does the image remain?

The question therefore arises: when the likeness of reflection yields to the likeness of replacement, does any authentic image of God remain? If the mirror is painted over with a self-portrait of its owner, can it any longer reflect the object at which it was once pointed? The debate about whether, to what extent, and in what way sinful humanity can still be said to be in the image of God started in the early church and continues to this day. Is the image lost or marred? Is most of it gone so that only remnants of it remain?

In the mainstream theological tradition it has always been difficult to give an unambiguous answer to that question. Those who hold that in sinners the image of God is destroyed have had to qualify that answer by saying that traces of it remain. Those who have maintained that, in spite of sin, humanity remains in the image of God in which it was created have immediately to add that although it remains, it has been spoiled or marred.

It is not surprising, therefore, that between these two extreme positions, there has been a third which affirms rather than avoids the ambiguity and holds, on the one hand, that sinners as God's creatures are made in the image of their Maker and the only way they can destroy that is by destroying themselves and ceasing to be, but on the other hand, precisely as sinners they are engaged in just that process of denial and destruction of that which makes their own being possible, of corrupting and resiling from the relationships with God and other people that are the source of their life. It is that third position that we will seek to clarify and explore.

Starting with Irenaeus

At the head of this tradition, as of much else in Christian theology, stands Irenaeus of Lyons who, we will remember, fastened on the two terms that are used to describe Adam's imaging of God in Genesis 1:26: "Let us make man in our *image, according to our likeness.*" As we have seen in our exegetical chapter, the two terms are nearly synonymous in the original Hebrew. Irenaeus, however, as Pannenberg points out, translates them with the Platonic terms *eikon*, meaning image or copy, and *homoiosis*, which means actual communion with the original and the reflection in humanity of the moral qualities of that original (Pannenberg, 1985, p. 48). Thus, according to Irenaeus, in sinners the *eikon*, the likeness to God which consists in human rationality and freedom remains, but the *homoiosis*, the assimilation of our character to his that results from our actual relating to him, is lost.

The compartmentalized solution – the medieval schoolmen

This distinction was translated into Latin and taken over by the medieval schoolmen who held that the *similitudo* that consisted of *iustitia originalis*, original righteousness, was lost in the fall but the *imago* remained, comprised as it was of rationality and self-determination. This was in conformity with the dominant understanding of the human person famously encapsulated in the formula of Boethius as *individua substantia naturae rationalis*, an individual substance of a rational nature. The tendency to understand sin in terms of *concupiscentia*, disordered desire, that left this rational core of humanity intact, easily led to a compartmentalized view of fallen humanity in which part of us, our reason, remained unfallen, but sin had its seat in our urges and desires.

Image lost – the Reformers

The sixteenth-century Reformers rejected this view because they saw that there was no part of our humanity that was unaffected by sin, least of all our mind and our thinking. They held, with Paul in Romans 1, that it was wrong thinking about God, others, and ourselves that was at the very root of all that was wrong with us. "For though they knew God, they did not honour him as God or give thanks to him, but they became futile in their thinking, and their senseless minds were darkened. Claiming to be wise they became fools and they exchanged the glory of the immortal God for images resembling a mortal human being or birds or four-footed animals or reptiles" (Rom. 1:21–23). The fallen human mind, instead of being responsive to the true God that it was made to image in its thinking, became itself a creator of false images of gods of its own making. Our reason is thus at the heart of our problem and it is in our minds that first and most we need to be renewed, "Be transformed by the renewing of your minds" (Rom. 12:2).

In negative reaction to what they saw as the failure of medieval Catholicism to be serious enough about the devastating effects of sin upon the whole of our humanity, Luther and Calvin, in Irenaean terms, tended to deny or at least play down the continuing image and to place all the emphasis on the lost likeness. Their intense christological concentration made them passionately aware of the contrast between the Christ, who in his human obedience was the perfect mirror of the Father's goodness and righteousness, and sinful humanity in its rebellion and disobedience. The moral difference between Christ and us is so overwhelmingly great that it dwarfs the similarities between his humanity and ours and leads to the inevitable conclusion that if he is the image of God, then in our sinfulness we are not.

> From the image of God, from the knowledge of God, from the knowledge of all the other creatures and from a very honourable nakedness man has fallen into blasphemies, into hatred, into contempt of God, yes, what is even more, into enmity against God
>
> (Luther, 1958, 1:60).

Calvin sees Adam as the mirror of God who is orientated toward his creator. In sin, that orientation is lost; when the mirror is no longer pointed toward God, it can no longer image God. So writing of fallen Adam, Calvin can say,

> Therefore, after the heavenly image was obliterated in him, he was not the only one to suffer this punishment – that in place of wisdom, virtue, holiness, truth and justice, with which adornments he had been clad, there came forth the most filthy plagues, blindness, impotence, impurity, vanity and injustice – but he also entangled and immersed his offspring in the same miseries.
>
> (Calvin, 1960, II.1.5, p. 246)

Calvin, ever more systematic than Luther, does rather grudgingly allow that sinful man is still distinguished from the rest of creation by his will and reason.

Even though something of understanding and judgement remains as a residue along with the will, yet we will not call a mind whole and sound that is both weak and plunged into deep darkness. And depravity of the will is all too well known. Since reason, therefore, by which man distinguishes between good and evil, and by which he understands and judges is a natural gift, it could not be completely wiped out; but it was partly weakened and partly corrupted so that its misshapen ruins appear.

(Calvin, 1960, II.2.12, p. 270)

To be fair to Calvin, he explains how in the realm of earthly things the will and understanding can still function, but the whole tone of the discussion is well represented by the talk of residue and misshapen ruins, depravity and darkness in the above quotations. Calvin and much of the Reformed tradition after him is much more concerned about the loss of the *imago* as a result of sin than with the persistence of the *imago* as the given structure of human creation. That is one reason why in this book we have sought to correct this one-sidedness by concentrating attention not in the first place on man the sinner who has lost his right relationship to God but on man the creature whose being is dependent on and expressive of his relationship to God, however much he has spoilt and distorted it.

Barth and Gunton – image retained

In making this correction we are simply following faithfully some of the leading twentieth-century representatives of the same Reformed tradition, who at this point have departed from the teaching of their sixteenth-century forefathers and insisted that even as sinners humanity has its being as the image of God and can have no other being. As Karl Barth puts it, commenting on Genesis 1:26,

For an understanding of the general biblical use of this concept [*imago Dei*] it is advisable to keep as close as possible to the simple sense of "god-likeness" given in this passage. It is not a quality of man hence there is no point in asking in which of man's peculiar attributes and aspects it exists. It does not consist in anything that man is or does. *It consists as man himself consists as the creature of God. He would not be man if he were not the image of God. He is the image of God in the fact that he is man.*

(Barth, 1958, p. 184, italics mine)

It follows from this that, if man as sinner is still man, then man as sinner is still in the image of God, and that is, in fact, Barth's position. Looking forward from the Genesis creation story to the future of biblical revelation, he says, "It will be revealed also that God is faithful to himself and his work and Word; that the creation of man as male and female, and therefore in the image and likeness of God, *is not overthrown by the episode of the fall, but remains even in face of the total contradiction between it and the being of man*" (Barth, 1958, p. 190, italics mine).

Barth can indeed offer a very positive picture of human life quite apart from Christian faith and discipleship.

> What we have called humanity can be present and known in varying degrees of perfection and imperfection even where there can be no question of direct revelation and knowledge of Jesus Christ
>
> (Barth, 1960, p. 276).

The same approach is echoed and its practical implications for penal theory are further explored by Colin Gunton.

> Even the apparently irremediably lost remain in the likeness of God because he continues in Christ to be Creator,

whether freedom to love is exercised or rejected. That means that, however horrible the deformity, however great the need for redemption in its broadest sense, those created in God's image remain so and hence Genesis' prohibition on killing one so created ... At the very least the human being, simply as created is the kind of being to which is due a certain radical moral respect, however sunk in villainy or depravity.

(Gunton, 1998, p. 204)

The difference in tone and content between these two representative latter day Reformed theologians and their sixteenth-century precursors can hardly be overstated and it is worth asking what accounts for the change. The answer is both clear and complex. Barth and Calvin share a central christological commitment, but for Barth Christ is Lord not just of redemption and new creation, but also of original creation. "All things were made by him and without him was not anything made that was made" (John 1:3). To be in the image of Christ, therefore, belongs not just to the transforming sanctification of believers, but to the ontology of created humanity. Even where Christ is far from the center of our faith, he is at the very center of our being. What he is in his relationships within the divine life, we are in our relationships within human life. If to be a person-in-relationship describes what he is, then it also describes what we are in our imaging of him.

Such an approach is quite explicit in Barth. For him also *imago Dei* is *imago Trinitatis*.

> God exists in relationship and fellowship. As the Father of the Son and the Son of the Father, he is himself an I and a Thou, confronting himself and yet always one and the same in the Holy Ghost. God created man in his own image, in correspondence with his own being and essence. He created

him in the image that emerges even in his own work as Creator and Lord of the covenant. Because he is not solitary in himself and therefore does not will to be so *ad extra*, it is not good for man to be alone and God created him in his own image, male and female.

(Barth, 1960, p. 324)

For Barth, the togetherness in difference of the man and the woman is the archetype for the relational structure that constitutes the image of God – a subject on which we will have more to say in the next chapter.

For the moment, we note that such an approach shifts the emphasis away from an understanding of the *imago* in terms of natural qualities in creation or supernatural virtues in sanctification toward an understanding in terms of the ontological relationality in which human life is constituted and of a shift in the same direction in the understanding of sanctification in Christ, as we will see later.

Furthermore, particularly for Barth, what God gives in grace has a reality and an objectivity that far exceeds the power of sin to destroy. The sovereign work of God in creating man in his own image cannot be undone by human rebellion against it or in contradiction of it. The work of God is too substantial and robust to be nullified by the sin of man. The sinner, just by being human, continues even in spite of himself, to provide evidence that he has made by and for the triune God.

All that said, the question still remains how we are to understand the relationship between Genesis 1 and Genesis 3. Are we to swing over from the hamartiological negativity of Calvin which insists that sin destroys the image, to an optimistic positivity that declares that the image is stronger than the sin and that even the worst sinner is secure in his dignity as a created child of God?

Formal and material image – Brunner

The Reformed theologian who has addressed this question most specifically is Emil Brunner and, as we will see the answers he offers, while greatly concerned to do justice to the insights of Calvin about the deadly results of sin, is clearly in the tradition of Irenaeus in affirming that the *similitudo* is lost but the *imago* remains.

Brunner insists, as against the dominant Western tradition, that the essence of being human is not rationality but being held in a relationship to God in which he calls us to a responsible response to his loving self-communication to us. Our reason enables us to recognize that relationship and to respond to it. "He [man] is not to be understood in himself nor from that reason which is in him. He can be understood only in terms of that which stands 'over against' him, the Word of his Creator ... Reason is, so to speak, only the organ of man's relation to God" (Brunner, 1939, p. 102).

This relationship to God in which God freely addresses man in love and calls upon him to respond freely to that address is at the heart of what Brunner calls the formal or structural image of God which persists when man becomes a sinner. He contrast this with what he calls the material image of God, which is man in free, positive, and obedient response to the God who addresses him, as he is in Christ.

Brunner takes with utter seriousness the fact that the material image of God, what the Latin tradition, following Irenaeus, called the *similitudo* is lost across the whole range of human existence. He will have nothing to do with what he calls the Catholic "two-storey" version of the situation in which the lower nature falls but the higher reason remains intact (Brunner, 1952, p. 58). The man who is a sinner is a sinner in every part of him. Till it is restored in Christ the material image is gone.

Marred Image

But even in the sinner, the formal or structural image that is constituted by his relationship to God remains.

> The biblical testimony on this point is ruthlessly logical; man is the being who stands "before God" even if he is godless. The fact that man, misusing his freedom and denying his responsibility, turns his back on God does not mean that he no longer stands "before God". On the contrary he stands "before God" as a sinner, he stands before God in a wrong attitude, hence he is "under the wrath of God"... the loss of the *Imago* in the material sense, does not remove responsibility from man; he still stands "before God" and he is still a human being. Only human beings can be sinners ... The loss of the *Imago* in the material sense, presupposes the *Imago* in the formal sense. To be a sinner is the negative way of being responsible.
> (Brunner (1952), p 60)

In this way of putting things Brunner is concerned to do justice to all the different ways of thinking about the image of God that have emerged in the theological tradition since Irenaeus. On the one hand he affirms the robustness of God's continuing relationship with us as his creatures made to respond to him and, on the other, the destructiveness that sin brings to that relationship and the tension between the two which is the burden of the teaching of so many of the Old Testament prophets. He rightly rejects quantitative ways of understanding this relationship, on the one hand, in the medieval theologians with their intact reason and corrupted desires and, on the other, with the Reformation talk of a surviving remnant of the image. He insists rather that over the whole range of our humanity we are simultaneously made by God and in rebellion against him.

The line Brunner takes gives a good basis on which to develop our understanding of how we can at the same time be formally or – better – structurally in the image of God but materially in rebellion against him. The following points will take us further.

The fall – analysis not history

The fact that our createdness and our sinfulness are in simultaneous co-existence in our relationship to God is basic to most modern theological anthropologies and certainly to those of Barth and Pannenberg. The first three chapters of Genesis are seen not so much as stages in a historical account of how we got where we are, but rather as an analysis of where we are.

In contrast with Augustine, who affirmed Adam as the first man made in a state of original perfection who then fell from it into sin, this understanding sees Adam rather as Everyman viewed in his relation to the God of Israel, so that what is said of him in the form of the Genesis narratives has authority because it rings true as a valid understanding of what we are constrained to say about ourselves when we see ourselves, as Brunner would put it, "before God." The fact that we are made as free persons-in-relationship to reflect his life is the presupposition for the understanding of ourselves as those who have rebelled against our Creator and his purpose in our creation. This analysis of humanity as it is now rather than a historical account of how it got like that is the nub of the Genesis story.

How this relates to evolutionary history is another question to which there is no certain answer. If the development of the first humans, about whom we know little, is analogous to the development of contemporary humans of whom we know much, then perhaps we have to say that our created exocentricity and our egocentric revolt against it emerge together side by side, that when we become conscious of the claims of others and supremely the claims of God upon us, there is that in us that makes a positive response to them, but there is also that in us that wants to defend ourselves and indeed assert ourselves against them, so that all our relationships are corrupted and resorted as a result. That is how it is now and therefore, most likely, how it was in the beginning as well – although by the mercy of God in Christ – not how it ever shall be world without end!

Our interest, however, is more in the acuteness of the analysis than in the accuracy of the history. Our perfect response to the divine intention in creating us in his own image to be his covenant partners is to be understood not protologically of a mythical past, but eschatologically of a redeemed future. We are made in such a way that that responsiveness is possible to us, we are those who can hear God's call and have the ability to answer it; but the reality with which we have to deal is that that possibility has been unrealized and that freedom has been misused so that in all sorts of ways we affirm ourselves against God.

The creature of Genesis 1 and the sinner of Genesis 3 are the same man, and in our self-understanding they are inseparable, in that we never encounter the one without the other. If there is a priority of creation over fallenness, it is not that one precedes the other historically, but that one is the work of God and the other the work of man and the second presupposes the first. As Brunner points out, if God had not made us to be responsible to him, we could not sin against him.

Our fall, therefore, is not from a state of innocence that preceded it, but rather a falling out of God's purposes for humanity, a refusal to be what God made us to be, a turning away of a summons and a calling to reflect God back to himself in our dealings with him and with one another. As Pannenberg puts it, "the essence of the human being is seen as a destiny that will be achieved only in the future" (Pannenberg 1985, p. 58).

Our fall is our refusal of that future for the sake of self-assertion and self-fulfilment in the present. Such an approach affirms the theological heart of the Genesis stories, the eschatological orientation of the New Testament understanding of sanctification (cf. 2 Cor. 3:18) and is consonant with the contemporary anthropological understanding of human development.

Image and fall – vertical and horizontal

Both Barth and Brunner, for all their celebrated conflicts on these issues, share the relational understanding of the *imago Dei* that we have been expounding. Each, however, has a characteristic emphasis. For Brunner we image or fail to image God primarily in the vertical relationship that we have with him just by being human, in how we answer his address to us and respond in our freedom to his loving call to us. This resonates well with what Pannenberg says about the engagement with the ultimate which is the final expression of human exo-centricity and the ineluctable sense of being rooted in a transcendent presence that places us under an unconditional obligation to which we have earlier drawn attention as characterizing in a multitude of different forms the whole of human culture.

Barth, of course, in his own terms affirms this. Within their covenant relationship to God, men and women are called to respond to God with a love and freedom that reflects his own. But what preoccupies Barth more in this context is the way in which the horizontal relationships of men and women on the human level are made to reflect the inter-Trinitarian relationships on the divine level. If Brunner's approach to the divine issue points in the direction of the first great commandment and tells us that we are like God when we love him with all our heart and soul and mind and strength, Barth's points more in the direction of the second great commandment and tells us that we are most like God when we love our neighbors as ourselves. While that difference of emphasis is interesting and significant, it is no more than that, and both our theologians would agree that imaging God involves reflecting him back to himself in our relationship with him and reflecting his love and freedom in our relationships with one another and that in the end the horizontal and vertical dimensions are so intimately connected that you cannot reflect the life of God with any fullness on the one without also reflecting it on the other.

In fact, on that basis we can go on to point out that it is at the heart of Christian revelation to hold that our vertical relationships with God are always mediated through our horizontal relationships with other people, as we saw specifically and somewhat ideally in our little case study of John Baillie.

At the heart of the doctrine of the incarnation is the claim that our vertical relationship to God is mediated by our horizontal relationship with the man Jesus, because that man Jesus is uniquely identified with God as his only-begotten Son. It is by a constant returning to the story of the man Jesus, made possible by the witness of the scriptures to him, that we maintain and renew our relationship with God. Where that specific link with the man Jesus is loosened or marginalized, the Church's relationship with God can be dominated and controlled by its own traditions and predilections or by whatever presuppositions are predominant in the culture of which it is a part.

The human relationships that mediate the divine relationship has for Christian faith, its prototype and model in the incarnation, but that prototype gives us a clue by which we can at least begin to make sense of what is happening in the complicated process by which human religion in all its diverse forms has developed.

Throughout, in conformity with the incarnational model, there is a divine origin and a human mediation. The authenticity of the result will depend on how much similarity there is between the divine source and the human reflection of it, whether the human medium is a well pointed and focused mirror that gives a faithful representation of the God who seeks to reveal himself through it, or whether the mirror is focused in the wrong direction and its glass so warped and distorted that it is unable to image God except in a highly distorted and one-sided way.

Paul on religion

This perspective casts new light on the way Paul deals with the phenomena of the religion of the Greco-Roman world as he encountered it in his missionary campaigns. His classic treatment of this is in the passage in Romans 1:18ff., which was discussed in Chapter 1.

At the root of all religion is the self-revelation of God to those he has made in his own image, so that they may know, honor, and worship him (1:20, 21). Jewish and Gentile religion alike give evidence that they spring from the same ultimate origin in this revealing activity of the one God who in different ways is at work in them both. Both are concerned about the invisible source of the created world and about human relating to it. They both spring from an awareness of the presence and pressure of that divine revelation upon them so that they cannot evade its claims and its calls, and the universal nature of religion witnesses to that fact. Simply as human beings made by God for himself, their common destiny is to know him and serve him, and their religion is the way in which they seek to fulfil that destiny.

For a Christian theology of religion, the difference between the relationship to God that emerges in human religion and in Christian faith is due to the way in which it is humanly mediated. In the case of Christian faith, as we have seen, the mediation is through the humanity of Jesus, which has been claimed and purified by God for a unique hypostatic union with himself, so that it can be a pure and undistorted mirror of God's triune divinity. It is uniquely through the mediation of the human story of Jesus that we can know and participate in the knowledge and the love of the true God.

According to Paul in the passage before us, the case is very different with Gentile religion, which for him is the presenting example of all religion that does not have its base in Christ's mediation of the saving knowledge of God. Instead of being mediated through the new humanity of Christ, that religion is mediated through a humanity that is so out of focus on its subject and so distorted in its egocentric sinfulness that it cannot receive or transmit the revelation of God from which its religion springs but in all kinds of ways distorts and denies that revelation. Faced at the depths of their being with God's self-disclosure in his creation, sinful men and women find a whole variety of ways in which they affirm themselves in their distortion and contradiction of it.

That is why in the light of the gospel Paul speaks in the severest terms of castigation of the human religion he encountered. Gentiles, precisely in their religious relationship to God, are subject to his wrath because by their wickedness, they suppress the truth (v. 18), they become futile in their thinking and their senseless minds are darkened (v. 21), they exchange the glory of the immortal God for images resembling a mortal human being (v. 23), they exchange the truth of God for a lie and worship and serve the creature rather than the creator (v. 25). That formidable indictment is the theological presupposition out of which Paul engaged in what we know as interfaith dialogue.

When we get a glimpse of Paul engaged in an actual encounter with the philosophers of Athens as we do in Luke's rendering of it in Acts 17, his starting point is that he comes to proclaim a God who, till now, is unknown to them (17:23), the religion that he finds among them is idolatrous and that it is what it is because human beings have projected their ideas on to God and made him what they wanted him to be (16:25). Against the gods that they have made he proclaims the God who has made them, and the whole world (17:24) and seeks to recall them to the revelation of that God who is the origin of their religious enterprise and who still, in the midst of their idolatry, presses his claims upon them, as witness the poetic quotations to which Paul appeals. (17:27, 28)

Religion as truth and lie

Just as a lie depends on the elements of truth within it to give it credibility, and yet so encloses these elements in its all embracing falsehood that part of the truth is used to resist and deny the whole truth, so, in spite of the genuine and noble insights that characterize the Greek religion Paul encountered at Athens, it is so held and controlled by its man-made and idolatrous context that it cannot and will not hear the message of Christ's judgement and resurrection that Paul brings to it from the heart of the Christian gospel (17:30, 32).

As Francis Watson puts it, writing of Paul's appeal to the Greek poets in this passage,

> It may tentatively be asserted that through God's prevenient grace a seeking and a finding has occurred among the Gentiles, and that certain symptoms of this may be discerned. But nothing much may be built upon this tentative discernment. It is not a foundation for the gospel, which must everywhere reckon not with a pure universal knowledge of God, given in and with human existence, but with idolatry, distortion, ignorance.
> (Watson, 1997, p. 255)[8]

It may be that in a very proper reaction to pluralistic approaches, Watson somewhat underplays what, in a continuation of the passage just quoted, he calls "the continuities between the age-long human quest for God, with its occasional though partial moments of finding and the moment of fulfilment through Christ". There is much in the teaching of the Dalai Llama which Christians can receive and admire; Muslim affirmations of the sovereignty of the one God have Old Testament resonances that Christians as well as Jews can share.

The main point, however, stands firm. The Dalai Llama approaches other religions in terms of an ultimate loyalty to the brand of Buddhism, of which he is the chief exponent and representative. Buddhism has a non-theistic, anti-personalist perspective and an understanding of the human situation and the means of salvation from it that is totally opposite to the that of Christian gospel, of such a nature that if the one is true, the other false; if the one is a faithful revelation of ultimate reality, the other must be seen as a human invention, and so, in Paul's terms, as an idolatrous projection and corruption of the truth.

Similarly, the Muslim affirmation of the sovereignty of God, right as it may be in itself, is made in a context which vehemently rejects the Christian affirmation of that sovereignty as being exercised supremely in the incarnation, death, and resurrection of God's only begotten Son, so that, for all that the two faiths may share, the accusation of idolatry with which each charges the other is the inevitable consequence of the central theological divide that at the center separates and divides them.

Christians who are committed to the gospel of the incarnation and the cross cannot but view the Muslim version of the divine sovereignty as the projection on God of human ideas of absolute power and therefore idolatrous. The universal revelation of the one true God is corrupted by its human receptors, so that our exocentric openness to God is distorted by the priority we give to our own ideas and predilections and is, in that way, ultimately egocentric – not in the sense of being selfish or self-seeking in the ordinary meaning of these terms, but in the sense of giving ultimate priority to our ideas about God that fatally circumscribe and limit the ability of our humanity to mediate and reflect his revelation of himself to us.

Such an approach in the current climate will inevitably be accused of an arrogant exclusivism that disqualifies its proponents from an open and respectful participation in interfaith dialogue, but as Gavin D'Costa has so clearly shown (D'Costa, 2000, p. 3 passim) all truth claims are exclusive to the extent that they reject what denies and contradicts them; for that reason pluralist approaches in their truth claims are every bit as exclusive in their rejection of and arrogant in their scorn for anyone who stands by the ultimacy of one religious claim over against all the others.

We may do well to speak in more dulcet tones than the Paul of Romans 1, but if, like him, we are not ashamed of the gospel and believe that it is the power of God for the salvation of everyone who believes in it, then we are bound to enter dialogue with other faiths with the sort of respect that Paul showed to the Athenian philosophers but with the same evangelistic intent to win them out of their sophisticated and sometimes noble idolatries to the grace and truth that are mediated uniquely by Jesus Christ.

We will do so very humbly, when we remember the intellectual, cultural, and personal idolatries that have marred the life of the Christian community itself down the centuries and how often then and now our own faith has been distorted by the cultural priorities and personal prejudices of those who have professed it. What mediates God's revelation is not the human nature of Christians, which, with far less excuse because it lives in the light of the gospel, has often been as corrupted and marred as anybody else's. The truth of God is mirrored in and mediated by not our humanity but that of Jesus and by us only in so far as our humanity is opened up and converted out of its corruptions by the Holy Spirit to that of Jesus and brought into such conformity to him that we also are able to receive and convey his truth. As Jesus said to Peter, "Flesh and blood have not revealed this to you, but my Father in heaven" (Matt. 16:17).

When, however, that revelation is both given and received by Christian sinners in an act of undeserved grace, we are bound to proclaim the sole lordship of Jesus and to deny as idolatrous the claims of any other to sit on his throne.

This whole discussion has shown the good biblical basis that Luther and Calvin had for rejecting the medieval catholic claim that the human reason somehow escaped the consequences of the fall, that we remained *capax Dei*, capable of a pure natural knowledge of God with our unsullied minds. Paul's whole approach in Romans 1 suggests that the mind is the central seat of sin, that when our minds focus on ourselves egocentrically rather than on God exocentrically and when they claim that what has its origin in ourselves is in fact an objective truth about ultimate reality beyond ourselves, our minds are the very factories of idols that Calvin described; the images of God have been contaminated by the images of self, and the truth has been corrupted into the lie from which it takes the truth of God incarnated in and mediated by the humanity of Christ to set us free.

Original sin

Having seen how our philosophies and theologies can be corrupted by the distortions of the humanity that receives, reflects, and communicates them, we can go on to see how the relational understanding of personhood that is at the basis of all we have been saying, brings the Western doctrine of original sin into a fresh perspective and makes it accessible to us in a new way. If in our created exocentricity we depend on others and upon the society that has shaped them for our personhood, it becomes, in principle, easier to see how it is from others that we are inducted into those wrong relationships with God and neighbor that we call sin. Our corruption is not something that we originate, but something that we receive and with which we then identify ourselves.

Augustine and Pelagius

In that last sentence there is encapsulated the conflict that dominated the famous debate between Pelagius on the one side and Augustine on the other. Pelagius argued from an individualistic basis that sin had its origin in the will of the sinner and that it could be undone by a simple act of choice that rejected what was evil and opted instead for what was good. Against this, Augustine held that the sin in human society was prior to and the cause of the sin of the individual whose will was shaped by that society, that it was therefore a binding oppression before it was a personal choice.

Furthermore, since the oppression was prior to the individual's assent to it, liberation from that oppression was not the work of the individual but had its origin in the grace of God incarnate in Christ, which was also prior to any act or choice of the individual and came to him as a gift he had no part in fashioning. Just as the individual person was enslaved by an oppressive power outside himself, so he was saved from that oppression by a liberating power that was also outside himself.

We have only to state the issue in the broadest outline to see that whatever hesitations we might have about the outworking of Augustine's position, his presupposition that sin is rooted in the human person in its relatedness to the culture and the society to which it belongs is very much in line with our own, whereas Pelagius bases his case on the contrary presupposition that the autonomous individual with his free choices is in control of his own destiny and is therefore the creator rather than the creation of the human context in which he lives.

Before we examine the position further, we do well to look at its biblical base. One thinks, of course, of Old Testament verses like Psalm 51:5. "Behold I was brought forth in iniquity and in sin did my mother conceive me," to which Augustinians have often appealed, especially as it seems to tie the inheritance of sin to sexual activity, one of the most ambiguous features of the Augustinian model.

Paul on sin

It is, however, to Paul and to the letter to the Romans that we must look for the beginnings of an orderly exposition of this whole matter. In recounting his own experience, whether as Jew or as Christian, in Romans 7, Paul speaks of sin as an invasive controlling force that overcomes the will's resistance to it and reduces it to a condition of impotent slavery. "For we know that the law is spiritual but I am of the flesh sold into slavery under sin. For I do not do what I want, but I do the very thing I hate ... Now if I do what I do not want, it is no longer I that do it, but sin that dwells within me" (7:14, 15, 20). The man created in the image of God for obedient response to God finds himself situated in a force field of rebellion and opposition to God – the flesh – that overwhelms his intention of obedience so that he acts against his createdness and yields to besieging sin. However difficult that situation may be to conceptualize coherently, it is easy to identify existentially with it; it is something that happens to us all.

What Paul describes in these existential terms in Romans 7 he explores more theologically in Romans 5, where he sees human sin in the context of our relationship with Adam, the prototypical sinner who is prior to us all and represents us all.

Adam and Christ

Central for Paul is the claim that we sin and die in virtue of our relationship to Adam and we obey and live in virtue of our relationship to Christ. Although the two relationships are completely different in nature and outcome, they both affirm that we are not the originators either of our downfall or of our uprising. The one comes to us in our solidarity with Adam and the other comes to us in our solidarity in Christ. "Therefore just as by the one man's disobedience the many were made sinners, so by the one man's obedience the many will be made righteous" (Rom. 5:19). Our status whether in sin or salvation is not individualistically but socially determined.

For Paul, in spite of 7:14ff., this does not mean that when we sin, our will is coerced or by-passed, so that we can evade responsibility for our actions by pleading that they are involuntary and so not really our actions at all. Paul's whole theological stance contradicts such a conclusion. Within this passage he insists that the purpose of the law is to expose and consolidate human responsibility. Sin is not reckoned till the law comes (7:13), but when it does come sin is exposed as voluntary and responsible disobedience to it (7:20). Although sin has its origin in Adam and to that extent is a fate that comes to us from outside ourselves, we internalize that sin by the active voluntary sinning by which we align ourselves with what has come to us from outside ourselves. All that seems to be implied by or at least to be consonant with what Paul says, "Therefore just as sin came into the world through one man and death came through sin, and so death spread to all *because all have sinned ...*" (5:12).

The sin of Adam is something we inherit, but the guilt that we incur comes not from the inheritance but from our personal affirmation and internalization of that inheritance as the principle and motivation of our own actions. As human beings created in the image of God, we recognize and affirm his claim upon us expressed in the obligations of the law, but we act against our createdness and in the fleshliness that comes to us from Adam when, in fact, we act in disobedience to that law.

In using this passage to support a relational and social understanding of sin, we are once more thinking of

Adam not so much as the first individual who precedes the rest of us in time, but as Everyman, who encapsulates in himself the flawed humanity into whose inheritance we are quite involuntarily born. The fact that Paul makes so much of his contrast between the one man Adam on the negative side and the one man Christ on the positive side suggests that he was thinking of Adam as a historical individual, but what matters about that individual is not what separates him from the rest of us but rather what binds us to him. Everything that Paul says about Adam is about his relatedness to the whole of humanity, so that it is legitimate to interpret the passage socially and relationally in the way that we have.

In essence Augustine's teaching about original sin affirms and develops this Pauline teaching, although his sexual obsessions lead him to emphasize sexual intercourse as the sinful channel by which the sinful inheritance is transmitted from one generation to another, in a way that has no parallel in Paul, who affirms the transmission without specifying the method.

The basic nature of Augustine's position is well summed up by Alistair McFadyen, whose groundbreaking reinterpretation of Augustine has been in the background of this whole discussion. He puts it in this way:

> Augustine may be interpreted as construing willing as the personal energy through which one's life is directed, committed, and oriented. But this personal energy is not directed by the power of a pure, autonomous self. Willing is rather situated and relational, influenced in its orientation by extra- and supra-personal fields of force within one's situation. Through willing, we incorporate ourselves into, internalise and redouble dynamics which are generally supra-personal and not of our own making, while adding

our own personal power to them. Thereby we achieve an internal integration in identity and orientation to match the external.

(McFadyen, 2000, p. 203)

McFadyen substantiates this analysis in a contemporary context by sociological case studies that show how pedophile child abusers corrupt the willing of their victims into a guilty consent to the sexual practices which have been forced upon them; and of how the whole German civil service was corrupted into enthusiastic participation in the efficient organization of the transportation of Jews to the concentration camps and the gas ovens of the holocaust that awaited them there. In both cases, evil force from outside was exerted not to override the will of its victims by sheer physical force but, by a process of psychological and moral manipulation, to corrupt the will into consent to that evil, however reluctant and guilt-ridden.

In the realm of drama, we can see the same process working itself out step by step in Shakespeare's *Macbeth*, where the protagonist's uneasy will to good is overcome by his encounter with the forces of darkness (expressive of his own lust for power), by his wife's determined ambition, and by ironic opportunity (Duncan's decision to visit him) all combining with irresistible force.

Just as our rationality can be corrupted to turn the truth into a lie, so our wills can be corrupted to assent to the egocentric orientation that controls the society into which we are born, so that we internalize that orientation and make its values and predilections our own, and thus share responsibility for them. Sin that overrides the will would be a fate that made us its unwilling victims; sin that corrupts and wins the will makes us its responsible accomplices who, by saying yes to it, make it our own.

Apartheid and liberation

So, to take a different example, to be born into the white minority in South Africa was to be born into a situation that was at every point dominated by the evil ideology of apartheid which pervaded every level of life from the political system of the country, to what beach you could swim from and what public toilet you could use. If you belonged to that white minority, it had much to offer you: unlimited privilege, black workers that provided subservient domestic service, and cheap labor that kept prices low. If you were born into that situation, although you had no part in creating it, you absorbed it with your mother's milk, took its benefits for granted, and moved almost inevitably into an implicit acceptance of its values. Only when it was challenged by internal and external voices that demanded liberation from it would you begin to see how personally implicated in it and responsible for it you had become, so that you had either to affirm and defend it or embark on a long process of emancipating conversion from it at every stage of which you became increasingly aware of how deeply the thing you wanted to reject had penetrated the fiber of your being and the way of life through which you expressed it.

And, of course, the situation is further complicated by the fact that the protest for justice and liberation on behalf of the oppressed majority is itself, like all human enterprises, compromised by its own kind of self-assertion: the violence and the hatred that are the invariable components of such struggles. It was, in this case, gloriously relativized by Nelson Mandela's will for reconciliation, which is so remarkable just because it is so unusual in such encounters between the oppressors and the oppressed.

The particular way in which apartheid worked in South Africa is an example of the way in which sin works universally in other quite different human situations. We are all born into societies that in all sorts of different ways are corrupted by human egocentricity and we are in all sorts of ways seduced and corrupted into implicit assent to it and compliance with it, so that the original sin that we inherit almost imperceptibly becomes the personal sin that we commit.

Most sin is by compliance rather than by decision. We know how committed we are to it when it is challenged at particular points by the moral demands that in every society press on our conscience the claims of the exocentricity in and for which we were created. It is, as Paul pointed out, when we encounter the law that implicit consent to evil is exposed as what we might call voluntary enslavement to its power – that corruption of the will described by McFadyen.

Sin and morality

This is in line with the further Pauline insight that even the moral life in which we respond positively to the ethical demands that are mediated to us by the society to which we belong can become the final bastion of our self-assertion and self-righteousness. For this becomes the basis for a condemning superiority over other people and a claim to an intrinsic worthiness which gives us a self-achieved standing with and a justified claim upon God, while in reality it throws us back on ourselves as the authors of our own salvation and fortifies the denial of our dependence upon him that is the very essence of sin.

The paradox of the Pauline gospel, which, from a Christian perspective, is the paradox of the moral life, is that obedience to God's law can make of us the enemies of God's grace in our denial of our need of it, so that, in Pauline phraseology, the law which is at least the proximate expression of God's will can become the very instrument of our rejection of and enmity toward God's purpose. The power of evil can corrupt even the righteous expression of God's will and turn it to its own purposes. As Paul himself puts it, "The very commandment that promised life proved to be death to me. For sin, seizing an opportunity through the commandment, deceived me and through it killed me" (Rom. 7:10, 11).

Behind the theology is the personal experience of Paul and the heart of the story of Jesus. It was the man who based his life on his good standing in terms of the law of Israel who for that very reason became the persecutor of the Messiah of Israel and his people. "... circumcised on the eighth day, of the people of Israel, of the tribe of Benjamin, a Hebrew of the Hebrews; as to the law, a Pharisee, as to zeal, a persecutor of the church; as to righteousness under the law blameless" (Phil. 3:5, 6). The whole paradox that we are expounding is contained in the juxtaposition of these last phrases – blameless under the law, but precisely as such, a persecutor of Jesus Christ and his people.

The sin that crucifies

Furthermore, the personal experience of Paul mirrors the public record about Jesus. From the start of his ministry to its end, the opposition to it is led by the high priests and the Pharisees, the religious establishment and the moral elite of Israel. The moral outcasts, the publicans and sinners of the gospel, were more receptive to him than those who were dedicated to the worship of Israel's God and the purity of Israel's moral response to God's covenant with them. To say the same thing in theological depth, when God's love becomes incarnate among God's people, those who are the guardians of that people's response to God are found to be the most unresponsive and implacably hostile to it and bend all their energies to having it violently done to death.

The crucifixion of Jesus exposes the fact that at the heart of human religion and morality, with all its revealed truths, valid insights, and noble intentions, there is an inbuilt corruption, a proud human autonomy that, deep down, denies its dependence on God and his grace and bases itself on its own religious and moral achievements, so that, at the end of the day, Caiaphas, as much as Adam, sets himself up as his own god, who arrogates to himself the authority to determine that what he stands for is good and what Jesus stands for is evil for Israel. The proponents of that kind of religion are, like the Pharisee in the parable, forever giving thanks that they are not as other men and rehearsing their own achievements in proof of their own superiority. What this kind of religion cannot tolerate is the challenge to its own self-respect by the revelation of the fundamental egocentricity at its own heart, which is brought about by its exposure to the exocentric graciousness of the person and ministry of Jesus.

When Jesus shows in word and action what it means to love God and neighbor with heart and soul and mind and strength, the leaders of Israel are faced with the intolerable ambiguity of their own situation, because what ultimately motivates and controls them is not, as they imagined, unsullied love of either God or neighbor, but their own self-preservation and the protection of the structures of moral law and religious power that secures it.

It is not that they do not genuinely care for God and neighbor, but that when the crisis comes in their encounter with Jesus the last and prevailing word is the word of self-affirmation and self-preservation, and so they crucify. It was the inheritors of the best revelation who committed the worst sin.

We are all crucifiers
We must immediately add that what became explicit in the Jewish leaders because of their unique exposure to the living God, is implicit in all of us and similarly becomes explicit when we, too, are exposed to God's self-revelation in Christ. What they did, far from being an excuse for anti-Semitic condemnation, is representative of the way all of us, apart from the converting action of God, also act all the time when we are brought into relation with the story of God's love in Jesus; what they did is exactly what we would have done in their situation, as the participation of Gentile Pilate in the perpetration of the passion clearly shows. He also, faced with Jesus, sacrificed his future to secure his own. Jew or Gentile, "we were there when they crucified the Lord."

When we encounter the incarnate and crucified Christ there is exposed in us, especially in our moral and religious commitments, the same sort of ambiguity. On the one hand there is a real desire for God and for what is good, but on the other we find ourselves at the deepest levels of our being in compromising collusion with evil forces that contradict and defy the will and the nature of the God we say we are seeking.

The cultures that crucify

The culture in which our personhood is constituted is itself warped in its thinking and corrupted in its willing by the egocentricity that, for all the marks of the Creator's generosity and goodness upon it, nevertheless skews it toward a basic rejection of God's truth and a basic hostility to God's purposes as they are revealed in Christ. At the end of the day, human culture is crucifying culture and human religion is crucifying religion, gobbling up all that God has given and twisting and turning it into a weapon with which to resist and reject the giver, just as the high priests of Israel did long ago. Our personhood is shaped by the goodness and the generosity of the God into whose creation we are born, but also by the egocentricity that corrupts that creation and therefore corrupts also our own thinking and willing in relation to our Creator, making him in our own image and projecting our will on to him.

That corruption is the original sin of which we are the inheritors. It comes to us a fate from outside ourselves but shapes and woos and wins our wills into personal connivance with it. We twist and distort the image of the triune God who made us to reflect himself in the ways we have been describing, so that the Father's initiative is corrupted into coercive domination that oppresses others; the Son's obedient freedom to respond to the Father becomes instead a freedom from God that distances us from him and from other people in our self-assertion; the creativity of the Spirit collapses into a sloth in which we conform to others or into a perverse creativity that diminishes others. All these perversions show themselves in different ways and to different degrees in different people, but they are all expressions of that corruption of mind and will that perverts our relationships with one another and with God.

The divided will

That brings us back, on the personal level, to the Pauline existential experience of the divided will from which we started. "For I know that nothing good dwells within me, that is in my flesh. I can will what is right but I cannot do it. For I do not do the good I want, but the evil I do not want is what I do. Now if I do what I do not want, it is no longer I that do it, but sin that dwells within me," (Rom. 7:18–20).

That Paul should will what is good and right in the authenticity of his created personhood is a sign that he is a man made in the image of God, by God, and for God. That he is unable to activate that will is a sign that his very willing has been seduced and corrupted because he lives within the malign dynamic of a force field of evil, so that what he activates is the exact opposite of what he desires, so that he is constrained to cry out in agony, "O wretched man that I am! Who will rescue me from this body of death?" The reality of original sin reveals itself in the fact that when the goodness in us struggles with the evil in us, it is evil in one form or another that prevails.

The knowledge of original sin

Pauline scholars have discussed at great length whether the man who speaks in Romans 7 is Saul the Jew or Paul the Christian. Without entering into the subtleties of the question we may perhaps say that this is Paul the Christian interpreting the experience of Saul the Jew, not as it looked when he saw himself in Philippians 3 terms as irreproachably righteous in terms of the moral law (3:6), but as his life then looks now in the light of Christ. As Paul Achtemeier puts it, "The situation Paul faced prior to his conversion was that he knew the law embodied God's will and he knew God's will was good, and he wanted to do it. The problem was sin's control over him through the law led him to oppose, rather than accept, God's will as expressed in Christ" (Achtemeier, 1985, p. 123).

In the same discussion, Achtemeier is more specific about what he takes Paul to mean when he speaks of sin's control over him through the law. "Part of that bondage is an unawareness of it! Paul the Pharisee actually thought, in the very moment he was opposing God's will, by persecuting Christ's followers, that he was obeying God's will! The problem is not only enslavement by sin, it is unawareness that that is even one's condition! There is no freedom there, only blind unacknowledged enslavement to sin" (Achtemeier, 1985, p. 125).

That understanding of Paul classically exemplifies how even our best human pursuit of what is God's good will is vitiated by the corruption of mind and will that is endemic to the societies, the cultures, and the religions that shape us, so that precisely in what we take to be our service of God we build ourselves up in our opposition to God. Because we are made in the image of God, we still implicitly or explicitly seek him, but our reflection of him is itself distorted by the corrupt humanity of the mirrors in which that reflection is borne.

A modern Pelagian

When I studied moral philosophy in Glasgow, just after the war, the professor there was a sincere and passionate advocate of a secular Kantian morality which held that I could clearly know what was my duty and that, because "ought implies can," I had the freedom and the responsibility to do it. That made him the equally passionate opponent of any revealed morality and any talk of the need for the intervention of redeeming grace to make goodness possible. These were dismissed as illegitimate intrusions into the realm of ethical autonomy where the individual had all the resources needed to know and to do what was required of him. In the most subtle and civilized way possible he was one with Paul in rejecting the gospel of redemption that has its center in Christ, and the doctrine of original sin as we have been expounding it he would have denounced as both false and immoral because it compromised and denied the individual freedom on which all genuine morality depends.

Conclusions

Karl Barth knew what he was doing when he expounded his doctrine of sin not before but after his doctrine of reconciliation. Apart from Christ, the knowledge of God and the service of goodness can be made to look naturally compassable and achievable, well within the competence of our reason and our freedom.

> Yet whatever gains I had these I came to regard as loss because of Christ. I regard everything as loss because of the surpassing value of knowing Christ Jesus my Lord. For his sake I have suffered the loss of all things, and I regard them as rubbish, in order that I may gain Christ and be found in him, not having a righteousness of my own that comes from the law, but one that comes through faith in Christ, the righteousness from God based on faith.
> (Phil. 3:7–9)

The moral law taken in isolation can be seen in terms of a series of commands that one by one we are able to satisfy, but the moral law radicalized in the teaching and even more in the utter self-giving of Jesus shows us that to love God and neighbor as he did is utterly beyond our capacity and that, in fact, the autonomous search for a goodness of our own has at the heart of it a closedness and opposition to the God of the Gospel. God's redeeming self-revelation in Christ shows up people whom everybody calls the guardians and the promoters of goodness to be the crucifiers of God's Son. In the very exercise of our vaunted moral freedom, we show ourselves to be the ignorant and therefore helpless servants of sin.

The doctrine of original sin has therefore no independent standing of its own, as though its truth was self-evident or could be established by disinterested observation. It is an insight that is derived from our exposure to Christ and his gospel. It does not claim that we are all immoral, but rather affirms that our morality, in which we reflect in many ways the image of the God who made us, can be and is deployed in the service of our basic egocentricity in such a way as to alienate us from the purposes of God as they are revealed in Christ.

Outside Christ such an estimate of the human situation will be indignantly repudiated, and I have to confess that there is much in me that is protesting against it even as I have been expounding it. That could mean that it is a false analysis, but it could also mean in its own terms that the enslaving corruption of which it speaks is so strong that even as believing Christians we are still to some extent under its spell.

The doctrine has a kind of negative empirical confirmation to the extent that the "ought implies can" of an autonomous morality has singularly failed to solve the problem of human evil, which suggests that the human will is itself the heart of the problem rather than the answer to it, and that answer will have to be sought not in ourselves but from beyond ourselves, not in something we do, but first in something that is done to us. To see that is to be taking the first tentative step toward an openness to what the gospel claims God has done for us in Christ and on that basis can do in us by his Spirit and his grace.

Outside Christ in the realm of human autonomy, in our religion and in our atheism, in our morality and in our immorality, in our relationships to God in our corporate societies and in our personal relationships, the good for which God has made us is corrupted and spoilt by the egocentricity that has everywhere its hold upon us, so that good people do bad things and their goodness is always under the shadow and the threat of the sin that gnaws destructively at the roots of all our relationships and threatens them with disaster and death.

The wages of sin is death, because, if our life has its basis in our relationship to God and to other people and if these relationships are corrupted, our very life is threatened to its core. That threat besets us on every side and it is due to nothing but the grace of God that the death sentence under which we live has not yet been executed upon us.

The claim of this chapter is that such a doctrine of original sin is an implicate of the Christian gospel and so of an anthropology that takes its bearing from that gospel. It is an anthropology that assumes that human beings are made in the image of God and that they continue to reflect that fact, but the mirror is so distorted that the image is inauthentic; we are made to picture him, but in all kinds of ways we have become people who cannot but mirror a world which does not know the God and Father of our Lord Jesus Christ and resists both his truth and his grace. A false picture is superimposed on the original image and the confusion threatens to crack the mirror and tear us apart.

7 Gendered Image

This is the chapter that I would have preferred not to write! It forces me into an area of debate that is characterized more by confusion than clarity, where passions run high and unexamined presuppositions abound, and where I have no reason to think that I am any more exempt than anybody else from all these distractions that make the truth so hard to discern.

That is why I have deliberately placed this chapter near the end of the book, when by the nature of its content it should have come much nearer the start. The question about how gender is related to being made in the image of God is raised in the very passage where the whole notion of the *imago Dei* is first introduced. "So God created humankind in his image, in the image of God he created them, *male and female he created them*" (Gen. 1:27 italics mine). Integral to our theme is the assertion that the image of God is a gendered image so that we have to face the question whether and how men and women participate in it in different ways.

I have, however, for tactical reasons, left that aspect of the matter in the background until now, so that it should not prematurely dominate the discussion, as is very possible in current circumstances, and thus obscure the central thesis of the book: that to be authentically human is to reflect in our relationships with one another the initiating love of God the Father, the responsive love of God the Son, and the creative love of God the Spirit, in interpenetration the one with the other. All that I have written to this point applies to men and women alike, because as the Genesis passage makes clear, both are created in and for the image of God and therefore both, in ways appropriate to them, reflect what is distinctive of the three Trinitarian persons.

The question we have to ask is about what ways of participating in the image of God are appropriate to men and what ways are appropriate to women. I am going to take a line on that with what I hope will be a properly tentative humility. But I also hope that those who take a quite different line will nevertheless be able to appropriate some of the insights of the first six chapters. We can, in other words, all agree that men and women find their true humanity in the reflection of the triune God, even if we disagree about what part, if any, our gender plays in the way that reflection comes into focus in mirrors that are male and mirrors that are female.

Making space for scripture

One of my central concerns here is to make space for what the biblical tradition, viewed in the context of Trinitarian theology, actually has to say about men-women relationships in the light of their shared relationship to the God who made them to be like himself. That space is quite hard to find in contemporary debate, which has been so crowded and controlled by egalitarian and feminist ideologies of one kind or another

Gendered Image

that the biblical witness is hard to hear amidst all the clamor.

To see this one has only to remember how seldom Ephesians 5 is read at modern weddings and how immediately suspect is all its talk of the headship of the husband as an unworthy remnant of a rejected and despised patriarchal culture that only the most incorrigible biblical fundamentalists could take seriously any more. More generally, any discussion of a differentiation between men and women will immediately be heard as implying an inferiority of women to men and therefore an attempt to justify the continued subjugation of women from which the feminist protest of the last thirty years has with real success begun to set us free.

As a result, much of the biblical tradition that deals with these things has been scornfully dismissed by neglect as much as by refutation, so that here if anywhere we play up the bits that chime in with the controlling ideologies and leave the rest alone. We are glad to hear from Galatians that in Christ there is neither male nor female (Gal. 3:28) but cannot understand how the very Paul who said that could also say to the Corinthians, "But I want you to understand that Christ is the head of every man, and the husband is the head of his wife and God is the head of Christ" (1 Cor. 11:3).

I want, as against this pick and mix approach to scripture, to give it a chance to say all that it has to say about the inter-relating of men and women without the dismissive presupposition that much of what it says obstructs rather than promotes the liberating fulfilment that God in Christ intends for women as much as for men. According to the biblical witness, that fulfilment will be reached not by denying the differentiation between men and women which is maintained all the way from Genesis to Ephesians, but by showing how the relationships that are shaped by that differentiation are the means by which men and women make each other complete and free.

In the same way that the initiating Father is differentiated from the responsive Son and yet neither Father nor Son can be who they are without relating to each other and without giving themselves to and sharing themselves with each other in the distinguishing and uniting mediation of the Spirit, so men and women in their differentiated humanity can only be themselves in their relationships with one another and in their sharing of themselves with one another in a human communion that mirrors the divine communion that constitutes the life of the Trinity.

We will not in this chapter become immersed in the discussion about same-sex relationships that is confusing and dividing us all as I write, but what we will elicit from the Bible about the way it understands the differentiation and relating of men and women will perhaps help to clarify what is involved in being a man and in being a woman, which will in turn elucidate the way people relate within and across the gender differentiation and show why man-woman relating has a centrality that man-man and woman-woman relating can never equal, however much we may want to affirm a place for them.

We turn now from such generalities to a more specific examination of some of the biblical texts, trying to hear them before we criticize them and in the expectation that if scripture is indeed the word of God it will speak, even in those parts that are least congenial to the culture that has shaped us, in a way that is corrective, liberating, and creative in areas in which it is hardest for us to find our way.

Adam and Eve in Genesis

It is not surprising that most biblical treatments of man-woman relationships take their bearings from Genesis 2, rather than Genesis 1.

Genesis 1 is to be valued because quite unambiguously it affirms both that men and women are made in the image of God and also that their differentiation is relevant to the understanding of what that means. In that way it is the Old Testament equivalent of the New Testament Galatians passage, because it affirms that, in the original creation, as well as in the new creation, men and women stand together in their relationship to God and in their calling to reflect what he is in what they are.

When we come to Genesis 2, the interest shifts from the equality of men and women as joint bearers of the *imago Dei* to the distinctive ways in which they relate to one another. In this it connects less with Galatians 3 than with 1 Corinthians 11, in which Paul uses this story as the key to man-woman relations in the churches of his own day. We will look in due course at how he did that, but in the meantime we can affirm that the main point of Genesis 2 is that the man cannot be fully human without the woman and the woman cannot be fully human without the man.

One nature, two persons

In terms of that Genesis story, the fact that Eve is made from Adam indicates that her human nature is identical with his and that the differentiation between them is not that he possesses one set of characteristics and she another. In early feminism there was a tendency to compile a list of qualities that were held to be distinctively masculine – and therefore suspect – and another list of qualities that were held to be distinctively feminine – and therefore highly approved. Men could then be urged to develop their feminine side and become more like women. Such an approach was soon abandoned because it totally failed to describe reality. There is no personal quality, whether good or bad, that cannot be found in both men and women; we have all met the bullying, aggressive woman and the craven, compliant man, as well as men of great sensitivity and women of drive and effectiveness.

Ray Anderson, in discussing the different approaches of Barth and Brunner to this matter makes the same point.

> Our assertion that gender identity is intrinsic to human personhood does not entail a set of stereotyped characteristics by which to identify masculinity and femininity. Such stereotypes almost invariably attempt to describe the female in terms of the male, either as the "weaker vessel" or as the "intuitive" one as opposed to the rationality of the male. Barth vigorously protests this categorisation of masculine and feminine traits, and labels Brunner's depictions of them as preposterous
> (Barth, 1960, p. 152ff.).
>
> But Barth is not much help when it comes to saying what it means to be male as opposed to female. Whatever it means, he suggests, must be determined by the man and woman in pursuing the concrete instance of their own humanity through their sexual identity, not by attempting to rise above sexual identity in search of true humanity.
> (Anderson, 1982, p. 113)

At any rate, there is no place in the Genesis picture for any attempt at a sexist picture of human qualities. Both man and woman are made by the God whose nature is love in freedom, and both are made so that that they also may be free to give and receive love in specific ways in their dealings with one another.

We come nearer to the biblical approach to the man-woman differentiation when, still speaking in terms of Trinitarian theology, we say that the distinction between them is one of person rather than one of nature.[9] Father, Son, and Holy Spirit share the same nature of love in freedom, but they express it in different ways because of the relationships in which they stand to each other. In the Father, love is initiating; in the Son, love is responsive; in the Spirit, love is creative. To speak for a moment with Karl Barth, the divine love has three distinctive modes of being in the three divine agents who exercise it.

Work and relationships
So, it is in line with the Genesis presentation to say that the same humanity in which both Adam and Eve are created has distinctive but inter-dependant modes of being in each of them. The distinction between them is not one of diverse qualities but of distinct vocation. The distinct calling of the man is the care of the garden; the distinct calling of the woman is the care of the relationships that make human life possible. Adam names the animals before Eve comes on the scene but cannot find in the exercise of his vocation the human fulfilment that he seeks.

To set the particularities of the Eden story within the wider creational context of Genesis 1, the vocation of the man in which he images God is the dominion over the whole creation in the same fostering and perfecting love in which it was made.

But that is not enough for him or for God. As a human individual engrossed in his work, his life still lacks that which will make it a valid reflection of the image of God who is who he is and does what he does only in virtue of the relationships that constitute his being.

In all the initiating activity in which Adam orders and categorizes the creation that has been committed to his care "there was not found a helper as his partner" (2:20). Only when human individuality is turned into human relationality do human beings begin to become like God, and that relationality is the gift of God that comes through the woman. "Then the Lord God said, 'It is not good that the man should be alone: I will make him a helper as his partner'" (2:18). It is not for nothing that we say that the woman humanizes the man, that the realm of human relationships is one that is given very particularly into her care.

Appropriate penalties[10]
That this is a credible interpretation of how Genesis 2 understands the distinct vocations of the man and the woman is confirmed by the account in Genesis 3 of the distinct punishments that God allocates to the man and the woman after they have sinned.

When the harmony of their relationship with God is broken, the consequence for the woman is the breakdown in the harmony of her relationship with her husband and her children. "To the woman he said, 'I will greatly increase your pangs in childbearing; in pain you shall bring forth children, yet your desire shall be for your husband and he shall rule over you'" (3:16). The pangs of childbirth may not unreasonably be taken as symbolic for the pain that human sin continually causes in the relationships between the generations that are a particular burden for women and for mothers.

Furthermore, it is sin that accounts for the male dominance that is at the root of the patriarchal oppression against which in our day feminism has made its justified protest. If in the purpose of God in creation there is a priority of the male over the female – a subject of the highest sensitivity that we will have to discuss later in this chapter – the patriarchal domination of the man over the woman, of the husband over the wife, is here seen not as the legitimate expression of that priority but as its sinful corruption. In this, at least, the author of Genesis and modern susceptibilities are at one.

In contrast, Adam's punishment is in terms of his vocation of work in the world.

> And to the man he said, "Because you have listened to the voice of your wife and have eaten of the tree ... cursed is the ground because of you; in toil you shall eat of it all the days of your life; thorns and thistles it shall bring forth for you, and you shall eat the plants of the field by the sweat of your face, you shall eat bread until you return to the ground, for out of it you were taken; you are dust and to dust you shall return."
>
> (Gen. 3:17–19)

The result of sin is both a wrong usurping dominance of the man over the woman and, as its obverse, a wrong servile subservience of the man to the woman. Adam should not in this case have surrendered the initiative to his wife. The resulting disharmony in his relationship with God itself brings about as its punitive consequence a disharmony between the man and the world in which he works so that, in a mysterious way that the text makes no attempt to explain, it becomes resistant and obstructive to his creational vocation within it. The world as it is is not the world as God made and meant it to be; the fallenness of man has somehow infected the creation over which he has been set. When he falls out of God's good purpose, his world falls with him; it has been in Paul's equally mysterious words in Romans "subjected to futility" (8:20). As he has become disobedient to God, so the world has become disobedient to him.

It is therefore in terms of their distinct vocations as man and woman that Eve and Adam suffer the consequences of their sin. As von Rad puts it,

> The woman's punishment struck at the deepest roots of her being as wife and mother: the man's strikes at the innermost nerve of his life: his work, his activity, and provision for sustenance
>
> (von Rad, 1961, pp. 93–94).

Thus, the negative impositions of Chapter 3 are imposed in the same areas as the positive vocations of Chapter 2; for the man in terms of his work in the world, for the woman in terms of her relations in the family.

Two Trinitarian analogies

If we look at what we have just been saying in a canonical context and relate it to the triune God of the New Testament gospel and the theology that explicates it, we can trace two possible parallels. Firstly, it is the special vocation of the man with its outward orientation to work in the world to mirror the work of the triune God *ad extra*, outside his own being as the creator of the world. As the Father by his work and word fashions a reality distinct from himself, so the man by his work and word maintains, explores, and realizes the potential of that world.

So it is the special vocation of the woman with her orientation to human relationships to mirror the personal relationships that constitute the life of God. Just as it is the business of the Holy Spirit to unite the Father and the Son in a way that both unites them and maintains their hypostatic distinctness the one from the other, it is the prime concern of the woman to foster inter-human relationships so that within families and in the wider society, harmonious relationships are maintained and the integrity of the people who engage in them is affirmed. In other words, work is the characteristic concern of the man, and love is the characteristic concern of the woman. On this showing her calling can properly be said to have a priority over his. God does his work in time but from eternity to eternity in the relationality of Father, Son, and Holy Spirit, God *is* love.

There is, however, an alternative way of relating our gendered vocations to the life of God. Within the life of God there is the Father who initiates, and there is the Son who responds to that initiation, so that the Son has his whole being and action rooted in what we have called the "from-ness" of the Father and in that initiation and response, which are equally divine, God has his being. All that is mirrored in human life, as Genesis 2 depicts it. Where the man mirrors the "from-ness" of God the Father, he is the originating source of the life of the woman. "Then the man said, 'This at last is bone of my bone and flesh of my flesh. This one shall be called Woman, for out of man this one was taken'" (2:23). As the Son depends on the Father for both his being and his vocation, so the woman depends on the man for her being and vocation.

It has immediately to be added that, as in a different way the Father depends on the Son for the relationship that will make him Father, so the man depends on the woman for the relationality that will rescue him from his individualistic isolation and loneliness and present to him the needed other in relationship to whom he can grow and be fruitful. To speak the language of Martin Buber, the Thou without whom he cannot be I and will be in danger of becoming It!

Equality and headship

There is here, both in the divine and the human orders of being, a real equality, in that Father and Son on the one hand and Adam and Eve on the other cannot exist without each other. It is, however, not the equality of undifferentiated sameness, but rather the equality of mutual dependence, in which, sharing the same, in the one case, divine and, in the other case, human being, the Father and the man are the source and origin of that being, and the Son and the woman receive that being from them and, in doing so, expand, consolidate, and complete it.

At this point we can hear the egalitarian and feminist protests rising to a crescendo all around us, because the approach that we are describing implies the unacceptable affirmation of male headship, which is indignantly and scornfully dismissed on all sides as a cultural entrapment that keeps the biblical writers from seeing the liberating potential of their own gospel and provides a basis for the patriarchal oppression of women that has prevailed right into modern times. On this showing, what is non-negotiable is the complete equality of men and women and, if that does not reflect the revealed Trinitarian relationships, then these must be "reinterpreted" in order to affirm a simple undifferentiated equality between the divine persons which can then be mirrored in the equality of the human persons.

But in the biblical presentation, be it right or wrong, neither the divine nor the human persons have that simple undifferentiated equality which these modern ideological presuppositions require, but are both related in the unique kind of ordered interdependence we have been describing.

In particular the male headship that is affirmed in Genesis 2 is reaffirmed in the main New Testament discussions in 1 Corinthians 11 and Ephesians 5, to which we will soon be turning, and, make of it what we will, there is no point in hiding that fact. Later we will suggest possible ways of dealing with that inconvenient fact in the contemporary context. However, before we assess we need to expound what the biblical witnesses are actually saying, so that we do not construct a caricature that can be easily dismissed and despised. It is clear that the biblical witnesses do affirm male headship, but it is by no means clear the way in which they affirm that it leads to or justifies the patriarchal oppression which is the target of largely valid feminist criticism. If we look at the passages concerned in a little more detail, we will be able to see why this is so.

The marital exchange
We must, however, first complete our exposition of Genesis 2. It is of the essence of the story that man in his initiating and the woman in her responsiveness are not left facing each other in the separation of their different vocations. From the start, each is open to and eager to participate in what the other brings to and elicits from the humanity that they share, certainly on a sexual level, but on all sorts of other levels as well. "Therefore a man leaves his father and his mother and clings to his wife and they become one flesh" (2:24).

The outcome of the differentiation of male from female, and of female from male, is the rich union in which each gives to and actualizes in the partner what he or she needs to complete his or her humanity. In his relationship to and union with the woman the man learns the sensitivity and the tenderness that make human relationships positive and creative; in her relationship with the man the woman, far from being confined to kids and kitchens, is brought into relationship with his world of work and activity and is enabled herself to make choices and exercise her own authority and initiative within it.

The one flesh of the marriage is a humanity in which the initiating vocation of the husband and the intuitive and sensitive relationality of the wife become available to both the partners who share that one life. The contemporary Church of England marriage service expresses in a single sentence the mutual participation of husband and wife in all that each brings to the marriage and its relationship to the love that constitutes the life of the triune God. "All that I am I give to you, | and all that I have I share with you, | within the love of God, | Father, Son, and Holy Spirit."

Genesis 2:24 is universal in form. It is concerned not just with a particular relationship of Adam and Eve in Eden, but exposes the essential nature of marriage in the plan and purpose of God. Its universality is recognized in the whole witness of canonical scripture, because every discussion of man-woman relationships is based on this verse. 1 Corinthians 11 and Ephesians 5 are, in fact, extended commentaries on and applications of this verse to the contemporary situations of the New Testament authors, and, more importantly, according to all three synoptic gospels, it from this verse that Jesus himself starts every time he speaks of marriage and divorce. The inmost nature of the man-woman relationship is revealed in its most intense and complete consummation in marriage. There each spouse in their gendered differentiation is, in a unique way and through a unique covenantal relationship, called and enabled to be the agent of the other's human flourishing and maturing.

Gendered Image

The union of the man and the woman in marriage is a reflection in the created order of the Trinitarian union of Father and Son in the divine life. In both cases, the initiator and the responder give themselves to one another in a mysterious unity that binds them inseparably together in a love that at the same time constitutes their unity and maintains and affirms their identities as distinct persons. These two become one flesh, where the two-ness and the oneness are equally essential to the relationship.

Within that relationship both partners share themselves. In his union with the responsiveness of the Son the Father is given the possibility and the actuality of a relationship in which he himself can be responsive; in his attentiveness and commitment to the initiating purpose of the Father, the Son participates in the authority and power of the Father. "He became obedient to death ... therefore God has given him the name that is above every name" (Phil. 2:8, 9).

So in marriage, the man whose calling is to reflect the initiating love of the Father in his work in the world and the woman whose calling is to reflect the responsive and attentive love of the Son in human relationships give themselves, the one to the other. In her openness to him she is to be stimulated and incorporated into his kind of loving; in his giving of himself to her he is to be sensitized by and incorporated into her kind of loving. To speak for once in the language of Jungian psychology, his predominant male *animus* stirs hers into initiating activity; her predominant female *anima* stirs his into sensitive responsiveness, so that each is moved by the other into an appropriately balanced male or female personhood. So the human union mirrors the divine; man and woman together image the God who made them and gave them each their distinctive calling.

Furthermore, just as the relationship between Father and Son becomes endlessly creative beyond itself through the creative power of the Spirit who himself is involved in that relationship and makes it life-giving for the whole creation, so the love of husband and wife expressed and sustained by their sexual union has, in the power of the same Spirit of life, the power to create the new life of the child who is the fruit of their union. In the initiating love of the father and in the responsive love of the mother, the child has its being, and in the home environment created by the shared loves of father and mother, that child has its wellbeing and the solid foundation of its growth into mature human personhood. The human relationships mirror the divine relationships. The human family manifests the initiating, the responsive, and the creative modes of love that characterize the life of God; like the life of God, it involves three distinct persons: a man, a woman, and a child.

Marriage in a fallen world
Set out in that schematic way, the pattern can look very formal and idealistic. In actual living, the intention of God that, according to the biblical witness, it expresses is constantly frustrated, marred, and annulled by sin and circumstance in their many different forms with the devastating results for marriage and family life that we see all around us. Marriages fail to fulfil their promise for all sorts of reasons. Divorce, distance, and death effectively deprive children of one or both of their parents so that they have to grow up without a father's challenge or a mother's empathy.

For all that and despite the fact that it may be written off as irrelevant or even oppressive by many people who have been shaped by a culture that is antipathetic to it, that biblical pattern of man-woman relationships and of marriage has been the basic framework of the lives of many people of my own now elderly generation. It has been the source of inspiration, stability, safety, and joy for a whole lifetime and it behoves us to bear witness to that fact before we finally depart from the earthly scene.

In over fifty years of marriage and Christian ministry my wife and I have sought to live out together a Christian calling that was originally mine but that, as she will tell all and sundry, she has found her fulfilment in making her own. Within that framework, far from simply presiding at coffee mornings, she has found her own authority, has brought to me pastoral insights, balance, and correction that I could not have found without her, and, from the basis of our togetherness, has branched out into personal evangelism and other highly responsible organizational tasks at both of which she was and is far more effective than I could ever be. This has been for both of us neither restrictive nor oppressive but rather liberating, fulfilling, and uniting. We might have lived it out better, but neither of us is in any doubt that to live this way has been for us to live within the good ordering of God.

Singleness and relationality
All this has been about marriage, but marriage is not for everybody. Some are unmarried by calling, some are unmarried by choice, some are unmarried by sexual orientation, and some are unmarried because the longed-for partner has been removed or never appeared. Among the unmarried is the person of Jesus as a standing reminder that it was a single man who was the full and final image of the triune God in human living.

It is, however, also true that that single man was not a solitary individual but was who he was in constant interaction with the men and women around him. He was not involved in marriage as a husband but he was nurtured within a marriage as a son. It is no accident that he whose humanity reflected the attentive responsiveness of the eternal Son to the eternal Father was shaped in the home of a woman whose own attentive responsiveness was expressed in the eager submission of her reply to the angel who announced his birth, "Let it be to me according to your word" (Luke 1:38).

We may conclude from all this that the ordering of man-woman relationships that has its most intimate, intensive, and permanent self-commitment in marriage is also reflected in the many creative and upbuilding ways in which men and women relate to and deeply influence one another. Like Jesus, we are also shaped and marked by the homes into which we were born long after we have left them, and happy indeed is the child who has grown up in a home where the purposeful commitment of a good father and the tender empathy of a good mother have been shared and combined in happy unity.

Biblical insights and contemporary culture

In fact, the biblical pattern of gender-specific relationships that we have been identifying does provide one way in which we can understand what has been happening in our culture. The world of work, of managing the affairs of the world and taking the initiatives that would provide for human needs and fulfilment has, indeed, long been a male priority, and the oppressive refusal to allow women their part in it has had its roots in sinful male arrogance and domination against which feminist protest had its full justification.

In the current penetration of the male world of government, business, the professions, and the arts by women, what is distinctively female has begun to correct, complement, and complete what has been exclusively male. In the gendered exchanges of shared enterprises, women are stimulated into demonstrating their proactive abilities and skills, and men have to come to terms with female human sensitivity, intuitive insights, and concern for people and for peace, and their exercising of their influence not just in the home but in the government ministry, the office, the school, the court, and the hospital as well. The interpenetration of the male desire to get a thing done efficiently, economically, and quickly with the female concern to get it done in a way that exercises care, compassion, and understanding for those involved in doing it and those affected by it, offers a combination whose full implications and effects we are still in process of discovering and that reflects in the outward world that same gendered ordering of life that is depicted in the intimacies and commitments of Christian marriage.

Men and women – the New Testament perspective

The understanding of that ordering of man-woman relationships that we have elicited from the Genesis creation story is confirmed and completed in the context of the New Testament gospel, and we turn now to the exposition of two central passages, both from the Pauline corpus, in which that becomes clear.

Ministry and authority – 1 Corinthians 11

The practical concern at the center of 1 Corinthians 11 is the prophetic ministry of women in the early church, and the hairstyles and the headgear are simply the outward and visible signs of the relationships within which that ministry functions properly and profitably. In looking at it we need to distinguish carefully between the permanent principles that underlie what Paul says from the cultural symbolism of a world that is very different from our own.

First, we may note that this passage is a clear affirmation of the ministry of women in the Church and that the ministry they exercise is one that is central to the wellbeing of the Church. The passage assumes that a woman as well as a man has a valid calling to "pray and prophesy" (11:5); Paul is discussing how she can do it rightly, not whether she should do it all. What exactly Paul meant by prophesying has been the subject of much debate, but since for him the prophets are second only to the apostles (1 Cor. 12:28; cf. Eph. 4:11) this for him is a ministry of central importance in the building up of the Christian community and here he recognizes that such a ministry belongs to women as well as to men.

Less congenial to modern sensibilities is his insistence that the authority of women to exercise this ministry is one that comes to them through men and, in that culture, the covering of the head is an acknowledgement of that fact. To establish the prior authority of the man, which he then communicates to the woman, he appeals to Genesis 2 but also uses the image language of Genesis 1. "A man ought not to have his head veiled since he is the image and reflection of God; but woman is the reflection of man. Indeed, man was not made from woman but woman from man. Neither was man created for the sake of woman but woman for man" (1 Cor. 11:7–10).

Commenting on this verse, Roger Beckwith says, "The image of God is in man directly, but in woman indirectly" (Beckwith, 1978, p. 57).

As will be obvious by now, I am no feminist, but I find that statement quite chilling and, more importantly, completely one-sided in its portrayal of New Testament teaching about the relationship of women to God. In this passage Paul is expounding Genesis 2 in its bearing on ministry in the church and it is in that specific context that he is insisting that the authority to minister is mediated to the woman through the man.

But even within the passage Paul seems to modify his position. After his unqualified assertion of male priority he goes on to recognize that in the light of Christ things begin to look a bit different. "Nevertheless *in the Lord*, woman is not independent of man or man independent of woman. For just as woman came from man, so man comes through woman, but all things come from God" (11:11–12, italics mine). Here the one-way dependence of woman on man is modified into mutuality by a recognition of the dependence of men on women. This mutuality is said to be "in the Lord," that is to be a result of the coming of Christ and his liberation of women from the male dominance that was the result of sin and his treatment of them as people who had the same capacity as men for direct relationship to God quite apart from any male mediation except his own. That Paul was aware of the new status of women inaugurated by Jesus's own attitude toward them is reflected clearly in his statement in Galatians that in Christ there is neither male nor female (3:28) and his move in this passage from one-way dependence toward mutual interdependence.

Nevertheless, for Paul, although the old man-woman relationship has been relativized in Christ, in relation to ministry it has not been abolished; the woman receives her authority to minister through the man and the way she dresses should bear witness to that fact. We can acknowledge as a sheer matter of fact that this is the way it has actually happened. Women have been made deacons and priests by the laying of male hands. Whether that is historical accident or has some theological justification, as Paul clearly thinks, depends on how one evaluates the biblical affirmation of male headship in the light of the new relationships that have been established "in the Lord." Before that affirmation can be evaluated, it must first be explained.

Headship – divine and human

In this passage we can see Paul struggling with how to reach a position in which he can affirm both the interdependence of men and women and the differentiated relationships in which they stand to one another, which for him and for the whole tradition out of which he speaks (11:1), like it or not, includes the priority of the male. In his opening statement in the chapter he enunciates the heart of the theological anthropology that underpins the whole discussion and in so doing introduces the notion of headship. "But I want you to understand that Christ is the head of every man and the man is the head of the woman, and God is the head of Christ" (11:3).

There is here a hierarchy of headship: God is the head of Christ, Christ is the head of the man, the man is the head of the woman. At this point we must ask what the word "head" means in such a context. C. K. Barrett, in his commentary on this passage suggests that the Greek word *kephale* is used here with a meaning that is more akin to *arche* than to *kurios* (Barrett, 1971, p. 248). As verse 8 makes clear, Paul is discussing origination rather than domination; the man is the enabling source (*arche*) of the woman's life and authority, rather than its overpowering lord (*kurios*).

That interpretation is confirmed by the context. To say that God is the head of Christ is to place the whole discussion in the realm of the relationships between the Father and the Son as they are revealed in the gospel. As we have been seeing throughout this book, the Father-Son relationship is one of originating and affirming love that results in the Son's reception of and participation in the Father's power and authority. This Father is no patriarchal oppressor, but the one who in his love enables his Son to execute the purposes of the divine love that they both share.

If that is the meaning of headship in the paradigmatic relationship of God to Christ, it retains that meaning as we move down the chain in the relation of Christ to the man and the man to the woman. Christ is the source of the life and authority that he receives from the Father and transmits to the man, and therefore the man is the source of the life and the authority that he transmits to the woman. At all stages, as the life and authority moves from one person to the other, a real transmission takes place. At all stages what is transmitted is not overbearing oppression but empowering liberation. In his receptivity to the Father, Christ receives the authority to save the world; in his submission to the Son, the man receives a share of that life and authority to free him to be what God made him to be; and, in the same way, in her receptivity the woman receives from the man the same life and authority that frees her to be the person God made her to be.

To understand what Paul is saying in that way does not, of course, solve our problems with the passage. It still has its main emphasis on the dependence of the woman on the man that is highly uncongenial to our way of thinking. That dependence may describe the way in which authority has, in fact, been transmitted to women authorized in ministry, but does it mean that the whole relationship of women to Christ depends on male mediation? We have seen that much in the gospel points in a quite different direction. We have also seen that Paul himself, having drawn that conclusion, resiles somewhat from it in favor of male-female interdependence. We might say that in the realm of work and ministry, the woman receives from the man, because in that realm he has the prior calling. We would, however, immediately have to say with equal emphasis that, in the realm of personal relationship to God in Christ, the woman has the prior calling and for the full development of his personal and intimate responsiveness to Jesus, the man has much to receive from her.

However that may be, we have perhaps shown that the Pauline teaching about headship in this passage is caricatured if it is made to support an exclusive and oppressive male domination of men over women in the church or in the world. It is about the transmission of life and authority rather than the imposition of self-assertive will.

Loving heads – Ephesians 5

When we turn from 1 Corinthians 11 to Ephesians 5, this interpretation of the New Testament understanding of headship is reinforced and confirmed. Here it is specifically husband-wife relationships that are in view and the context is christological rather than Trinitarian. Central to the passage is the claim that the relationship of Christ to the Church is analogous to the relationship of a husband to his wife. Paul[11] pursues the analogy from both ends. He uses the nature of marriage to clarify the relationship of Christ to the Church and indeed, according to 5:32, this is his central purpose, but he also uses the Christ-Church relationship to elucidate the husband-wife relationship in a way that is relevant to our present concerns.

Like all New Testament teaching about marriage, this passage bases itself on the union of husband and wife in one flesh, which has its classic expression in Genesis 2:24.

The two, without ceasing to be two have yet become one so that in loving his wife, a man loves himself (5:29). This union reflects the union of Christ with his church. That means that it is a differentiated union in which there is one who gives and one who receives, and again the language of headship is used both of Christ in relation to the Church and of the husband in relation to his wife.

Here also it is clear that, in both cases, the headship commended here consists of a liberating bestowal of life which elicits a grateful response from its recipients rather than a coercive imposition of an oppressive and overbearing will, however distorted this may have become in Christian practice over the centuries. Husbands are to love their wives in the way Christ loves the Church, not to exploit and subjugate them for their own pleasure or purpose but to give themselves to them in order to affirm them, nurture them, and enable them to grow into God's designed completion for them (5:25ff.). In the way he gives himself to her, the husband is to be subject to his wife, and in the way she receives and responds to that love in caring for him, the wife is to be subject to her husband.

There is thus a mutual submission (5:21) both of the giving husband and the receiving wife to the claims of the love that unites them. In her receiving of his love for her, she is enabled to give her love to him; in his giving of his love to her, he is enabled to receive what her love can give to him. The relationship is thus constituted by a participation by both partners in the giving and receiving that creates and sustains their union, just as in the triune relationships the giving love of the Father and the receiving love of the Son are shared in their unity, and just as in the relationship of Christ with his people, he becomes the giver of the love that he receives from the

Father and the recipient of the response that by the Spirit that love elicits from his people.

The exchanges of love

The exchange of love that constitutes marriage is far removed from the issuing of instructions by the husband and the compliant obedience to them by the wife, which is the way in which this passage is popularly misconstrued. Markus Barth in his classic exposition of this passage says, "Ephesians 5 supports anything but blind obedience or the breaking of the wife's will" (M. Barth, 1974, p. 714). Rather,

> He who is the "head" (and goes ahead) is the husband, whenever the Christological basis and model of marriage are maintained ... The subordination of the wife is now characterised as her response to the husband's love. It is a matter of the heart and conscience – an attitude of self-giving, of radiating warmth and above all an expression of insuperable love. How else can love be requited than by love? The wife's response to the husband's conquering love is her joyful and freely accepted subordination.
> (M. Barth, 1974, p. 713)

There we have it, the New Testament's culminating word about husband-wife and man-woman relationships, clearly in opposition to all patriarchal domination by its insistence that the love of men and women should mirror the love of Christ, and yet by virtue of the same christological reference, insisting on the headship of the husband as the giver and the responsiveness of the wife as the receiver of that love, so that, although each is subordinate to the other, that subordination is expressed differently in his giving and in her receiving.

Some tentative affirmations

What then will we say to these things? To speak personally once more I have to confess that it is this model that has been implicit in the way my wife and I have lived for over fifty years. She has more than once intimidated me by insisting that when life-changing decisions had to be made the ultimate responsibility for making them rested with me as the head of the family, to which I have responded by saying that I would exercise that headship by deciding that unless we both were agreed to make a change of job, or location, we would stay where we were. Fortunately we have always been agreed at these crucial points, so that the exercise of that kind of headship has never been required!

But of course the questions are far wider and deeper than such matrimonial understandings. The picture of marriage in Ephesians 5 is an ideal one that can guide but is never fully reflected in any actual marriage. The sin we identified in the last chapter is at work here as everywhere else, and marriage is easily corrupted by the dominating self-absorption or self-assertion of one partner and the resentment at such treatment and the counter-assertion of a right to independence by the other.

Here also, across the whole field of man-woman relationships, the initiating love of the Father can be distorted into the selfish domination of men and provoke the bitter protests of women claiming denied rights in an attitude in which a justified demand for justice and a different form of self-assertion are inextricably entwined. So the complementarity of the sexes becomes the battle of the sexes, and in the midst of that fray what Ephesians 5 is saying about man-woman relationships has little chance of being heard, and its teaching about the initiative of men and the responsiveness of women are ideas that are totally alien to the "good as you" competition in which men and women easily become involved. I hope enough has been said in our attempts at a proper exegesis of Ephesians 5 to show that it offers no justifications at all for such confrontations and conflicts.

The approach of Karl Barth

To speak more theologically, the point at which we have arrived is very similar to that reached by Karl Barth fifty years ago in his own treatment of gendered relationships (Barth 1960, p. 285ff.) He also wants to find a way of affirming the differentiation of the initiating male and the responsive female expounded in Genesis as belonging to God's order and intention in his creation of humankind in his own image and not simply as the cultural clutter of an exploded patriarchy.

He offers a christological base for that differentiation in that the man reflects the Lordship of Christ and the woman his servanthood and that there can be no question of superiority of the one over the other, since in Christ the lord is the servant and the servant is the lord.

For Barth the responsiveness of the woman has its own priority, because it is in submissive responsiveness to the lordship of Christ that men and women alike are remade in the image of God. This connects with his understanding of the virgin birth of Jesus in which the male initiation of Joseph is excluded and the submissiveness of Mary is the means of the incarnation.

Back to perichoresis

My own reaction to that position is that I would want to align myself with its attempt to take seriously and to do justice to the way in which biblical teaching understands the man-woman differentiation rather than simply dismiss it as outmoded and exploded, but I would like to suggest that to interpret it in fully Trinitarian rather than a christological context may make it more accessible and bring it into closer relationship with man-woman relationships as we actually experience them.

The Trinitarian approach does that by bringing into play the notion of inter-personal *perichoresis* which has accompanied us throughout this study and which may be helpful here also. Just as Christ in his obedience as servant comes to participate in the lordship of the Father, so men and women, in their inter-relating, share with each other that which is distinctive of the male and female humanity that constitutes their differentiated gendered existence.

In their inter-relating with women, men, in their distinctive calling to initiating work in the world, are inducted into the realm of empathetic attentiveness to the other which male humanity needs for its completion but which is the distinctive calling and gift of women. In their inter-relating with men, women, in their distinctive calling to that responsive relationality, are inducted into the realm of initiation and authority which female humanity needs for its completion but which is the distinctive gift and calling of men. This happens with special concentration and passionate intensity in marriage in which the two become one flesh, but with equal authenticity and appropriate creativity, as sons relate to mothers, daughters to fathers, brothers to sisters, teachers to taught, friends to friends, colleagues to colleagues, helpers to helped.

Such an approach avoids forcing actual men and women into stereotypes of authoritative proaction and intuitive relationality, which is perhaps not wholly overcome in Barth. The men and women we meet are, in fact, both proactive and responsive in a whole series of combinations and permutations as they are shaped by all the relationships with other men and women that make them what they are.

For all that, a man is not a woman and a woman is not a man. The personhood of the one, however modified and matured by the personhood of the other, has its own calling. The man is to be responsive as he remains faithful to his distinctive calling to image the initiating love of the Father; the woman is to be proactive as she remains faithful to her distinctive calling to image the responsive love of the Son.

The appropriate integration of the image of the Father and the Son in men and women, so they are both true to their calling and yet mature in their humanity, is itself the work of the creative Spirit who does in the realm of gendered humanity what he also does in the realm of ungendered divinity, by relating men and women as he relates Father and Son, so that each shares what they have with the other and yet remains in the distinctiveness that constitutes their being. When, in all these interchanges, affirming and enabling love is given and received in expressions appropriate to them, the true complementarity in the creation and perfecting of our humanity begins to be realized.

Conclusion

In this whole realm I, like everybody else, am feeling my way, and any conclusions have to be provisional and tentative. My impression is that the biblical material we have surveyed is itself provisional and in process as it tries to do justice to the Old Testament material, which it rightly respects as the authoritative word of God, and to the new creation in Christ and its liberating and renewing power in the lives of men and women and in the relations between them and to do this in a cultural context that is alien to them both. The same three factors have shaped what I have tried to say here, and here also unresolved tensions remain.

An understanding of the relationships between men and women is basic to any discussion about the primacy of marriage, same-sex relationships, the relative priority of work and home in the lives of contemporary men and women and many other issues, My central suggestion in this chapter is that the notion of *perichoresis* which has proved so fruitful in Trinitarian theology may also be productive here, precisely in line with my central thesis that human relationships and in particular the relationships of men and women are created and renewed in Christ in order that they may reflect the relationships within the life and being of the triune God.

8 Incarnate Image

The husband-wife relationship and, indeed, the whole rich network of man-woman exchanges we have just been discussing are not the primary or normative expressions of the *imago Dei* in human life. They are, in fact, images in a second mirror that owe their reality and authenticity to the image that is reflected in the first mirror. That becomes clear precisely in Ephesians 5.

At the heart of that passage is the point-by-point insistence that the marriage relationship is to be ordered and lived out in faithful reflection of the relationship between Christ and his people. He is the original and model bridegroom whose love is set not on any woman but on the Church which is his bride. He is the original and model of all headship; he joins the Church to himself in one body, in his love he seeks its purity and its maturity, and in submission and conformity to that love his Church gladly acknowledges him as its head.

The image of God that is revealed in Christ's relationship to his people has its secondary reflections in the human relationships that constitute the created reality in which all people live. How could it be otherwise if the eternal Word who is incarnate in Jesus is identified with the triune creator by whom all things were made? In most of this book we have been identifying these reflections in every nook and cranny of human experience and seeing that they are still identifiable even where sin has corrupted, distorted, and threatened totally to destroy them. From start to finish the human creation is christologically orientated; he is the Alpha and the Omega, the first and the last, the beginning and the end of all that is. Only to the degree that our living reflects his living do we live at all; to begin to lose his likeness is to begin to die. Sin threatens not just moral condemnation but ontological disintegration. In an exocentric openness to God and to others we become so far like Jesus; in the egocentric inversion which is the essence of sin his image in us is dimmed and obscured and our lives are at stake.

The christocentric orientation of human life and the Trinitarian implications that it incorporates have been the central interpretative framework within which we have looked at the various manifestations and corruptions of the *imago Dei*. Now in this final chapter the searchlight that has been sweeping widely across the whole range of human experience must be narrowed and concentrated in its focus so that it shines on Jesus himself. In the rest of us the image of God is blurred, compromised, and rendered ambiguous in a thousand different ways. To learn finally and unambiguously what it means to be human in the *imago Dei* we have to accept the unintended invitation of Pontius Pilate, to look at Jesus standing before the judgement seats of Israel and Rome in the majesty of his humiliation and there behold the man – the ultimate human being as he was made and meant to be – going out to give himself to the uttermost in glad obedience to his Father, in unconditional love and acceptance to his fellow men. Here, as nowhere else, "Behold the Man!" (John 19:5).

Karl Barth, commenting on Paul's teaching on the Christ-Adam relationship in Romans 5, makes the same point.

> The primary anthropological truth and ordering principle ... is made clear only through the relationship between Christ and us. Adam is, as is said in v.14 *typos tou mellontos*, the type of Him who was to come. Man's essential and original nature is to be found, therefore, not in Adam but in Christ. In Adam we can only find it prefigured. Adam can therefore be interpreted only in the light of Christ and not the other way round.
>
> (Barth, 1956a, p. 29)

Because we are working within the hermeneutical framework that Barth outlines, we must in this chapter home in on the humanity of Jesus, not only to emphasize that it has been normative for us throughout, but also because in him we can see our human destiny prefigured and the energy to realize that destiny released. In that way he is the key to the understanding of the human past and the promise of the human future; in what he is we have insights into what we used to be when we were out of relationship with him, what is happening to us now that he has called us into his company, and what he promises that we will ultimately be as we go on relating to him. As John's first letter puts it:

> See what love the Father has given us that we should be called children of God; and that is what we are. The reason that the world does not know us is that it did not know him. Beloved, we are God's children now; what we will be has not yet been revealed. What we do know is this: when he is revealed, we will be like him, for we will see him as he is. And all who have this hope in him purify themselves, just as he is pure.
>
> (1 John 3:1–3)

Our past is controlled by the fact that although we were made by and for him, we did not know him and therefore did not know ourselves. Now by the love of the Father reaching us through him we know ourselves to be God's children who have been adopted into a share of Christ's Sonship. Our one clue to our ultimate future is that we will be like him. Seeing him in his humanity will be transformative and purifying for our humanity; what he is will be reflected in what we are.

Therefore the program for this chapter is that we should identify his humanity to confirm what we have said about the relationship of all men to this one man, to see what it means to belong to him and, as Christian people, to be called by his name and to identify the future which comes to us from his hands.

Christ – converted humanity

The first thing to say is that the humanity of Jesus Christ is a *converted* and a *converting* humanity. The man that Pilate invites us to behold is the man who is in the final stages of his utter identification with us, not merely in our createdness but in our sinful alienation from God. The Word has not just become human, in the way that unfallen Adam might have been human, intact in his relationships with his Creator and his fellow-creatures. The Word has taken to himself not just humanity but flesh (John 1:14).

In Pauline terminology, he who knew no sin has been made sin that we might become the righteousness of God in him (2 Cor. 5:21). He has entered into our life not only in its created finitude, but in its frailty and in its ingrained propensity to egocentricity that has brought upon it the destructive disruption of the very relationships with God and other people that are the sources from which it springs. In other words, he has taken upon himself the death sentence that is at once the consequence of sin and also God's righteous judgement upon it. All the pressures of original sin that assault us have also assaulted him (Heb. 4:15); all the crucifying propensities of human nature have marshaled themselves against him and, in the freedom of his love, he has submitted himself to them so that he might deliver us from them.

An adequate theology of the cross needs many dimensions even to begin to do justice to the cosmic significance of what was happening there; but one way of looking at it is to see it as a great conversion of our humanity, so that, as it is taken by the Son of God to be his own humanity, it is extricated from the network of sinful and destructive relationships in which he found it and is brought back into the force field of the triune God to mirror at last the divine love by and for which the world was made.

According to Martin Luther, 2 Corinthians 5:21 describes a great exchange: in joining himself to us, Christ takes our sin to himself and gives his righteousness to us. The same thing could equally well be described as a great conversion; on the cross, bearing in his humanity the judgement of God upon our humanity, Jesus shows himself to be the man who fulfils God's covenant by reflecting back to him his own divine love. From the gallows on which he suffers the defiant No of the old humanity, Jesus speaks the obedient Yes of the new humanity and in the resurrection the Father speaks his own Yes to him. In that decisive act on Calvary, the Man who is the victim of sin is converted into the Man who is the agent of righteousness who, out of the midst of his agony, shows that he is the Man who loves the Lord his God with all his heart and soul and mind and strength and his neighbor as himself. In the self-offering of Calvary the crucified Jesus is the restored *imago Dei* who mirrors in human life on earth the triune love of God in heaven.

Christ – converting humanity

The *eschatos Adam* became *pneuma zoopoioun*, life-imparting Spirit (1 Cor. 15:45). The humanity that Jesus converted back to God on the cross has, through the activity of the Spirit in exposing and joining us to it, the power to convert others. What he did for us alone on Calvary, once and for all, is progressively applied to us and made actual in us by the Spirit, who makes us what Jesus is, reflecting in our relationships with God and with others the attentive self-giving responsiveness that characterized his own relationships with his Father and with his others in his life and supremely in his death.

As Ephesians 5 shows, we are called and enabled to become in the concrete and specific relations of our lives, including marriage, the mirrors of the humanity of Jesus, which is itself the prototypical mirror of the love and being of God. That is the message of 2 Corinthians 3:18, which is one of the classic New Testament descriptions of our sanctification: "And all of us with unveiled faces, seeing the glory of the Lord as though reflected in a mirror are being transformed into the same image from one degree of glory to another; for this comes from the Lord who is the Spirit." The Trinitarian distinctions are not clearly defined, but the Trinitarian purpose of making us like Christ is crystal clear.

Trinitarian sanctification

This process of sanctification has indeed to be understood not only in a moral but in a fully Trinitarian context. To be like Christ is far more than to be made good or righteous: it is to be fashioned into the image of the triune God, so that in the attentive submissiveness that constitutes our relationship to Christ we, like him, come into a participation in the proactive authority of the Father and the innovating creativity of the Spirit.

That threefold relationship to the threefold God is anticipated in the discussion of charismatic gifts in 1 Corinthians 12. "Now there are varieties of gifts, but the same Spirit, and there are varieties of services but the same Lord and there are varieties of activities, but the same God that activates all of them in every one" (12:4–6). The "activities" (*energemata*), the proactive authoritative initiatives, relate us to God (the Father); the "services" (*diakoniai*), the attentive responses that we make to the needs of others, relate us to the Lord (the Son), and the "gifts" (*charismata*), the words and deeds by which we interpret and apply the gospel in fresh ways to the new situations we encounter, relate us to the Spirit.

The fact that 1 Corinthians 12 is followed by 1 Corinthians 13 and 14 is of course an immediate reminder that the activity in which we become like the Father, the service in which we become like the Son, and the charismatic endowments in which we manifest the creativity of the Spirit are all different ways of manifesting the one free, self-giving love that binds Father, Son, and Holy Spirit in one. To mirror them is to act, to serve, to exercise the gifts we are given in the same love. The endowments we are given are sanctifying if they are used exocentrically; destructive and sometimes perhaps even demonic if they are used egocentrically, as they were at Corinth and can be still. As charismatic Christians might put it, it is when we mature the fruit of the Spirit as we exercise the gifts of the Spirit that we can at last begin to reflect the humanity of Jesus in whom the power and the love were always one.

The humanity of Jesus in its participation in the image of the triune God is thus the norm and the goal of our sanctification. In him the human mirror is converted back to God, redirected and refocused on its divine original and becomes transforming to those who enter into the union with Christ that is effected through our submission to him in faith and that brings us into the beginnings of a human life that reflects the life of Father, Son, and Holy Spirit in their distinctiveness and in their union of love.

Christ's humanity – the man for others

At the heart of Jesus's humanity, as witnessed in the gospel narratives, is his calling and his will to devote himself entirely to the needs of other people. He manifests in his own life the paradox that he expounds; in giving himself, he finds himself. He is most himself when he is most for others. In their service he finds his own significance and his own fulfilment. He is never at the beck and call of the people he helps; when he is most servant he is most Lord.

He is the Man for others only because first of all he is the Man for God; his responsiveness to others is the consequence of his primary obedience to and identification with his Father's saving love. According to Karl Barth, the basic relationships within which Jesus lived and worked in his relationship to God, on the one hand,

and in his relationship to people, on the other, can be described by the three prepositions "from," "with," and "for." On the divine side, he is the Son *from* the Father, the eternal Word who, according to the Johannine prologue, is *with* the Father, and who in his earthly obedience acts *for* the Father.[12]

On the human side the same prepositions apply. He is *from* his fellow humans. The whole history of Jesus is determined by the needs and claims of other people, a giving of himself to their healing, a bearing of the consequences of their sins, the offering of himself on their behalf. To speak for a moment the language of the theology of the sixties, the world sets Jesus's agenda, although how he deals with the various items of that agenda is determined by his obedience to his Father; just because he is the servant of God, he is the servant of all.

That means that Jesus is *with* his fellows. Immanuel, God with us is the central message of the incarnation. Where people are around, he is around so that he relates to them willingly and gladly, seeks them out, sits at their tables, and cultivates their company. Whenever we see Jesus it is *with* his disciples, *with* the crowds in Galilee, *with* his crucifying enemies, and even when he is alone *with* his Father.

Jesus is *with* his fellows in such a way that he is *for* them. He is for them in a way that affirms their human integrity and their freedom. He does not seek to manipulate or control them or make them compliant to his purposes, but rather provokes them into personal insights, responsible decisions, free responses so that they may be liberated from all manipulation, bondage, and control and be able to become the real people that God made them to be: "I am come that they may have life and have it more abundantly" (John 10:10).

Jesus and the restoration of relationships

In so far as Jesus can be categorized at all, he does not belong with the great thinkers and philosophers. He gave the world more to think about than any of them, but their complicated theories and abstractions are not the language he speaks.

Nor can he be easily numbered with the mystics and the masters of the inward journey so much prized in contemporary spirituality. The journeys that Jesus takes are the journey from God to us, the journey to Jerusalem and the cross, and the journey from death to life and from earth to heaven. It is in terms of these outgoing metaphors of journey that his story can best be told. The inwardness of Jesus is never revealed or explored from one end of the New Testament to the other. He is the teller of stories, the teacher of crowds, the trainer of disciples, who engages one by one with the people who come to him, sustained not by a retreat into the inner resources of his own personality, but by his personal interaction in prayer with his Father and his reception of the Holy Spirit the Father gives.

Nor does Jesus sit easily with the moralists with their principles, their rules, and their duties, although he is often so located. His whole career, and especially the controversies that ultimately crucified him, provide ample evidence that he did not subscribe to an autonomous ethical system with its deontological prescriptions of oughts and musts. He identified with those in Israel who saw that God's *Torah* was the spelling out of the implications of his covenantal relationship with his people, that the law and the prophets were all about what it means to love God and neighbor, that they existed to promote human liberation and not to inhibit it because the Sabbath was made for man and not man for the Sabbath. In other words moral law is the framework for right relationship, it shows us how people can live from and for and with one another and with God.

Jesus, therefore, is not primarily a legislator but a restorer of relationships. The kingdom whose arrival he announces and indeed incorporates in himself is to be understood less in terms of law and more in terms of reconciliation. "God was in Christ reconciling the world to himself" (2 Cor. 5:19). and in so doing calling us into reconciliation with one another. That Pauline summary of the gospel sits well with the story of Jesus, which is the basis of that gospel. If you want to know how human you are, measured by the humanity of Jesus, you have to ask and answer questions about the state of your relationships.

Karl Barth puts it like this:

> The fact that I am born and die; that I eat and drink and sleep, that I develop and maintain myself; that beyond this I assert myself in the face of others and even physically propagate my species; that I enjoy and work and plan and fashion and possess; that I have and acquire and exercise powers, that I take part in all the works of the race either accomplished or in process of accomplishment; that in all this I satisfy religious needs and can realise religious possibilities; and that in it all I fulfil my aptitudes as an understanding and thinking, willing and feeling being all this as such is *not* my humanity.
>
> (Barth, 1960, p. 249)

All these facets of human life are the field in which authentic humanity in the image of Jesus either does or does not happen. To be human as Jesus was human one has to live in all these fields as one who is rightly related to other people; we have in them all to be from, with, and for our fellows. If we are not, all our "participation in scholarship and art, politics and economics, civilization and culture" (Barth, 1960, p. 249) will not make us human. In christological perspective, right relationships and the community they make possible are the measure of humanity; the state of our relationships show whether and how far we are imaging Jesus who is the image of God.

The point that Barth is making so strongly here has implications for our understanding of how people with mental handicaps or learning difficulties can be seen to be fully human and made like the rest of us in the image of God. If that image is understood in terms of sophisticated rationality, as it has been in the dominant Christian tradition of the West, then the participation of such people in it becomes highly problematic and one would have to resort to saying that even if they were not made in the image of God on earth, they might ultimately be remade in the image of God in heaven.

But if imaging God, as Barth is saying here, has to do with the quality of our relationships rather than with our ability to participate in the full range of human culture, then things begin to look very different. As the experience of communities like Jean Vanier's L'Arche movingly demonstrate, those who are disabled in terms of discursive reason often have, almost in compensation, an innate and well tuned sensitivity in terms of human relationships and an ability to give and receive love that can put the rest of us to shame, as well as a responsiveness to Christ and his gospel that, in its genuine wholeheartedness, more than makes up for the cerebral complexity that can inhibit as well as enable our faith. By this criterion, disabled people are more certainly in the image of God and can have a very real ministry in reminding the rest of us what that means. They are to be numbered among the little ones who, on the word of Jesus himself, are to be envied rather than patronized. "Take care that you do not despise these little ones; for, I tell you, in heaven their angels continually see the face of my Father in heaven" (Matt. 18:10).

Jesus and his Church

All of this is, of course, immensely challenging to our own much more rationalistic understanding of what it means to be human, but, as well as that, its ecclesiological implications can shake to the core thinking about what it means to belong to the people of God who belong to Jesus and this, at least in outline, we must now explore.

There is an ongoing exegetical discussion about how much evidence there is in the gospel story that Jesus envisaged or intended to found anything like the Christian church, and books have been written on both sides of the question. Whatever the outcome of that debate, if the picture of a Jesus whose priority in his earthly ministry was right relationships, then it seems inevitable that in his new risen humanity he would gather round himself a company of people whose priorities were the same and who were constituted into a community that lived out of and for the relationships with himself, with his Father and with other people that he lived, died, and rose to inaugurate.

It is very much along these lines that the first letter of John, in one of the central ecclesiological statements in the New Testament, describes the community that was gathered round the incarnate Lord. Speaking of the story of Jesus and claiming first-hand apostolic contact with it, the writer goes on, "We declare to you what we have seen and heard so that you also may have fellowship (*koinonia*) with us; and truly our fellowship (*koinonia*) is with the Father and with his Son Jesus Christ" (1 John 1:3).

Christian *koinonia*

The word "fellowship" in English does not do justice to the word *koinonia*, which means a having in common, a sharing of life. It is, as we have already noted, the word used to describe the distinctive activity of the Holy Spirit in the Trinitarian blessing at the end of 2 Corinthians – "the *koinonia* of the Holy Spirit be with you all" (13:13). Read in that context, the 1 John verse which names the Father and the Son is implicitly Trinitarian because the vertical *koinonia* with them and the resultant *koinonia* with one another can be seen as the work of the perichoretic Spirit who comes to induct us into a sharing of God's life as it is offered to us from the Father through the Son and, as a consequence to draw us into an interdependent relationality with one another.

It is interesting that in the book of Acts in which the coming of the Holy Spirit at Pentecost inducts the disciples into a sharing of the life, the power, and the mission of the ascended Jesus, the almost immediate result is the formation of a community in which the sharing of life that we have been describing begins to happen not just on a spiritual or religious level but across the whole range of living of the people involved.

> All who believed were together and had all things in common (*koina*); they would sell their possessions and goods and distribute the proceeds to all as any had need. Day by day as they spent much time together in the temple,

they broke bread at home and ate their food with glad and generous hearts, praising God and having the goodwill of all the people. And day by day the Lord added to their number those who were being saved.

(Acts 2:44–47)

There is more than a hint here that what was attractive to all, and indeed converting to many, was the quality of the relationships that that first community had with God in Christ and consequently among themselves. There was deep down in people a hunger for fulfilment through this kind of holistic sharing, and they were drawn to that first Christian community by the promise that in it their hunger could hope to be satisfied.

In the theology of 1 John and the practice of Acts 2 we have the seeds of an ecclesiology which is consonant with the Trinitarian and anthropological presuppositions that we have discerned as deeply embedded in the biblical story and its culmination in the New Testament gospel. As Jesus is the human image of the love of the triune God who made the world to be like himself, so the community that Jesus gathers round him to share his life, is called and enabled by his Spirit to image his kind of love in its own lifestyle and thus to offer to the world a way to the renewal, restoration, and completion of the image that sin has so marred. The church has, therefore, a pivotal place in the saving purposes of God for his whole creation. In their relationship to Christ his people have access to the relationality of love, and in their community that new relationality starts to overcome the egocentricity and individuality that is the source of the woes of the human world.

Paul was aware of the strategic place of the Christian community as the first fruits of the new creation, the first installment of the life of the new age that made God's promises credible and real in the midst of the old creation. The Church, he dares to say to the Ephesians, is "his body, the fullness of him who fills all in all" (1:23). The church is the visible expression in the world of the life of Jesus and what the church is witnesses to the reality of a power which has in it the ability to transform the whole creation.

The Church as mystical communion

What we have been expounding is the understanding of the Church which Avery Dulles in his book *Models of the Church* designates as "The Church as Mystical Communion." He shows that this approach has deep roots, not only in scripture but in the theological tradition, and, as a contemporary witness to this, he points to the work of Heribert Mühlen (not available in English) who especially relates the human communion that is the Church to the divine Communion that is the Holy Trinity, and points to the Holy Spirit as the link between the two who, both in the life of God and in the life of his people, creates what Mühlen calls a "personalogical" union, by which he means a real unity of persons in which their distinctness and freedom is affirmed and preserved – almost exactly what we have called a perichoretic union (Dulles, 1976, pp. 51–52).

Koinonia threatened

Such a union is subject to corruption at many points, and the history of the Church bears dire witness to corruptions with which we are already familiar. On the one hand, the freedom of the members of the Church can be lost in the overbearing domination of a central power, whether it be the infallible Pope in Rome, a fundamentalist representation of scripture as an equally infallible authority demanding unquestioning submission to every verse of every chapter, or a charismatic leader in one of the new churches claiming a divine right to shepherd his flock by exercising a dictatorial control over every aspect of their lives. These have been threats to different parts of the Church at different times in its history and they are threats still.

If the fellowship of the Church is threatened on the one side by authoritarian domination, it is equally threatened on the other by individualistic independence, where the ways in which people relate to one another and to God are determined not by the gospel but by the individual members of the church and the degree of commitment that they are prepared to offer to one another and to the purposes of God. When our basic egocentricity remains unbroken, our participation in the life of the Church is limited to its ability to meet our perceived religious needs, and our commitment to the gospel is relativized by the personal priorities that dominate our opinions and our choices, and there are whole areas of our lives to which our membership of the people of God is seen as irrelevant and where the writ of the gospel does not run. The churches and their gospel are today largely marginalized in the life of individualized Western society because they are first of all very near the margins of the lives of many of their members – and most of us have only to look at our own hearts and our own lifestyle to see that this is so.

The lordship of Jesus

But in this situation it belongs to the ministry of the Holy Spirit to bring the Church back to its basic confession that

Jesus is Lord, that, on the one hand, the relationships and the priorities in which we live are determined by him and not by us, and on the other, that lordship is confessed and not imposed, that he is the Lord who is confessed with our lips because, not by his authoritarian demands but by his self-giving love, he has won and goes on winning the allegiance of our hearts (cf. Rom. 10:9, 10). His lordship is total and not partial, but it does not suppress our freedom, rather it engages and imparts it. The free and willing submission of the Son to the Father is imaged in the free submission of believers to the crucified and risen Lord.

Within that balance between authority and freedom there will be those in the church whose specific concern is with the maintenance of the authority of the given gospel and there will also be those whose specific concern is with the freedom and integrity of those who confess that gospel. The mutual challenge that those of a more conservative orientation and those of a more liberal orientation present to one another is for the health of the body, provided that each remembers that the *koinonia* of the Church requires both submission and freedom in the relation of the body to its head.

Koinonia – vertical and horizontal

Dulles raises questions about how our sharing of life with Father and Son on the vertical level relates to our sharing of life with one another on the horizontal level. The ecclesiology of John 1, enacted in the pentecostal experience of Acts 2, clearly affirms the interdependence of the two. We have here once again a mediated immediacy. It is when two or three are gathered together in his name that Christ will make known his presence to them. And on the other side, if any one says he loves God and hates his brother, he is a liar and the truth is not in him (1 John 4:20).

There can be much solitariness but no aloneness in our relating to the triune God. Even when we go into our own room and shut the door on the world, if we take the Bible with us, we are by that very action affirming that our relationship to God is mediated to us by the apostolic witness of the first Christians and by the interpreting tradition of the whole Church. It is by being in a receptive exocentric relationship with our fellow members in the body of Christ and the ministries of word, sacrament, and care that they offer that we can come in to a receptive and exocentric relationship to the risen Christ and through him to God.

On the other hand the corporate activities of the Church, its liturgy, its gatherings, all the activities in which its members interact with one another miss the mark and never pass beyond the social to the spiritual, from fellowship with people to fellowship with God, unless they are open to those graciously granted moments of immediacy when through human speaking God speaks, when through the giving of bread from human hand to human hand Christ feeds us with his body and blood, when through what we receive from and give to others we are brought into a new receiving from and a new giving to God. That divine immediacy through human mediation is what the Church is for and what it lives by, and where either factor fails the Church begins to die.

As a possible objection to all this, Dulles says, "But it is not clear that outgoing friendliness in point of fact leads to the most intense experience of God. For some persons, perhaps it does, but not for us all" (Dulles, 1976, p. 56). In other words, there are introverts as well as extroverts in the body of Christ, those for whom closeness to other people looks more demanding than renewing and whose instinct is to keep a good personal distance between them and their fellow members.

But what we are talking about here is not informal "happy clappy" chumminess or a "groupy-gropey" kind of intimacy which can be not only quite uncongenial to many people but so overwhelming in its emotional intensity that there is no silence in which God can speak, no disengagement from the closeness of others in which we can enter into our closeness to God. The horizontal can indeed distract from the vertical; our happy meeting with one another can become a substitute from our awesome encounter with God.

What matters is not emotional closeness but ontological inter-dependence, that in our gifts, our ministries and all our inter-relating, we should be the images and the mirrors out of which God's truth and love can shine, that we should be addressed by him as we are addressed by one another and served by him as we serve one another, that we should recognize in our fellow Christians people in such union with Christ that in meeting them we meet him and the one meeting facilitates and enriches the other. That is the message of the Eucharist, that not outside but within the togetherness of God's people and the distinctive ministries that each offers to the others, each enters through that mediated immediacy into a sharing of life with Christ the Lord.

Koinonia for the world

The most powerful objection to this model of the Church is that it can easily be developed in a sectarian and isolationist way. Here in a little ghetto of its own is the Church nurturing and cherishing a privileged two-dimensional *koinonia* that separates it off from the rest the world. In our own day with the collapse of Christendom and the marginalization of the Church, there is a real temptation to see it in that way.

It is here that we need to emphasize again that the *imago Dei* which is the humanity that Christ shares with us has to be viewed in the creational and eschatological contexts that are native to it. The Christ who is the head of the Church is also the *eschatos Adam*, the ultimate human being who is the culmination and goal of the whole human creation. Through him and for him all things were made; his mission is not accomplished with the gathering round himself of a believing minority in an untouched world but only when "all things are put into subjection to him" (1 Cor. 15:27) and at the name of Jesus there should bow down, not a few Christians but every knee in heaven and earth and under the earth (Phil. 2:10).

In our context, that means that everybody is called to be human in the way that Jesus Christ is human, that all men and women are to find their fulfilment in relationships with one another that reflect the love of the triune God and that thus the divine purpose in creation should be accomplished. The fellowship of the Church is therefore for the sake of the mission of the Church; the *koinonia* of believers is at its best a preliminary, provisional, and plausible adumbration of the relationships that will characterize the coming kingdom; the calling of the Church is to witness to the promise and the power of the new humanity of Christ in marriage and families, in work and leisure, in the just ordering of society, and to call people into that relationship with him in which that new humanity can begin to become reality in all the human inter-relating that constitutes our lives.

Our calling is not to hide our humanity in a churchy ghetto, but to give it full and free expression in the life of the world, because this is the humanity that the world was made for, is looking for and cannot find, and it is there, redeemed, renewed, fulfilled for everyone in Christ.

The Trinitarian commission

It is, in fact, in the conjoinedness of its fellowship and in its mission to the world that the Church reflects the *imago Dei* which it has received from Christ. The new humanity in Christ that the Church offers in its mission is plausible outside the Church only if it can be seen to be effective within the Church. As Leslie Newbigin used to say, a church riven by bad relationships and yet preaching reconciliation is like a Total Abstinence society all of whose members are permanently drunk! On the other hand, if the central relationship out of which the Church lives is its submission to the Christ who is its head, it can never rest content with any self-contained internal *koinonia*, but will be caught up in his passionate commitment to establish God's kingdom in God's world and create a society that is held together by the same kind of love that holds God together.

An impressive witness that such a commitment can actually be lived out in the contemporary world is contained in the life of Petre Tutea, a Romanian orthodox Christian who suffered imprisonment and torture at the hands of the communist regime, but of whom it could be said that through every chapter of his story "... there shines out Tutea's faith in the God who creates human persons in his own image and likeness, and destines them to share in the Trinitarian life through deification by the uncreated grace of God. Such faith sustains a life of prayer and practical love, even for one's torturers through which the Christian believer can experience the presence of God."[13] It is in the inspiration and resources of such a life that a Trinitarian theology of sanctification finds its practical and costly confirmation.

A church that is motivated by the obedient responsiveness to Christ that it has learned from Christ will, like him, also begin in its mission to be caught up into the initiating love of the Father, so that it will know itself to be sent and authorized for its mission as Jesus was sent and authorized for his. That is implicit in the great commission of Matthew 28, "All authority in heaven and on earth has been given to me. Go therefore into all the world and make disciples of all the nations, baptising them in the name of the Father and of the Son and of the Holy Spirit, teaching them to obey everything that I have commanded you" (28:18–20). This verse, which contains the most explicitly Trinitarian statement in the whole Bible, is also Trinitarian in the shape of the mission to which it calls us. Not only is it to be undertaken in obedience to the Son but, as the word "go" makes clear, it is a call to an initiating intervention in the life of the world which reflects the intervening love of the Father in the sending of his Son. We are not to live alongside the cultures of the world, claiming for ourselves and allowing to them an autonomy that sets up tacit or explicit borders between us. We are not either to sit in our Zion and wait for the nations to come knocking at our doors. "As the Father has sent me, so send I you" (John 20:21). The church that is in obedience to Christ, will, like the first church at Pentecost, have the boldness to stand up in a world that may be hostile to it and announce what it means for that world that a new humanity has arrived with the resurrection of Jesus from the dead.

Furthermore, the going is followed up in the discipling, in the creative and imaginative application of the gospel to the reconstruction of the life not just of individuals but of all nations into the likeness of the new man, Jesus Christ, "teaching them to observe all that I have commanded you" (Matt. 28:20). That creative reconstruction of life in specific applications to it of the love of the Father and the Son is the work of the Holy Spirit and it is in the power of the Spirit that our mission will be faithfully and relevantly accomplished. The mission of the Church, executed in the power of the love of God, is to baptize people into the relationships with Father, Son, and Holy Spirit that constitute the new humanity so that they become as initiating as the Father, as responsive as the Son, and as creative as the Spirit and so bring to fulfilment what has been implicit in creation, marred in sin, and restored, renewed, and completed in Christ.

Renewal for mission

To be the witness and the bearer of that new humanity the Church, especially as we know it in the weary West, is itself in need of a great renewal. As we have been looking again at the magnificent New Testament affirmations of the centrality of the Church to the fulfilment of the purposes of the triune God, many of us will have been thinking of the actual local congregations to which we belong, and have become agonizingly and even despairingly aware of the disparity between the ecclesiology we are asked to believe in and the actuality we encounter.

Our churches do, indeed, live in that *koinonia* with God that leads to *koinonia* with one another. We receive that communion as God's gift to us week by week in the sacrament. There is no grudging in his giving, but much interference with our receiving. The life of the fellowship is restricted on the outside by antiquated structures and our continuing collusion in clerical domination and on the inside by individualistic independence that hold us aloof from deep commitments to God or one another, the marginalization of the gospel in the priorities that rule our lives with the resultant lack of conviction about the centrality of Christ that holds us back from the missionary engagements with our culture to which we are called. And yet, underneath all that, we are held to Christ by the awareness that what he offers is what we need, if we had but the courage to open ourselves to it.

A church in such a condition is, indeed, in great need of a renewal that goes far beyond charismatic personal experiences of the Spirit and his gifts. God's method of renewal is by death and resurrection, and it is into that scary, risky agenda that all our churches are being drawn today. How and when we will have died enough to start living again is in God's hands, but his promise and our prayer is that we will be converted and restructured in quite new ways into that perichoretic participation in his own life so that we can credibly and committedly offer that life to the world.[14]

There are many secular people who think that you can be fully human without God; there are many religious people who think you can be fully human without Jesus. We have to ask God to reshape his Church so that we can tell and show that it is only in communion with the Father, the Son, and the Spirit that the new humanity can be born. Lord, let it be soon.

The mirrors that shine

There is much darkness in the world and in the church. But the last word about the church and the world can never be about their darkness. "The light shines in the darkness and the darkness has never conquered it" (John 1:5). The men and women that God has made never entirely cease, albeit with much dimness and blurring, to reflect what is still recognizable as the image of the God who made them. But it is in the initiation of the Father, in the incarnation of the Son, and in the effulgence of the Spirit, that light has its victory. Through that Spirit Christians have seen "the light of the gospel of the glory of Christ who is the image of God ... For it is God who said, 'let light shine out of darkness' who has shone in our hearts to give the light of the knowledge of the glory of God in the face of Jesus Christ" (2 Cor. 4:4–6).

The final thing to be said about the new humanity in Jesus and in us is that it is doxological humanity that both receives and reflects the glory of the one true God. When our little mirrors are trained and focused on his great mirror which is the light of the world, they in turn become brilliant with his reflected glory. Upward toward God in joyful worship, outward to the world in the beaming of the gospel of love they SHINE!

Notes

1. From 'Meditations' (Thomas, 1993, p. 275).
2. In *The Giving Gift*, 2002, p. 54ff.
3. This whole matter is discussed in greater detail in Chapter 6 below.
4. Gavin D'Costa interestingly argues that there is no ultimate religious pluralism, because even the most liberal and tolerant attitudes to other faith systems – like that, for instance of the Dalai Lama – are based on commitments to fundamental presuppositions in the light of which everything else is adjudicated. If Christians do this, so does everyone else (D'Costa, 2000, pp. 74–90).
5. Hamartiology (from the Greek word *hamartia*, sin) is the technical term for the doctrine of sin in Christian theology.
6. This chimes in well with the modern psychotherapeutic emphasis on an assertiveness that is neither combative aggression or passive submission, but an ability to intervene and to insist on being taken seriously in subsequent negotiation.
7. This reflects on the large scale the problem with which Paul had to deal on the small scale in the church at Corinth.

Genuine gifts of the Spirit were being used in ways that destroyed rather than built up the relationships of Christians with one another.
8. Watson's whole discussion of this passage is an impressive exposition and defense of this way of understanding Paul's missionary strategy in Acts 17 over against the approaches that are much more accommodating to non-Christian religion and that have been in vogue in much interfaith theology.
9. I owe this suggestion to a personal discussion with Professor Andrew Walker.
10. For much of what follows I am indebted to a conversation with Professor Christopher Seitz of St. Andrews.
11. I am, of course, aware that the Pauline authorship of Ephesians is subject to much debate in New Testament scholarship. For my purposes here it is enough that the theology of Ephesians is clearly Pauline, whether the apostle or a disciple is its immediate author, and, in the area of our specific concern, affirms and develops the approach of 1 Corinthians 11.
12. In what follows I am indebted to Barth's detailed discussion of the humanity of Jesus in the section entitled "Jesus, Man for other men" in Church Dogmatics III.2 p. 302ff.
13. Reported in *Church Times*, August 6, 2004, p. 19.
14. I have discussed these matters more fully in my essay "The Ethics of Exile and the Rhythm of Resurrection," a contribution to *On Revival* (Walker, ed., 2003, p. 57ff.).

Select Bibliography

Achtemeier, Paul. *Romans* (in *Interpretation* commentaries). Louisville, KY: John Knox Press, 1985

Anderson, Ray S. *On Being Human: Essays in Theological Anthropology*. Grand Rapids, MI: Eerdmans, 1982

Baillie, John. *Invitation to Pilgrimage*. London: Oxford University Press, 1942

Barrett, C. K. *A Commentary on the First Epistle to the Corinthians*, 2nd ed. London: Adam and Charles Black, 1971

Barth, Markus. *Ephesians* (in *The Anchor Bible*), Garden City, NY: Doubleday, 1974

Barth, Karl. *Christ and Adam: Man and Humanity in Romans 5*. New York, NY: Harper and Brothers, 1956a

Barth, Karl. *Church Dogmatics IV.1: The Doctrine of Reconciliation*. Edinburgh: T & T Clark, 1956b

Barth, Karl. *Church Dogmatics II.1: The Doctrine of God*. Edinburgh: T & T Clark, 1957

Barth, Karl. *Church Dogmatics III.1: The Doctrine of Creation*. Edinburgh: T & T Clark, 1958

Barth, Karl. *From Rousseau to Ritschl*. London: SCM., 1959

Barth, Karl. *Church Dogmatics III.2: The Doctrine of Creation*, Edinburgh: T & T Clark, 1960

Barth, Karl. *Church Dogmatics I.1: The Doctrine of the Word of God*, 2nd ed. Edinburgh: T & T Clark, 1975

Select Bibliography

Beckwith, Roger. "The Bearing of Holy Scripture." In *Man, Woman and Priesthood*, ed. Peter Moore. London: SCM, 1978
Bettenson, Henry. *The Later Christian Fathers*. London: OUP, 1970
Bonhoeffer, Dietrich. *Letters and Papers from Prison*, enlarged ed. London: SCM, 1967
Brunner, Emil. *Man in Revolt*. London and Redhill: Lutterworth, 1939
Brunner, Emil. 3 vols., Vol II, *Dogmatics: The Christian Doctrine of Creation and Redemption*. London: Lutterworth, 1952
Busch, E. *Karl Barth: His life from letters and autobiographical texts*. London: SCM, 1976
Calvin, John. 2 vols, *Institutes of the Christian Religion*. Philadelphia, PA: Westminster Press, 1960
D'Costa, Gavin. *The Meeting of Religions and the Trinity*. Edinburgh: T & T Clark, 2000
Dulles, Avery. *Models of the Church*. Dublin: Gill and Macmillan, 1976
Grenz, Stanley. *The Social God and the Relational Self*. Lousville: Westminster John Knox Press, 2001.
Gunton, Colin E. *The Promise of Trinitarian Theology*. Edinburgh: T & T Clark, 1991
Gunton, Colin E. (ed.) *God and Freedom*. Edinburgh: T & T Clark, 1995
Gunton, Colin E. *The Triune Creator*. Grand Rapids, NY: Eerdmans, 1998
Kimel, Alvin F. (ed.). *Speaking the Christian God*. Leominster: Gracewing, 1992
Küng, Hans. *Does God Exist?* Translated by Edward Quinn. London: Collins, 1980
Luther, Martin. "Lectures on Genesis." In *Luther's Works*. St Louis, MO: Concordia, 1958
McFadyen, Alastair. *Bound to Sin*. Cambridge: Cambridge University Press, 2000
MacKinnon, D.M. Themes in Theology: The Three-Fold Cord. Edinburgh: T&T Clark, 1987.
Moltmann, Jürgen. *The Trinity and the Kingdom of God*. London: SCM, 1981

Pannenberg, Wolfhart. *Anthropology in Theological Perspective.* Philadelphia, PA: Westminster Press, 1985

Pannenberg, Wolfhart. 3 vols., Vol. 1, *Systematic Theology.* Edinburgh: T & T Clark, 1991

Patzia, Arthur G. "*Colossians, Philemon, Ephesians.*" In *Good New Commentary.* San Francisco, CA: Harper and Row, 1984

Porteous, N. W. "Image of God." In 5 vols., Vol. 2, *Interpreter's Dictionary of the Bible.* Nashville, TN: Abingdon, 1962

Thomas, R. S. *Collected Poems 1945–1990.* London: J. M. Dent, 1993

Torrance, Alan J. *Persons in Communion.* Edinburgh: T & T Clark, 1996

Tutu, Desmond. "Restoring Justice." In *The Tablet* (21 February 2004). London, 2004

Vanhoozer, Kevin J. *First Theology: God, Scripture & Hermeneutics.* Downers Grove, IL: IVP, 2002

Volf, Miroslav. *After our Likeness: The Church as the Image of the Trinity.* Grand Rapids, NY: Eerdmans, 1998

von Rad, Gerhard. *Genesis: a Commentary,* revised ed. London: SCM, 1961

Walker, Andrew (ed.). *On Revival: A Critical Examination.* Carlisle: Paternoster, 2003

Watson, Francis. *Text and Truth: Redefining Biblical Theology.* Edinburgh: T & T Clark, 1997

Westermann, Claus. *Genesis 1–11: A Commentary.* London: SPCK, 1984

Wright, N. T. *The Resurrection of the Son of God.* London: SPCK, 2003

Zizioulos, John. *Being as Communion: Studies in Personhood and the Church.* New York, NY: St. Vladimir's Press, 1985

Index

Achtemeier, Paul 235
Adam and Eve 44ff, 244ff
Anderson, Ray 39, 41,57, 245
Arianism 78
Augustine 75, 81ff, 110, 212, 222ff

Baillie John 148ff
Barrett, C. K 261
Barth, Karl 27,155
   Christ as *imago Dei* 273, 278, 281f
   God's love in freedom 155
   God's obedience 76ff
   image and sin 206ff, 211
   image and Trinity 208
   man/woman relationships 245, 267
   on the Trinity 86ff
Barth, Markus 265
Basil of Caesarea, 94ff
Boethius, 110, 204
Bonhoeffer, Dietrich, 119, 131
Brunner, Emil 51, 210ff, 214

Calvin, John 22, 205ff
Cappadocians 93
Christology 57, 68, 72
Church 263, 283ff, 294
Creation
   and Christ 57ff, 273ff
   and covenant, 136ff
   and cosmology 40ff
   and gender 244ff
   and human mandate 161
   and sin 202ff
Conversion 188ff

Dalai Llama 219
Dawkins, Richard 126
D'Costa, Gavin 220
Descartes, René 111
Donne, John 156
Dulles, Avery 286, 289

Fall 212ff, 247ff
Feuerbach, Ludwig 5ff, 11ff, 112, 174
Freedom & Determinism 125, 128ff, 288

Freud, Sigmund 7ff, 16, 125
God
  his covenant faithfulness 134ff
  creation and covenant 136ff
  as Father 12, 35, 159ff
  his inescapability, 119ff,
  as love in freedom 154ff
  in natural theology 13ff
  as obedient 76ff
  as product of projection, 5ff
  in revelation 19ff
Grenz, Stanley 47, 63, 130
Gunton, Colin 82, 93, 94, 174ff, 207—8,

Headship 251ff, 261ff
Hegel, G.F. 113
Holy Spirit
  in Augustine 85ff
  in Barth 91f
  his creativity 183ff
  in culture and controversy 195ff
  and human development 193ff
  his personal distinctness 183ff
  in the East 94ff
  and *koinonia* 284ff
  as perichoresis 100ff
  his relationship to Jesus 67
  in revelation 27
  and the resurrection 187ff

Image of God
  and human autonomy 113ff
  as body, soul and spirit 151ff
  as dominion 43, 44, 161ff
  eschatological character 62ff
  its exocentricity, 123ff,
  imaging the Father 159ff
  formal and material 210ff
  in Genesis 40ff
  imaging the Spirit 186ff
  and language 140
  as likeness 47
  male and female 44, 51ff, 240ff
  in natural theology 15
  in New Testament 57ff
  in Old Testament 38ff
  as representation 45
  as obligated responsiveness 137ff, 145ff, 173ff, 181ff
  in revelation 19ff, 27ff
  imaging the Son 172ff
  as affected by sin 55, 158ff, 202ff
  its triune structure 153ff, 243
Individuality and Relationality 84ff. 109ff, 116ff
Irenaeus 203

Jensen, Robert W. 12
Jesus Christ
  in relation to the Church 263, 283ff
  his covenant faithfulness 134ff,

relationship to creation
   57ff, 273ff
his cross as revelation of sin
   230ff
his humanity 274ff
as image of God 57ff, 104ff,
   272
the man for others 278ff
teaching on marriage 253ff
his free obedience as Son
   76, 169ff
as restorer of relationships
   280ff
as Son 61
his trinitarian relationships
   66ff
as Word and Wisdom 60f
Justice, restorative 179ff

Kant, Immanuel, 112, 125, 236
Kelber, Gerhard 61
Koinonia 284, 286, 290
Küng, Hans 5, 8, 25, 121

Liberation 228ff
Luther, Martin 205, 275

Marriage 252ff, 263ff
Marx, Karl, 6
McFadyen, Alistair 226ff
Modalism 79
Modernity, 3ff
Moltmann, Jürgen, 89, 90, 92, 99
Mühlen, Heribert, 286

Newbigin, Leslie 292

Nietzsche, Friedrich, 120ff,
Pannenberg, Wolfhart, 203
   on human development,
      138ff, 174,
   exocentricity, 123ff
   on the Holy Spirit 184, 192
   the implicit ultimate, 121ff
Patzia, Arthur 5
Paul, 286
   on male/female relation
      ship 258ff
   on religion 31, 216ff
   on sin 224ff, 233ff
Pelagianism 222ff, 235ff
Perichoresis 97ff
   reflected in man/woman
      relations 268ff
Peterson, Eugene 2
Porteous, Norman 57
Post-modernism 24ff

Rahner, Karl 80, 118,
Ramsey, Ian 23
Religion
   in Paul 216ff
   as projection 5ff
   as implicit ultimate 216ff
Renewal and Revolution
   189ff, 294ff
Robinson, John 117,

Sanctification 277ff
Sartre, Jean Paul, 124,
Schleiermacher, Friedrich, 113
Self
   in biblical perspective 134
   in post-modernism, 130,
   in relationships 131ff, 142ff,

its survival 133
Sin, 118, 158ff
  as autonomy, 182
  as cultural crucifixion 232ff
  as destructiveness 199ff
  as egocentricity 124, 220ff
  in relation to Fall 212ff
  and the image of God 202ff
  and morality 229ff
  as oppression 164ff
  original sin 222ff, 234ff
  its penalties in Genesis 247ff
  as sloth 197ff
Singleness 256

Thomas, R.S. 20
Torrance, Alan 101
Torrance, T.F. 79
Trinity, doctrine of
  in Augustine 81ff
  in Barth 86ff
  biblical roots 69ff
  basis in revelation 35
  as community 93, 102ff, 156ff, 264
  deviations 77ff
  doctrinal development 73ff
  in East and West 80ff, 95ff
  in Genesis 43
  and man/woman relations 249ff
  and mission 292ff
  persons and relationships, 83ff, 102ff
  primacy of the Father 101
  single subject in repetition 88ff
  Son as image of Father 59
  unity and differentiation 76ff, 95ff, 157,
Tritheism 77
Tutea, Petre 292
Tutu, Desmond 139, 180

Vanhoozer, Kevin 140,
Vanier, Jean 282
Volf, Miroslav 98
von Rad, Gerhard 39, 47, 49

Watson, Francis 219
Wenham, Gordon 46
Westermann, Claus 52
Wright, N.T. 151

Zizioulos, John 101

www.ingramcontent.com/pod-product-compliance
Lightning Source LLC
Chambersburg PA
CBHW070232230426
43664CB00014B/2273